For James

7·7·

Michael Wardle

EDWARDIAN
HERITAGE

EDWARDIAN HERITAGE

A STUDY IN BRITISH HISTORY
1901 — 1906

BY

WILLIAM SCOVELL ADAMS

M.A.

LONDON
FREDERICK MULLER LTD.
29 GREAT JAMES STREET
W.C. 1

FIRST PUBLISHED BY FREDERICK MULLER LTD.
IN 1949
PRINTED IN GREAT BRITAIN
BY PILLANS AND WILSON
EDINBURGH

For my friends in adult education, students, tutors and officials, and particularly for my colleagues, whose sympathetic understanding of the strains of research alone enabled me to complete this volume.

For they have sown the wind, and they shall reap the whirlwind. — *Hosea, VIII,* 7.

CONTENTS

CONTENTS

CHAPTER I

THE SEVENTH EDWARD

The Queen died. The nation was still; its tumult ceased with the sudden jerk of a checked cinematograph film. The decline had been speedy. On 14th January she received for a final interview Lord Roberts, back from South Africa, but without the news of victory for which her weary spirit yearned. On the following day the plans for her annual visit to the Riviera were cancelled, and a fine of £800 paid to the hotel proprietor at Cimiez.[1] On 18th January she became the longest lived British monarch. On 22nd January, in the arms of her grandson, the German Emperor, she died.

Comment broke the momentary hush. The considered opinion of the *Annual Register* is a fair summary of the general trend: " The feeling of forlornness, which pervaded the country, was alike in its diffusion and its depth of a kind such as has not been known in England since the death of King Alfred a thousand years before." Lord Salisbury, the last of her ten Prime Ministers, more shrewdly remarked: " She had an extraordinary power of divining what her people, and especially those of the middle classes, would think." [2] There was scarcely a corner of the world where the event passed unrecorded. A New York divine contributed the supreme hyperbole: " I believe that no throne since the throne of David, the throne of Hezekiah, the throne of Esther has been in such constant touch with the throne of Heaven as the throne of Queen Victoria." [3]

Curious minds turned to the future. " This is notable news," wrote Wilfrid Scawen Blunt in his diary. " It will mean great changes in the world, for the long understanding among the Emperors that England is not to be quarrelled with during the

[1] Sir A. Fitzroy, *Memoirs*, Vol. 1, 38.
[2] House of Lords, 25th Jan. 1901.
[3] Dr. Dwight Talmadge, *The Times*, 24th Jan. 1901.

Queen's lifetime will now give place to freer action. The Emperor William does not love his uncle, our new King." [1]

By the time that the funeral took place a careful observer recorded that " the people were not on the whole deeply moved, whatever journalists may say, but rather serene and cheerful." [2]

The Queen was dead. The Queen was buried. The nation, almost ashamed by the ease with which the transformation had been effected, moved into the new reign.

The son, who now stepped into his mother's shoes, had waited long for the inheritance. He had been born in the " Hungry Forties," whose marks were still deep on the physique and minds of many of his subjects. His own generous contours showed that Edward, the second of Queen Victoria's nine state-subsidized children, had taken no harm. Yet there may be childhood recollections reflected in the scene in the Royal box at the gala performance for President Loubet in 1903, when the King expressed such vehement views against Chamberlain's food-taxing proposals in the hearing of the Unionist Free Traders that the Duke of Devonshire suggested sending him on the stump.[3] It is the only recorded instance of that very correct monarch voicing his political opinions in public.

His education had received the intense concentration of his parents, and perhaps cost his father his life.[4] Three Universities claimed him as their son,[5] while in his art studies the advice of Ruskin had been sought, and the answer returned that " one of the main duties of Princes is to provide for the preservation of perishing frescoes and monuments." [6] Extreme care had been lavished, particularly by his mother, on training in deportment. " A gentleman," reads a *Memorandum for the guidance of the gentlemen appointed to attend on the Prince of Wales*, " does not

---

[1] W. S. Blunt, *My Diaries*, Part 2, 1.

[2] Arnold Bennett, *Journals*, Vol. 1, 1896–1910, 110.

[3] Fitzroy, *op. cit.*, Vol. 1, 146. Lord Askwith, *Life of Lord James of Hereford*, 277. Edward valued food highly. When Baden-Powell visited him at Balmoral he presented the Chief Scout with a haunch of venison. " I have watched you at meals," he said, " you don't eat enough. When working as you are doing you must keep up your system. . . . Don't forget—eat more." E. E. Reynolds, *Baden-Powell*, 124.

[4] An urgent visit to his son at Cambridge, 25th Nov., was the last time Prince Albert left home before his death, 14th Dec. 1861.

[5] Oxford, Cambridge, and Edinburgh.

[6] Sir Sydney Lee, *King Edward VII*, Vol. 1, 60.

indulge in careless, self-indulgent, lounging ways, such as lolling in armchairs or on sofas, slouching in his gait, or placing himself in unbecoming attitudes, with his hands in his pockets, or in any position in which he appears to consult more the idle ease of the moment than the maintenance of the decorum which is characteristic of a polished gentleman." [1]

Academic studies had been supplemented by foreign travel. At the age of thirteen he had visited with his mother the Invalides, and paid homage on his knees at the tomb of Napoleon while a thunderstorm raged overhead and the tears streamed down the cheeks of the French generals present.[2] When he was seventeen he saw the Pope wash the feet of thirteen pilgrims in the Sistine Chapel, which he " thought very ridiculous, as the Pope did not even wet the feet of the pilgrims, who were all seated in front of him, but only touched them with a towel, and then gave each of the pilgrims a medal ".[3] From the time of these early tours few years passed without his leaving the country. Paris, a part of Paris, particularly appealed to him.

On the eve of the Civil War he visited the United States.

His interest in Foreign Affairs was further fostered by his marriage to the Princess Alexandra of Denmark, shortly before Bismarck seized Schleswig-Holstein. Queen Victoria sternly warned her daughter-in-law not to seek to interest her husband in the affairs of her unhappy country, but without effect. " This horrible war," he wrote to a friend, " will be a stain for ever on Prussian history, and I think it is *very* wrong of our Government not to have interfered before now. As for Lord Russell's everlasting Notes, nobody cares twopence about them on the Continent, and the Foreign Ministers to whom they are addressed probably only light their cigars with them." [4] Later he was to be accused of partiality for France during the Franco-Prussian war.

Alexandra, Tennyson's " Sea-King's daughter," proved a suitable consort. She possessed beauty and charm, also that patient consideration for human frailty so essential in the wife of Edward Guelph, while she was always willing to play the part of a leader of Society, and to set those changing fashions, which

[1] Lord Esher, *The Character of King Edward VII.* Quarterly Review, June 1910.
[2] Lee, *op. cit.*, Vol. 1, 37.   [3] *Idem*, Vol. 1, 61.   [4] *Idem*, Vol. 1, 250.

filled the leisure of the aristocracy, and the pockets of the industries dependent on them.[1]

The King was quite uninterested in the athletic pursuits such as cricket, tennis and golf, in which so many gentlemen of his period, including statesmen, spent their time; but racing on the turf remained a keen enjoyment up to the victory of his horse Witch of the Air at Kempton Park on the day of his death, and yacht-racing at least until the defeat of *Britannia* by the Kaiser's *Meteor* in 1896. The usual pursuits of a country gentleman he followed. He told Lord Rosebery that he liked nothing so much as seeing churches;[2] but the card table seems to have appealed to him more. Gladstone, who had played with him, thought that he had " an *immense* whist memory ";[3] but Gladstone was not an expert at the game. Baccarat he eschewed after the notorious Tranby Croft case. Late in life he became an enthusiastic but not a first-class bridge player, and it was an invitation to make a bridge four with him that earned a young lady at Marienbad a place in the chronicle of kings, when she refused with the words: " Sir, I don't know a King from a Knave."[4]

The punctilio of his mother he considerably relaxed. It was no longer necessary for the German Ambassador to lie on the floor of his bedroom at Windsor Castle, puffing the smoke of his cigarette up the chimney;[5] but the training of his childhood bore its fruit in his intense interest in uniforms and in correct dress. Criticism was voiced at the new tone he set to Society. The Kaiser complained of its looseness,[6] and was angered by an incident at a country house, at which the Crown Prince was staying, " where there had been unseemly romping in unlighted corridors, and one lady had even gone so far as to take off her slipper ".[7] But the English Sunday, fighting a rearguard action in the new century, continued to be officially observed at Court. When a clergyman, reading in the newspapers a report that the King was to see Maud

---

[1] E.g. fancy Japanese spaniels, or Pekinese. " The great popularity of these boudoir pets originated in the desire to imitate her." W. R. H. Troubridge, *Queen Alexandra*.
[2] Marquess of Crewe, *Lord Rosebery*, Vol. 2, 640.
[3] *Gladstone Journal*, 30th Sept. 1871. Quoted by Lee, *op. cit.*, Vol. 1, 206, 207.
[4] Fitzroy, *op. cit.*, Vol. 1, 266.
[5] Baron von Eckardstein, *Ten years at the Court of St. James's*, 43.
[6] Prince von Bulow, *Memoirs*, Eng. Trans., 1903–9, 182.
[7] Lord Newton, *Lord Lansdowne*, 330.

Allan in a play on Sunday evening, appealed to him not to go, he at once put off the entertainment, and resolved not to break the Sabbath in future.[1]

" Bright society of the opposite sex always attracted him," declares Sir Sydney Lee, his official biographer, and compares him with

> ". . . our courteous Antony,
> Whom ne'er the word of ' No ' woman heard speak." [2]

Blunt refers to " his pleasant little wickednesses "[3] and " a Philistine tolerance for other people's sins, which endear him to rich and poor from archbishops down to turf bookmakers and the man in the street." [4] *The Times* discreetly remarked at his accession: " We shall not pretend that there is nothing in his long career, which those who respect and admire him could not wish otherwise." [5] The leaders of the Established Church were even more discreet, and said nothing, until the King was convalescing from the operation for appendicitis, which postponed his coronation. Then the Archbishop of Canterbury spoke to him of " the lessons which such an illness at such a time might teach." [6]

He was an extrovert. Company was a necessity to him. His

---

[1] Lord Esher, *Journal*, Vol 2, 324. [2] Lee, *op. cit.*, Vol. 1, 182.
[3] Blunt, *op. cit.*, Part 2, 320. [4] *Idem*, Part 2, 2.
[5] *The Times*, 23rd Jan. 1901.
[6] G. K. Bell, *Life of Randall Davidson, Archbishop of Canterbury*, Vol. 1, 372.
It seems generally to have been agreed by the Churches that the appendicitis came from God, although there were differences of opinion regarding the reason. Cf. the following extracts from sermons given by *The Times*:
Bishop of Stepney at St. Paul's: May it not be that we were all advancing to this solemn act with undue levity and that the call has come in this postponement to remember the Lord Our God.
Cardinal Vaughan to his clergy: The finger of God has appeared in the midst of national rejoicing, and on the eve of what promised to be one of the most splendid pageants in English history. This is in order to call the thoughts of all men to Himself.
Dr. R. F. Horton at Intercession Service, National Council of Free Churches: He did not understand that the event necessarily meant that God was angry with us, for whom the Lord loved He chastened. This might be a signal instance of the unfailing love of God to our race and people. . . . Their lips were not shaped to adulation, and though on the one hand they made no impertinent conditions, on the other hand they felt compelled to judge a King by his acts, being unable to regard as good on the throne what they did not regard as good in their own homes.
Bishop of Southampton at Petersfield: It might be that we had been too much absorbed in thoughts of Imperial greatness and earthly prosperity.
Bishop of London at Chapel Royal, St. James's: Every inquiring mind must ask why it happened. It was our duty to profit by experience. Were we going

own anecdotes lacked subtlety,[1] but he liked amusing talk. He was an adroit public speaker, and could be depended upon to say the right thing in the right place. He did not often open a book, and preferred of all the authors of his time Marie Corelli,[2] but he carefully perused *Reynold's Newspaper* every Sunday.[3] He had what is described as a knowledge of the world. Referring to the King and the Kaiser, Bulow remarks: " When the uncle talked politics with the nephew I had the impression of a fat malicious tom-cat playing with a shrewmouse." [4] " I'm not sure that he could do the rule of three," wrote Lord Fisher, " *but he had the Heavenly gift of Proportion and Perspective.*" [5] He was aware of his own weaknesses, and was not more of a hypocrite than the Royal estate inevitably compels.[6]

As a constitutional monarch his conduct was impeccable. He often disagreed with his official advisers, but always bowed to proper pressure. His " passion for pageantry and ceremonial and dressing up " commended itself to his people. " He was never tired of putting on uniforms and taking them off . . . opening museums and hospitals, and attending cattle shows and military shows and shows of every kind, while every night of his life he was to be seen at theatres and operas and music halls." [7] He did not however neglect official business, and returning from an evening of pleasure with his cronies, would sit late into the night at the red dispatch boxes on his desk.

He had curiously little interest in the Empire, although in his younger days he had visited both Canada and India; but he was at home with the intricacies of Continental politics. It was however in his links with the business world that the most appropriate feature of his Kingship consisted. " He was acquainted

to the Coronation too much as a great show, too little as a great national sacrament?

Bishop of Durham at Foundling Hospital Chapel: A will that asked no leave of Crown or Senate had laid its hand upon us, and a voice said: Be still and know that I am God.

The historian must point out that the result of the incident was to make the operation for appendicitis fashionable and therefore profitable to the doctors. It might therefore be argued that the purpose of God in the whole perplexing matter was to assist the Royal College of Surgeons.

[1] Lee, *op. cit.*, Vol. 2, 411.   [2] Amy Cruse, *After the Victorians*, 181.
[3] Edward Legge, *More About King Edward*, 132.
[4] Bulow, *op. cit.*, 1897–1903, 339.   [5] Lord Fisher, *Memories*, 12.
[6] For a different view see Lord Newton, *Retrospection*, 116.
[7] Blunt, *op. cit.*, Part 2, 320.

with eminent business men of all nationalities, and he was inti-
mately conscious of the novel conditions of that international
commercial struggle for the open markets of the world, which was
slowly but surely taking the place of the somewhat aimless national
rivalries of the years immediately following the making of the
German Empire."[1] The leader writer in *The Times* significantly
makes the same point: " If he had been born in a humbler station
he might have become a successful business man."[2] We need
not take too seriously the Kaiser's statement that the King's visit
to Reval in connexion with the Anglo-Russian rapprochement
brought him " colossal profits ";[3] but it is improbable that his
friendship with Sir Ernest Cassel, the prominent financier, who
was made K.C.M.G. 1899, K.C.V.O. 1902, Privy Councillor 1902,
G.C.M.G. 1905, G.C.V.O. 1906, G.C.B. 1909, adversely affected
the royal investments. In his interventions in business he was
admirably patriotic. He asked the Tsar to receive Cassel, but
refused to speak for Sir Henry Burdett, who was acting for an
American firm.[4] The Directors of the Chartered Company,
created by Cecil Rhodes, included his son-in-law the Duke of
Fife, and his old friend the Duke of Abercorn. He was an admirer
of Rhodes,[5] and supported the employment of Chinese Labour
in the Transvaal.[6] There is a not so very faint odour of the Stock
Exchange about the life of Edward the Seventh.

Considerable satisfaction was felt when no application was
made to Parliament to discharge debts incurred before he became
King.[7] Informed gossip stated that these had been paid off privately
by his friends, with the honour of knighthood playing a part in
the transaction.[8]

In his views on public affairs he had become conservative.
The Morley-Minto reforms in India horrified him. He was a
confirmed opponent of Women's Suffrage.[9] He was only with
difficulty persuaded to consent to the appointment of two women
to the Royal Commission on the Marriage Laws.[10] Only a personal
liking for Campbell-Bannerman, whom he had met at Marienbad,

---

[1] Lord Esher, King Edward and Foreign Affairs, *Deutsche Review*, 1910.
[2] *The Times*, 23rd Jan. 1901.   [3] Bulow, *op. cit.*, 1903-9, 309.
[4] Lee, *op. cit.*, Vol. 2, 594.   [5] F. Whyte, *W. T. Stead*, Vol. 2, 107, 108.
[6] Lee, *op. cit.*, Vol. 2, 180.   [7] Askwith, *op. cit.*, 264.
[8] Blunt, *op. cit.*, Part 2, 8.   [9] Lee, *op. cit.*, Vol. 2, 468.
[10] J. A. Spender and Cyril Asquith, *Life of H. H. Asquith*, Vol. 1, 243.

reconciled him to the advent of a Pro-Boer Prime Minister in 1905. What his attitude would have been to the Parliament Act of 1911 we can only conjecture. His relations with Asquith were never cordial,[1] and the only time that he approved of Lloyd George was when the threatened railway strike of 1907 was averted by the Welshman's " cleverness." [2] But only on one occasion did he allow his feelings to influence his conduct: When attacks in Parliament were made on his visit to the Tsar, he omitted the chief offenders from his next garden party.[3]

His influence on Foreign Policy was often exaggerated by his contemporaries. In the first number of his new paper, *John Bull*, Horatio Bottomley wrote: " With Your Majesty on the throne a Parliament is almost a redundancy. You are our Foreign Minister, our Ambassador to all the Courts. . . . So long as you live European War will be impossible." [4] Both British and continental opinion over-estimated the part played by the King in the policy of alliances, which was attributed wrongly to his personal authority. But although it is certain that he could never have pursued a Foreign Policy contrary to that of the Government, the fact that his own views coincided with those of his ministers assisted more than once the efforts of the Foreign Office, from which Charles Hardinge, later Viceroy of India and on his retirement from official life " something in the City," was seconded to accompany him on his continental journeys. The famous visit to Paris in 1903 was made on the King's own suggestion, and was apparently not approved by some members of the Cabinet.[5] His conversation with Ivolsky, the later Russian Foreign Minister, at Copenhagen in April 1904, encouraged that ambitious diplomat to work for the Anglo-Russian agreement.

In the nation he was popular. " He had just the character that Englishmen at any rate thoroughly understand, thoroughly

---

[1] Lee, *op. cit.*, Vol. 2, 658.   [2] *Idem*, Vol. 2, 475.   [3] *Idem*, Vol. 2, 588.
[4] J. A. Farrer, *England under Edward VII*, 88.
For another example of sycophancy, see the verses on the coronation in *The Times Literary Supplement*, 20th June 1902, in which James Rhoades appears to hint at a comparison with Jesus Christ:

> For though, with Heaven and loyal hearts to add,
> This weight of Empire may be bravely borne,
> Purple is weary wear when all is said,
> The crown, though golden, edged with golden thorn.

[5] Lee, *op. cit.*, Vol. 2, 223. Lord Newton, *Lord Lansdowne*, 279.

like, and make any quantity of allowance for. It was odd how he managed to combine dignity with bonhomie, and strict regard for form with entire absence of spurious pomp." [1] Thus Lord Morley after his death. Even before his accession he had been favourably compared with his father. " Prince Albert was unloved," remarked Lord Granville, " because he possessed all the virtues which are sometimes lacking in the Englishman. The Prince of Wales is loved because he has all the faults of which the Englishman is accused." [2]

[1] Viscount Morley, *Recollections*, Vol. 2, 331.
[2] Bulow, *op. cit.*, 1897–1903, 336.

CHAPTER II

AN EMPIRE IN PERSPECTIVE

The people over whom Edward VII reigned constituted the greatest aggregate ever owing allegiance to a single crown. Gibbon estimated the subjects of Imperial Rome at one hundred and twenty millions. Reasonably reliable statistics gave the total over whom Edward ruled as more than four hundred.[1]

The newspapers of the new reign, " drunk with sight of power," or hot in the pursuit of circulation, regaled their readers with highly coloured comparisons of the Empire to which the girl Victoria had succeeded, and the Empire which she handed on to her mature son. " His Majesty," proclaimed the *St. James's Gazette*, " rules over one continent, a hundred peninsulas, five hundred promontories, a thousand lakes, two thousand rivers and ten thousand islands. Queen Victoria ascended the throne of an Empire embracing 8,329,000 square miles; she handed it down to King Edward with three million miles added to it. The Queen found the revenues of the Empire at £75,000,000; she left them at £225,000,000. The Army has twice as many men as in the first years of Victoria's reign, and the Navy has quadrupled itself. Seventy out of every hundred ships on the seas fly the British flag. The Empire to which Victoria acceded in 1837 covered one-sixth of the land of the world; that of King Edward covers nearly one-fourth. The Union Jack has unfolded itself, so to speak, over two acres of new territory every time the clock has ticked since 1800." [2]

These stupendous facts were ever present in the minds of the King's Ministers, and of Cromer, Curzon and Milner, the formidable Proconsuls.[3] They had begun, as the above extract shows,

---

[1] *Census*, 1901. Cd. 2174; 1904, 188.
[2] From an undated press cutting, presumably January 1901.
[3] Lord Cromer, Consul-General, Egypt, 1883–1907. Lord Curzon, Viceroy of India, 1898–1905. Lord Milner, High Commissioner, South Africa, 1897–1905.

to be absorbed into the clichés of journalists. They provided ready-made perorations for Tory and Liberal-Imperialist politicians. They were carefully and more critically noted by some foreign observers. But it is doubtful whether the ordinary British citizen was fully conscious of belonging to such a mighty grouping.

The Empire was so scattered. It spread over the five continents, and across the seven seas. It comprised so many races and creeds, such uneven economic and political developments. Three-quarters of the inhabitants dwelt in India. Only one in eight of the King's subjects was white, and of these four-fifths were crowded into the United Kingdom, which occupied only one-eightieth of the land area.

The historian of Edward's reign at once faces a problem. What is to be his perspective? Are the lives and deaths, the acts and thoughts, the hopes and disappointments of all the four hundred millions equally important? Or is there some special significance in the record of the forty millions of the United Kingdom? In one sense surely all are equally important. To deny this (and the most respectable historians have sometimes done so) is to set ourselves up as Herrenvolk. The rule of Edward was over them all. His reign should be judged on its total record. The Empire's Gibbon will no doubt point out (if only in a footnote) that Christianity, the official religion, viewed all men as brothers, and that leading politicians were fond of using the word " family " in their speeches on Imperial questions. The fact that Old Age Pensions were not obtained by the aged labourer in the West Indies in 1908 is as significant as the fact that they were by his fellow-subject in the United Kingdom. The difference in the infant mortality rate between Britain and Hong Kong is as important as the difference between Hampstead and Aberdare. The starvation in Bengal should not be ignored while the subnormal condition of English recruits during the Boer War is stressed.

But if the description of the condition of the people cannot stop short at the Straits of Dover, it remains true that when History moves on to an analysis of change and decision, the United Kingdom inevitably becomes the focal point. In this respect the forty millions in our islands have a special significance. For in Britain lay the supreme seat of power. Whatever other influences might indirectly affect the policy of the British Government (and these indirect influences were not always the least important), only the British Electorate was capable of direct constitutional pressure. Herein lay at once the symbol and the cause of the Empire's inherent inequality.

CHAPTER III

PROBLEMS OF POPULATION

The inhabitants of the United Kingdom, from whose enterprise or " absent-mindedness " the Empire had sprung, now numbered nearly 41½ millions, of whom about three-quarters dwelt in towns, and over one-seventh in Greater London.

Since 1801 the population had almost quadrupled, and during Edward's reign more babies were to be born than ever before or since; a fact which later historians may consider the most significant of the decade. Warning voices were beginning to be raised of the possibility of the British people following in the steps of the French towards decline and ultimate extinction. In 1895 Edward Cannan had startled the readers of the *Economic Journal* by his article on " The probability of a cessation of the growth of Population in England and Wales during the next century." He thought that the statistics indicated cessation in 1991, but expected it earlier, and mentioned the possibility of a decline. Sidney and Beatrice Webb in *Industrial Democracy*, published in 1897, appealed for funds for research into this " of all problems the most momentous for the future of the civilized races."

The Census of 1901 confirmed without stressing the position. And although the Royal Commission on Coal Supplies, 1903, accepted an estimate of 130 millions as the population of the United Kingdom for 2091, the facts were being widely discussed in informed circles. The Fabian Society, under the inspiration of the Webbs, carried out a survey. H. G. Wells in his statement on Socialism, *New Worlds for Old*, published in 1908, pointed out that " parentage is treated as a private foible, and those who undertake its solemn responsibilities are put at every sort of disadvantage against those who lead sterile lives," and soon was advocating Family Allowances.[1]

[1] *Le Matin*, 25th Nov. 1909.

The general public remained unmoved, the more easily as the decline in the birth rate was more than matched by the fall in mortality.

Informed opinion on the subject reflected the conditions of the time, and in particular the extension of Democracy, and the rise of new Great Powers with larger populations.

The successive franchise acts of the nineteenth century had drawn attention to the quality of the electorate, and to the unbridled reproduction of the lower classes. According to Sidney Webb, John Stuart Mill had become a Socialist largely because he thought " it was hopeless to expect to spread a Malthusian prudence " among the depressed workers existing under Capitalism on the barest livelihood.[1] Most of the members of the new Eugenic Society [2] disagreed with Mill. For them Social Reform was scarcely compatible with a sound population policy. If taxation was increased to provide Social Services, the ruling class —the " best people "—would have fewer children. Having rejected the implications of Democracy, of progress towards a classless society, they moaned and wriggled on the horns of their dilemma.

But not only the maintenance of a ruling class in Britain was reflected in Eugenic discussion, but the maintenance of a ruling British race, that " Imperial race," as Lord Rosebery described it, bearing " the white man's burden " without complaint and not without profit. Eugenics in the reign of Edward VII was strongly influenced by the Imperialist creed, the creed of an Empire now menaced by the rise of new Great Powers with larger populations and war potential.

" If the prophets were right," declared the Bishop of Ripon

---

[1] S. Webb, *The Difficulties of Individualism.* Article in *Economic Journal,* June 1891, reprinted in *Problems of Modern Industry,* 242 (1902 edition).

[2] Founded 1907. Cf. Karl Pearson, F.R.S., Lecture to Newcastle Literary and Philosophical Society, 19th Nov. 1900. " Social sympathy and state aid must not be carried so far within the community that the intellectually and physically weaker stocks multiply at the same rate as the better stocks. . . . You may hope for a time when the sword shall be turned into the ploughshare, when the American and German and English traders shall no longer compete in the markets of the world for their raw material and their food supply, when the white man and the dark shall share the soil between them and each till as he lists. But believe me when that day comes mankind will no longer progress; there will be nothing to check the fertility of inferior stock; the relentless law of heredity will not be controlled and guided by natural selection."

at a Diocesan conference, " the time when we must sink to a second-rate power was not by any means so distant as people imagined. Forty years might be given as the value of English authority if the diminution continues." [1]

But why had the birth rate fallen? The historian cannot neglect this important though perplexing question.

A recent writer has quoted a letter of Queen Victoria to her uncle Leopold.[2] Written in 1841, this is a *cri de cœur* which one is surprised to find so early in the century. " I think, dearest Uncle," she writes, " you cannot *really* wish me to be the ' maman d'une nombreuse famille,' for I think you will see with me the great inconvenience a *large* family would be to us all, and particularly to the country, independent of the hardship and inconvenience to myself. Men never think, at least seldom think, what a hard task it is for us women to go through this *very often*." [3]

The underlining which always expressed agitation in the royal breast is to be noted; also the grounds on which the Queen argues against a large family. First, the financial, because of course " the great inconvenience . . . particularly to the country " would be in their having to provide family allowances for those expensive luxuries, the younger children of the monarch; and secondly the burden of childbirth on herself.

If this letter could be considered in isolation it would be possible to form a picture of a change of opinion at Buckingham Palace gradually influencing the nation, first through the Court, and then through the matrons of the middle class, who took their cue in so many matters of fashion and thought from the Queen. It is however necessary to point out that Victoria gave birth to nine children in less than sixteen years, a performance which is an eloquent fact, and in striking contrast to the situation at the Imperial Court in Paris, where Napoleon III and Eugénie faced the problems of an only child.

But we must go further. If the year in which the letter was written is significant, the precise date also should be noted, 5th January 1841.

[1] Bishop of Ripon quoted in *Eugenics Review*, Vol. 1, 221.
[2] A. M. Carr Saunders, *World Population*, 109, 110.
[3] The letter is to be found in *Queen Victoria's Letters*, Vol. 1, 321.

Victoria had married on Monday, 10th February 1840. The nation at once speculated on when she would become a mother. Greville was alarmed to notice that " she and Prince Albert were up very early on Tuesday morning, walking about, which is very contrary to her former habits. Strange that a bridal night should be so short, and I told Lady Palmerston that this was not the way to provide us with a Prince of Wales." [1]

On 21st November 1840 the Queen's first child was born, the later Empress Frederick, and the letter of 5th January 1841 was therefore written at a time when mothers normally resolve not to go through their ordeal again. It cannot therefore be taken as the considered opinion of Queen Victoria. Indeed only a month later the future King Edward VII was conceived, the birth taking place on 9th November 1841.

But if too much stress must not be laid on this letter, in view of the circumstances in which it was written, the first ground on which the Queen rested her argument is worth attention: the expense of a large family.

The nineteenth century saw a vast accumulation of capital, and the addition to the landed gentry of a considerable middle class. For both the marriage settlement was an essential preliminary to matrimony. Late weddings were frequent for this section of the community. Evelyn Baring, the future Lord Cromer, then an army officer, fell in love with Miss Errington when he was 21. His private resources, with the addition of his army pay, gave him an income of £400 a year. " Marriage on this pittance," remarks his biographer, " was clearly out of the question; what then was he to do? Neither of them doubted; he would work and she would wait." He worked and she waited for fourteen years, and the marriage seems only to have taken place then (with Baring now 35), because the girl's father had died and left her a small income.[2] The case is an extreme one. The proportion of the population who would have considered £400 a year a " pittance " was not large (the average earning of men over 20 in the Cotton industry was under £80 a year), but [3] among the aristocracy and a large section of the middle class, marriage had to wait while

---

[1] *Greville Diary*, 13th Feb. 1840.
[2] Marquess of Zetland, *Lord Cromer*, 33, 54.
[3] *Earnings and Hours Enquiry*, Report 1, Textile Trades, xv. Cd. 4545, 1909.

wealth accumulated, and late marriages usually mean small families.[1]

Even while economic progress continued unchecked for these groups, the multiplication of purchasable amenities and opportunities, in an unequal and competitive society, was affecting their birth rate, which began to decline in the eighteen-sixties.[2] And then economic progress was halted. The arrival of the wheat of the American prairies in the seventies, coinciding with two successive bad harvests, lopped the profits of the landed gentry. Foreign competition threatened ever more severely Britain's industrial monopoly. Cyclical trade depression deepened. " The beneficent private war which makes one man strive to climb on the shoulders of another and remain there "[3] was leading inevitably to the ruin of many a private man of business and the rise of a small number of great economic empires.

Similarly in the new suburbs, where the increasing number of clerks (reflecting Britain's transformation from an industrial to a commercial society) made their homes, there was " limitation of the family pursued as a deliberate method of adjusting expenditure to income."[4] The birth rate of suburbia was below the average for urban areas.[5] On earnings often little more than those of the working class the clerk carried on the desperate struggle to achieve identification with the gentry. " It is intelligible," declared *The Times*, " that the growth of luxury in modern times should tend towards the limitation of families by reason of the desire of parents, from considerations either of selfishness or of prudence, to educate and maintain their children not only in their own rank but if possible in one somewhat in advance of it."

The new fashion in smaller families spread, as is usual in a class society, from the top downwards, with similar economic pressures producing similar results. An unequal and competitive

[1] Cd. 5263, 1910, 52. " The number of minors to 100 marriages has declined among husbands from 8 in 1876–80 to 4 in 1908, and has declined among wives from 22 in 1876–80 to 14 in 1908."

[2] *Census*, 1911, Vol. 13. T. H. C. Stevenson, " The fertility of various social classes in England and Wales from the middle of the nineteenth century to 1911." Royal Statistical Society, 1920.

[3] Sir H. Maine, *Popular Government*. Quoted by S. Webb, " The Difficulties of Individualism," *Economic Journal*, June 1891.

[4] C. F. G. Masterman, *The Condition of England*, 85.

[5] *Cost of Living of the Working Classes.* Cd. 3864, 1908, 173.

society in a competitive world, producing increasing quantities of purchasable amenities and opportunities, presented desperate choices. The charge of selfishness should not be made against the people of this time. The equipment of children for the struggle of life required greater sacrifices from parents than ever before. A chance for one child in a family might disappear if another was added. Later historians will surely declare that it was not the wish for greater amenities that was at fault, but the society which, while producing these amenities, was incapable of making them available on equal terms.

CHAPTER IV

THE STATE OF THE NATION

Mortality rates had fallen in Britain during the last quarter of the nineteenth century, and the expectation of life for males was about 44 years at birth in 1901, and for females slightly higher. In the same year the expectation of life in India was 26,[1] a figure which was probably equalled in other parts of the coloured Empire, but statistics are not available in many of the territories, even of the precise numbers of the population, a fact in significant contrast to the careful surveys of trade prospects and foreign competition carried out under the direction of Mr. Joseph Chamberlain by the Colonial Office.[2]

Infant mortality had not shown the same improvement. In Durham and Northumberland one out of every 30 infants died within seven days of birth.[3] It had remained almost stationary for fifty years;[4] but now startling events were to occur. In 1899 the first English milk dispensary had been opened at St. Helens.[5] In 1901 Liverpool established milk depots for infants whom their mothers were unable to feed.[6] In 1907 the first Infant Welfare centre was opened at St. Pancras, while at about the same time in Birmingham " to combat the mortality among infants during the hot weather, cards containing medical directions as to their care were circulated in the artisan districts and posters were affixed to the walls of courts." [7] It was not an easy campaign. " Attempts to reduce infant mortality were regarded by many as

---

[1] *General Report of the Census of India, 1901.* Cd. 2047, 1904, 479.

[2] See *Trade of the British Empire and Foreign Competition, Despatch from Mr. Chamberlain, 28th Nov. 1895, to the Governors of Colonies and the High Commissioner of Cyprus, and the replies thereto.* Cd. 8449, 1897.

[3] *Thirty-ninth annual report of Local Government Board, 1909–10. Supplement to the report of the Board's Medical Officer containing a report by the Medical Officer on Infant and Child Mortality.* Cd. 5263, 1910, 19.

[4] J. H. Clapham, *An Economic History of Modern Britain,* Vol. 3, 452.

[5] Ibid., 438.

[6] Ibid., 438.

[7] Ibid., 438.

an interference with natural selection, which must be inimical to the average health of those surviving. According to this school of thought efforts to save infant life merely prevent the weeding out of the unfit and ensure the survival of an excessive proportion of weaklings "; but the little group of doctors and social workers, aided in their fight by a " quickening of the public conscience " due to the decline in the birth rate, triumphed over all obstacles, and between 1900 and 1910 the infant mortality rate in England and Wales fell by one-third.[1]

Recruiting for the Boer War had revealed an alarming number of unfit among the applicants.[2] Those who knew the Elementary schools were aware that many of the children were too badly nourished to profit by the education they received,[3] in classes which averaged over 50 pupils even under the progressive London Board.[4] The surveys of Charles Booth in London and Rowntree in York had reached remarkable agreement in their estimate of the number of persons living in conditions of poverty, measured by a far from generous standard of human needs: nearly one-third.[5]

The Booth and Rowntree surveys were the more formidable for their lack of bias. They provided facts, which were not easily brushed aside as *ex parte* statements on the Condition of the People. *The Times* in its attack was compelled to a less direct approach. " The impatience with the imperfections of the Social Order," it declared, " which Mr. Rowntree expresses and in a great degree justifies, while it is the salt of public life, is apt to be mischievous if it merely prompts to hasty action and is not restrained by a sense of the slow operation of truly effective reforms and the might of self-help." [6]

The Booth and Rowntree approach was scientific. They related the realities of existence to the needs of a happy and a healthy life. From the moment of the publication of these surveys

[1] Cd. 5263, 1910, 9. (For a statement of the opposition to the campaign see Karl Pearson, *Social Problems: their treatment, past, present and future*. Lecture, 19th March 1912.)
[2] See Reports of Director-General of Recruiting.
[3] See Reports of the Board's Inspectors, e.g. H.M.I. Eicholz.
[4] *New Survey of London Life and Labour*, Vol. 1, 264.
[5] C. Booth, *London Life and Labour*. B. S. Rowntree, *Poverty, a study of Town Life*, London 30·7%, York 27·84%.
[6] *The Times*, 23rd Aug. 1902.

the Economic and Social system was put on the defensive. The cobwebs of Victorian complacency were blown away. Those who came after have but improved the weapon and extended the field; for this is not a method that can be applied only to the United Kingdom.

During the reign Mr. Chiozza Money followed up the attack, more deliberately, by an analysis in popular language of the distribution of the National Wealth. Almost half the total income he found went to a ninth of the population, more than one-third to a thirtieth. Half the capital of the country belonged to one-seventieth of the citizens. These facts he claimed were the explanation of the findings of Booth and Rowntree.[2]

The Britain therefore whose throne Edward VII ascended was a country in which more than one-quarter of the population lived in want, and in which the distribution of the national income and the ownership of capital was most uneven. It was also a country in which Social Services were practically unknown. Elementary Education there had been since 1870, free after 1891. There was too a Poor Law, based on a philosophy which attributed poverty to moral failure. But there was no National Health Insurance, no Unemployment Insurance, no Old Age Pension. Indirect taxes still amounted to half the total revenue, a heavy burden on the poor. On the rich taxation weighed lightly, and, relatively to the rich, heavily on the intermediate class. Income tax after abatements reached a maximum rate of 1s. on all incomes over £700 a year. There was no sur-tax or super-tax. The Death Duties introduced by Sir William Harcourt in 1894 were only a portent, since deceased millionaires, who, as Mr. Gladstone had remarked, couldn't take their wealth with them, still contributed only 8% of their total estate, and when Mr. Philip Snowden declared that a Socialist budget would include a rate of 50% for such aggregates[3] he was considered a dangerous lunatic. Meanwhile in the last two years of the Queen's reign 21 millionaires, moving their

[1] L. Chiozza Money, *Riches and Poverty*, 1905. Ten editions were published by 1910.
[2] See A. L. Bowley, *Wages and Income in the United Kingdom since 1860*; also the same author's *The Change in the Distribution of the National Income, 1880–1913*. Money's estimates are broadly confirmed.
[3] P. Snowden, *The Socialist Budget*, 1907, 81.

domicile from this earth, left between them nearly forty-two million pounds, of which the nation received not much more than three.[1]

The occupations of the people were the occupations of an industrial nation in the process of a new transformation. Agriculture languished. In 1851 of every hundred males over 10 nineteen worked on the land. In 1901 the number was only six. Since the grain of the Western Prairies had become available in the seventies the wheat area had been halved, and the nine hundred thousand men still working on the land were among the lowest earners in the country, with a weekly wage of perhaps 16s.[2] Among the larger increases shown by the 1901 Census, however, was a 20% rise in the number of Gamekeepers, who now numbered nearly 17,000.

Large quantities of food were imported. Four-fifths of the wheat, two-thirds of the eggs, one-half of the mutton and lamb and of the pig's meat, two-fifths of the butter, the beef and the veal, and the barley, one-fifth of the cheese and the oats.[3]

Britain remained a great industrial nation, although there were now anxieties about the future. Already in 1883 Mr. Inglis Palgrave, the President of the Economic section of the British Association, had expressed the view that " the country might almost be said to be entering the non-progressive state." [4] In 1888 Lord Goschen, then Chancellor of the Exchequer, remarked in his Rectorial address at Aberdeen University: " Our position in the race of civilized nations is no longer what it has been. We have had a great start in industry and commerce, and by virtue of that start we have attained to a station of unprecedented and long unchallenged supremacy. That supremacy is no longer unchallenged. Others are pressing on our heels." [5]

An increasing number of the population were finding employment as commercial clerks. The Census figures of England and Wales show a 47% increase between 1891 and 1901, and a further 31% by 1911. In the same periods the population grew by only

[1] Snowden, *op. cit.*, 55.
[2] Clapham, *op. cit.*, Vol. 3, 97.
[3] Ibid., 119.
[4] Quoted by F. Engels, 1892, Preface to *The Condition of the Working Class in England in 1844.*
[5] Hon. A. D. Elliot, *Lord Goschen*, Vol. 2, 253.

12% and 10%. This increased clerical employment, the mark of the new economic status of Britain, was more significant than the natural growth in the number of those occupied in Public Utilities, Chemicals, and in the new Electrical industry. Women particularly participated. In the last decade of Victoria's reign the proportion of female clerks had grown from eight in every hundred to eighteen, and by 1911 the number was to be thirty-two. The typewriter had arrived and the telephone, and with them the typist and the telephone girl. Nor was the clerical occupation the only new work opened to women. By 1901 there were already 212 doctors and 140 dentists. Teaching was becoming more and more a woman's profession. When Edward VII was crowned there were already three women teachers to every male. There were even 2 female accountants in 1901, 223 behind the counter of the banks (although a long way behind), and 382 commercial travellers. The 54 female chimney-sweeps of 1901 would seem to have been mostly relicts; at least the profession did not continue to attract women, the number falling to 32 by the end of the reign. In the Potteries it was noted that women were " now actively in competition with male labour, and as they are able to do similar work for lower wages they are gradually driving men from certain sections of the trade." [1] In the watchmaking trade at Coventry, where boys would not " serve the required apprenticeship seeing that they can earn much more in the cycle and motor factories, where apprenticeship is not required, girls were taken from school to learn watchmaking, beginning at a wage of about 4s. per week and earning 16s. by the time they are 24 years old." [2]

Women's labour was cheap. Although the Trades Union Congress had resolved as long ago as 1888 that " where women do the same work as men they shall receive equal pay," [3] the pronounced difference was maintained, and it was partly as cheap labour that women pushed open the door of more extensive employment. The Prudential Life Assurance Company began in 1872 to substitute women clerks for the lower grades of men clerks, at about half the wages paid to men, and the substitution

[1] *Cost of Living of the Working Classes.* Cd. 3864, 1908, 441.
[2] Cd. 3864, 1908, 160.
[3] B. Drake, *Women in Trade Unions*, 227.

31

was found profitable, in spite of an absence through sickness twice as frequent as that of the higher paid men.[1]

But it was not only their cheapness which recommended the women to the keen employer, but their " docility and want of combination." Women struck less, " a fact recorded, at the time, of the negro in the manufacturing districts of the Southern States of the U.S.A." [2] " Trade Unionism means rebellion, and the orthodox teaching to the woman was of submission." Further, as Will Thorne remarked: " When a man has done his day's work he becomes free, and that is not so with women." [3] But it is to be noted that trade-union organization was always difficult among low-paid workers, so that " docility " must not be completely separated from " cheapness." Food manufacturing (including cocoa and chocolate,[4] where the total workers more than doubled in the Edwardian decade) drew on large numbers of women; also the Catering trade, which extended even more considerably under the impetus of improving transport. But, if these new forms of employment received women, the old established industries of Textiles and Dressmaking continued to be the main form of women's work outside their own or other people's homes.

The domestic industry employed one-third of the occupied female population. It was probably not only the largest women's industry, but the largest single industry for either men or women.[5] But the situation was changing as alternative forms of employment became available. Between 1881 and 1901 the number of female domestics had it is true increased by 8%, but the population had grown by 25%. Worse still, there was evidence that the young women were seeking other forms of employment. " It is probable that London servant girls of fair intelligence," warned a writer in the *Quarterly Review* in July 1895, " will not for long consent to spend their days in cellar chambers and their nights in . . . inhuman attics. . . . Women of the middle class, who need domestic

[1] B. Webb, *Women's Wages*. Paper read to Economic Section of British Association, 1891, printed in *Problems of Modern Industry*. She suggested that women might work better if they ate more. But how could they on their wages?
[2] B. Webb, *op. cit.*   [3] B. Drake, *op. cit.*, 41.
[4] The production of cocoa in the Gold Coast rose from 1,200,794 lb. in 1900 to 50,692,949 lb. in 1910; and in Nigeria from 452,689 lb. to 6,567,181 lb.
[5] Miss C. Collet, *Report on the Money Wages of Indoor Domestic Servants.* Cd. 9346, 1899.

help, had better therefore become wise in time." In the Census of 1901 the phrase " standard of comfort " was coined, which was stated to be the number of female domestic servants to 100 separate occupiers or families (excluding hotels). But what if the women refused to support the comfort standard? Lord Esher, faced by a domestic revolt in his household, was moved to inquire: " Are we going up or downhill as a nation?" [1]

The figures showed remarkable differences in the " standard of comfort " within the United Kingdom. In Hampstead there were 80 female domestics to every hundred separate occupiers. In Oxford the number was 33; in Rochdale only 7; and in Oswaldtwistle less than 3. The average for England and Wales was 18. The unwillingness of the young woman to enter domestic service led to an increasing employment of males by those who could afford them, and in Westminster there were over 12 man-servants per hundred occupiers.

For a butler more than £58 per annum might be paid. The average for a female domestic was about £18 in London and rather less in the rest of the country; but for a girl of under 16 a wage of under £8 was normal, and even at 19 little more than £14. [2]

In London, of the families keeping servants in 1891 not quite half had more than one servant and nearly one-tenth had more than three. [3] Such figures are of important social significance, and illustrate the inequality of the comfort standard within the group of those who had attained it.

The housing conditions were mostly unsuitable, but working conditions were improving, as servants became more and more difficult to obtain (the average length of service based on the inquiry of 1891 was three years). Holidays were variable, rising to a maximum of " a fortnight in summer, one day monthly, half-day every Sunday, evening out weekly." [4]

The hours of work in factories were on the average 55 hours a week, with longer hours worked in many trades not covered by the Factory Acts. [5] The miners worked a nine-hour shift, and their agitation for the eight-hour day was resisted with the arguments of bankruptcy customarily used by employers, and most particularly by coal-owners.

---

[1] Esher, *Journals*, Vol. 2, 310.　　[2] Collet, *op. cit.*　　[3] Collet, *op. cit.*
[4] Collet, *op. cit.*　　[5] *Earnings and Hours Enquiry.* Cd. 4545, 1909.

Holidays with pay were practically unknown except for fore-men and those on a standing wage. What was the annual holiday for the wage-earner? The Factory and Workshop Act of 1901 gave six whole days to women and those under eighteen—a clear sign that the minimum was not being generally reached. It may be accepted as a reasonable estimate that the average for *all* workers was about ten days.[1] The decrease in working hours, particularly for women and children, during the nineteenth century appears in statistics and is noted by the historian. What statistics do not reveal is the effect of " speeding up " and com-petition on the general conditions of the workers.[2] The Editor of the Census of India, 1901, arguing a different case, thus commented on the relative rareness of mental disease in India with a population seven times as great as that of Britain, but with only one person of unsound mind to thirteen at the Empire's centre: " the main reason is doubtless to be found in the very different conditions of life in the East. In Europe the competition between man and man is severe, and is yearly becoming more so. The mental wear and tear is very great, and the strain on the nervous system deranges many feeble intellects, which in the calm and placid East would escape the storms to which they succumb." [3] The Registrar-General for England and Wales had written in 1885 of " the increasing severity of competition among adults. That the struggle for existence is daily becoming more and more severe and that feverish excitement and reckless expenditure of energy are rapidly encroaching on repose and leisure are matters of common obser-vation." [4] Herbert Samuel in his book *Liberalism*, published in 1902, with an introduction by Mr. Asquith, declared with emphasis: " if the hours of labour are shorter, the labour itself is more intense. If there is more leisure, work is more monotonous, . . . the worker has to keep pace with the machine; he is often subject to a more tiring strain; at an earlier age his powers become unequal to the demand made on them, and a man is dismissed as superannuated at a time of life when the easier conditions of the past would have regarded him as still in his prime. The greater intensity of labour has made the difficulties of old age far more

[1] *Earnings and Hours Enquiry*, Cd. 4545, 1909.
[2] B. L. Hutchins, *Women in Modern Industry*, 110, 184.
[3] *Census of India*, 1901. Cd. 2074, 1904, 133, 134.
[4] Quoted by R. and K. Titmuss, *Parents' Revolt*, 58.

acute." W. J. Davis (Brassworkers), in his Presidential Address to the Labour Representation Committee Conference in February 1902, remarked that " men are now thought to get older sooner than years ago " and referred to the " wrong side of 45." The decrease in working hours did not mean unqualified improvement in the lot of the working class.

What were the earnings in Edwardian Britain? To assess them it it necessary to adopt a standard of subsistence. Rowntree, in his survey of York in 1899, found that the minimum required to maintain in a state of physical efficiency a family of two adults and three children was 21s. 8d., or if there were four children 26s.[1] A family existing on this scale " must never spend a penny on railway fare or omnibus. They must never purchase a half-penny newspaper, or spend a penny to buy a ticket for a popular concert. They must write no letters to absent children, for they cannot afford to pay the postage. They must never contribute anything to their church or chapel, or give any help to a neigh-bour, which costs them money. They cannot save nor join sick-club or Trade Union, because they cannot pay the necessary subscriptions. The children must have no pocket money for dolls, marbles or sweets. The father must smoke no tobacco, and must drink no beer. The mother must never buy any pretty clothes for herself or for her children, the character of the family wardrobe as for the family diet being governed by the regulation: ' nothing must be bought but that which is absolutely necessary ' for the maintenance of physical health, and what is bought must be of the plainest and most economical description. Should a child fall ill it must be attended by the parish doctor; should it die it must be buried by the parish. Finally the wage-earner must never be absent from his work for a single day." [2]

The Government's Earnings and Hours Enquiry of 1906 showed that in the cotton industry the average weekly wage for males over 20 was 29s. 6d., and in jute 21s. 7d. with nearly half of those employed earning under 20s. In the clothing trades men averaged 30s. 2d.; in Public Utilities 28s. 1d. The agricultural labourer may have received 20s., when the value of pay in kind is taken into account. In engineering and boiler-making the average was 32s. 5d.; in shipbuilding 35s. 11d. The earnings of

[1] Rowntree, *op. cit.*   [2] Rowntree, *op. cit.*

women were of course on a lower scale. In the cotton industry the average for women over 18 was 18s. 6d., with nearly a quarter below 15s., but this was a well-paid occupation. In the clothing trades two-thirds of the women employed earned less than 15s. a week. In silk the average was 11s. 2d., with nearly 40% below 10s.

The combination of Rowntree's minimum scale of subsistence, of Rowntree's picture of life on this minimum, and of the official earnings figures gives in broad outline the money conditions of the working class.[1] The majority at any one time were above the minimum scale, but few indeed were above it all their lives; the margin was never enough to allow for the accidents of life, for the failure of ordinary folk to spend their money as prudently as experts thought they should, for the recurrent spells of unemployment. What a great gulf of experience lay between the wage-earner with his 20–30s. a week and those who were paying 1s. in the pound income tax on incomes of £12–£13 and more.

Real wages had risen during the latter part of the nineteenth century, and were now perhaps 50% higher than in 1850. The reign of Edward VII was to see the end of this rise, the rate remaining stationary, and perhaps declining.[2]

The ugly towns built during the reign of Queen Victoria, which had led Ruskin to declare: " The two most frightful things I have ever yet seen in my life are the south-eastern suburbs of Bradford, and the scene from Wakefield Bridge by the chapel," [3] remained as a legacy for Edwardian Britain. The statistics suggested that overcrowding was less than it had been, though there were still black spots in such cities as London, Gateshead, Newcastle-upon-Tyne, South Shields and Devonport, and particularly north of the Tweed.[4] Will Crooks was understood when he told a working-class audience: " They say: don't you know you belong to an Empire on which the sun never sets? . . . what's the good

---

[1] Those with incomes below 30s. were estimated to spend two-thirds on food. *Cost of Living of Working Classes*, B.O.T. report. Cd. 3864, 1908.
[2] Clapham, *op. cit.*, Vol. 3, 466. Cf. J. Kuczynski, *A Short History of Labour Conditions in Great Britain and the Empire from 1750 to the present day.*
[3] Quoted by C. F. G. Masterman, *The Condition of England*, 110.
[4] *Census of England and Wales*, 1901. Cd. 2174, 1904, 37, 38. In Finsbury over one-third of the people were living in overcrowded conditions, i.e. more than 2 per room.

of talking like that? Why, the sun never rises on our court."[1] Sanitary improvement was proceeding unevenly. At Liverpool and Coventry water-closets were to be found in most houses by the beginning of the century, but in Bradford only in 9000. At Burton-on-Trent house sewerage was largely non-existent. At Blackburn and Wigan less than half the houses had water-closets, and enteric fever and diarrhœa were rife, the latter a potent cause of infantile mortality.[2]

Transport was undergoing a new transformation. The railways were reaching the end of their development, and the last improvements were being made. The London and North-Western lit its principal trains with electricity in 1895. In 1899 the Cornish express of the Great Western received a luncheon car. With the new century metal footwarmers were gradually being replaced. In 1904 the North-Eastern introduced automatic signalling.[3] But in March 1901 *Punch* was suggesting a new form of taxation: " For every motor car £4. 4s. 0d. If with smell £5. 5s. 0d. Extra offensive smell £6. 6s. 0d. Motor car proceeding at over ten miles an hour, for each additional mile £1. 1s. 0d." [4]

Already in 1901 King Edward made the journey from Windsor to London in an hour by car,[5] and there were 623 professional drivers registered in the Census. In London five persons were killed in motor accidents, and the horse had soon to yield to the new machine in lethal efficiency. In 1901 one hundred and seventy five people were killed in horse accidents in London; by 1911 the annual figure had fallen to 116, while the motor car accounted for 291.[6] The horse was passing from the roads, and the reign saw the introduction of the motor bus. The motor car remained a monopoly of the rich.[7] Rolls-Royce was founded in 1906. It was suggested that " a large proportion of those who have employed motor cars in habitual violation of the speed limit and in destruction of the amenities of the rural life of England have done

[1] Quoted by Masterman, *op. cit.*, 147.
[2] *Cost of Living of the Working Classes.* Cd. 3864, 1908, 95, 109, 163, 279, 483.
[3] Clapham, *op. cit.*, Vol. 3, 349–51.
[4] *Punch*, 20th March 1901.
[5] *Annual Register*, 1901.
[6] *New Survey of London Life and Labour*, Vol. 1, 312.
[7] It is, however, worth noting that W. Crooks in his memorable election at Woolwich in 1903 was assisted by forty motors, presumably Liberal support. *The Times*, 11th March 1903.

so, either because their neighbours have employed motor cars, or because their neighbours have not employed motor cars." [1]

But although criticism of the motor car was now being voiced (a member of parliament complained that " harmless men, women and children, dogs and cattle, had all got to fly for their lives at the bidding of one of these slaughtering, stinking engines of iniquity "), it is interesting to note that it was of the bicycle that the novelist Ouida was thinking when in 1900 she declared: " Man has created for himself in the iron beast a greater tyrant than any Nero or Caligula. . . . The helot of Greece, the gladiator of Rome, the swashbuckler of medieval Europe . . . were dignity, purity, courage in person beside the Cad of this breaking dawn of the twentieth century; the Cad rushing on with his shrill scream of laughter as he knocks down the feeble woman or the yearling child, and making life and death and all eternity seem ridiculous by the mere existence of his own intolerable fatuity and bestiality." [2]

Drink, particularly beer, stronger than the following generation obtained and relatively cheap, remained the chief recreational expenditure of the working class.[3] The Cinema was still a curiosity. Broadcasting had twenty more years in the womb of time, although in December 1901 Marconi succeeded in transmitting a message across the Atlantic from Poldhu, Cornwall. But professional football was attracting increasing crowds. In 1902 the last hour of Saturday's work was cut off " so that the men could attend football matches." [4] The case of a young lad, who, knowing that he would soon die, had used his last energies to attend a cup final, and in place of the *sacramentum mortis* had asked to kiss the colours of the Sheffield Wednesday club, was much discussed, and received unfavourable criticism. It was asked " whether that congestion of grey small people with their facile excitements and their little white faces inflamed by this artificial interest " would " in a day of trial " show " tenacity, courage and an unwearying devotion to an impersonal ideal?" [5]

[1] Masterman, *op. cit.*, 23. See criticism in *Spectator*, 5th June 1909, 896–7.
[2] Y. French, *Ouida, a study in ostentation*, 144. Kipling's story, *The village that voted the earth was flat*, in which a favourable attitude to the motorist is taken, was written in 1913.
[3] Rowntree, *op. cit.*
[4] Bowley, *Wages and Income in the United Kingdom since 1860*, 25.
[5] Masterman, *op. cit.*, 132, 133.

Attendance at Church had fallen in all classes, an increasing proportion of the population being not so much hostile to organized religion as indifferent.[1] The Churches, however, remained important political pressure groups.

Interest in the world to come was steadily giving way before interest in the world in which people lived. This applied to all classes, and by the working class increasing interest was particularly being directed to the problem of Unemployment, which was presented session after session to Parliament by Keir Hardie, whose cloth cap had shocked the last Gladstonian parliament, and was the symbol of a new era.

[1] E. Halévy, *History of the English People. Epilogue.*

CHAPTER V

POLITICS AND THE PEOPLE

Only males had the vote in Edwardian Britain. The House of Lords could still reject bills passed by the Commons, and did. According to Lord Spencer, the Liberal leader in the " gilded chamber," [1] it could even reject the Budget, though it could not amend it; [2] but this interpretation was not universally accepted, even by his fellow-peers, and the power of the purse was generally held to rest with what was with some appropriateness still called the lower house.

Members of Parliament were unpaid, a fact of considerable importance in an unequal society. It is significant that Britain and Germany, both with strong working-class movements threatening the men in possession, were to be among the last European countries to pay their Members. [3]

Power in Britain was stated by the text-books to lie with the King in Parliament, but the definition is inadequate. So much of the decision that affected people's lives lay outside the accepted province of Government, and private enterprise remained the general pattern of industry. Although Chamberlain had declared in 1891 that " the State is justified in any law, or even in doing a single act, which in its ulterior consequences adds to the sum of human happiness," [4] Victorian individualism died hard, and the sum of human happiness was added up differently in Park Lane and in the one-roomed house at Legbrannock, in which Keir Hardie was born. The Bank of England continued its autonomous career,

---

[1] E. Harford (General Secretary of the Amalgamated Society of Railway Servants), 1894: " It is a golden rule that no workman ever enters the precincts of that gilded chamber." *Liberal Monthly*, July 1894, 208.

[2] House of Lords, 29th July 1904.

[3] France had paid members since 1875. An appendix to the *Report of the Labour Representation Conference*, 1903, lists Austria, Belgium, Holland, Switzerland, Denmark and Sweden as paying members; also many of the self-governing colonies.

[4] Clapham, *op. cit.*, Vol. 3, 397.

framing its policies according to the unquestioned rules of the Gold Standard. The Press, now becoming popular in the sense of cheap,[1] expressed the views of a few individuals or of limited groups. The uneven distribution of wealth permitted the existence of a ruling class.

The stratification of British society was complex. The income figures can be divided in many different ways. The existence of a ruling class is reflected in the presence in society of a group, with a separate educational system, a different " standard of comfort " through the keeping of servants, and a power over the lives of the rest of the nation, which found expression in a variety of ways perhaps symbolized most simply by the fact of sometimes a small number, sometimes a large, calling them " Sir." Its roots were in the over £13 a week group, with some addition from the inter-mediate group according to the number of dependents over which the income was spread.[2]

This ruling class was not a caste. Entry was possible to the possessor of exceptional attainments of the appropriate type. New entrants were absorbed, so that although the structure of the ruling class was in itself complex (no such victory over the landowners by the industrialists had been won as the annihilation of the plantation owners in the American civil war) the group was held together by a self-interest which, except under unusual stress, preserved effective harmony.

The Edwardian period was to provide an instance of such a stress. The Lloyd George budget of 1909, and the subsequent House of Lords controversy, led to such disharmony within the ruling class that adherents of the two opposed sections would not sit down at meat with each other. It is when the ruling class splits that the mass of the people makes its advances.

For the ruling class it was an age of conspicuous expenditure. Professor Bowley attributes " the increase of luxury and abundance of wealth, which many people believed they observed . . . to illusions fostered by the newspapers," to " diversion from other objects to the motor car . . . and to the possibility that wealth was passing into the possession of persons who enjoyed ostentatious

[1] In another sense far from cheap. Bernard Shaw complained that " it costs a quarter of a million to start a London daily paper with any chance of success." Preface to *Fabian Essays*, 1908.
[2] See Bowley and Money, *op. cit.*

expenditure." [1]   Certainly the Stock Exchange users (a larger group than the members of the Stock Exchange, which reached its maximum numbers in 1905) [2] were inclined to spend freely on entertainment, particularly that section whose Kaffir share speculations were saved by the successful issue of the South African war and the introduction of cheap Chinese labour. Edward himself was a free spender. Lord Curzon thought £100,000 not an excessive charge upon the population of India for the Coronation Durbar; [3] and even a Liberal Prime Minister was said to have spent £1000 on flowers alone at one of his receptions. [4]

If the rich were not spending more money, they were certainly spending it more conspicuously, and the accent of the prophet Amos was heard in the land. " We have converted half of the Highlands into deer forests for our sport; and the amount annually spent on shooting, racing, golf, on apparatus and train journeys and service, exceeds the total revenue of many a European principality. We fling away in ugly white hotels, in uninspired dramatic entertainments and in elaborate banquets, of which everyone is weary, the price of many poor men's yearly income." The ruling class " can compete for the pictures of great masters, but it leaves the men of genius of its own day to starve. It continues now, as always, garnishing the sepulchres of the prophets which its predecessors have stoned. It maintains large country houses, which offer lavish hospitality; but it sees rural England crumbling into ruin just outside their boundaries. . . . It fills vast hotels, scattered round the coasts of England. . . . It has annexed whole regions abroad, Biarritz and the Riviera coast, Austrian and German watering-places, whither it journeys for the recovery of its lost health, and for distractions which will forbid the pain of thinking." Thus C. F. G. Masterman, a young Liberal of whom great things were expected; [5] but criticism was not confined to Liberals. George Wyndham, a rising star in the Conservative firmament, declared that " a life of polyglot restaurants and international

[1] *The Change in the Distribution of the National Income, 1880–1913*, 20.
[2] Clapham, *op. cit.*, Vol. 3, 295.
[3] Marquess of Zetland, *Lord Cromer*, Vol. 2, 232.
[4] Lord Rosebery, Prime Minister, 1894–5. See Elizabeth Haldane, *From one century to another*, 175. Sir G. Kekewich, Secretary of Education Department, 1890–1902, found that the cost per head at the banquet of a City Livery Company was £6. *The Education Department and after*, 136–7.
[5] Masterman, *op. cit.*, 26, 28.

sleeping cars does not conduce to civic virtue. It laps us in the listlessness of cosmopolitan luxury." [1]

Political action still largely found its outlet through the two historic parties, which so far had been able to adjust themselves sufficiently to changing conditions to prevent serious competition.

The Conservative party was still based on the landed interest and the Established Church. The important liquor influence had been added, and when Gladstone launched Home Rule, the party had been elastic enough to absorb Chamberlain, the Duke of Devonshire, and the other Liberal Unionists. The sanctity of the family was beginning to occupy a prominent place in the new Tory propaganda. Meals for school-children were declared to mean the destruction of the home, although as was pointed out in a Fabian Tract " the Eton or Harrow boy is kept at school not only for meals but for the whole of the term, yet no one fears for the home life of the plutocracy." [2]

The Conservative Campaign Guide of 1909 quotes approvingly Bishop Westcott: " The popular estimate of the family is an infallible criterion of the state of society. Heroes cannot save a country where the idea of the family is degraded; and strong battalions are of no avail against homes guarded by faith, reverence and love." [3] Progressive writers complained that " if it be a question of providing work for the unemployed, meals for children, pensions for the old; if it be a matter of municipal trams, municipal wash-houses, municipal dwellings, in every instance they raise the cry that the independence of the family is threatened, and exhort their friends to fight the measure to the death." [4] Socialism was equated with the breaking up of the family.

Research on the nature and ideology of the family is still required. One may indeed wonder whether the root of the new preoccupation, which had not been visible when the Industrial Revolution was indeed breaking up the family, did not reflect a threat to the national family with a ruling class in the role of the dominant father, and to the imperial family with the British people in a similar position.

[1] G. Wyndham, *The development of the state*, address to students of Glasgow University, Nov. 1904.
[2] Fabian Tract, 120, *After Bread, Education*.
[3] See article *Socialism*, 334 f.
[4] R. Bray, *The Town Child*, quoted by Masterman, 139.

The Liberal party had its root in the new manufacturing class produced by the Industrial Revolution; it had pushed aside with Free Trade, but it had not destroyed, the landed gentry. Its philosophy of Liberty had drawn to it all who felt themselves under-privileged. It derived important support, in a state with an Established Church, from the Nonconformists, who, at a time when organized religion still moved men to corporate action, supplied much of the party's driving force,[1] as well as the stern censorship of the Nonconformist conscience.[2]

But how long could the party preserve its broad base? Its wealthy industrialist supporters had obtained their objective. Only the power of an ideology that had lost its roots kept them in the Liberal fold, while their interests became more and more conservative. There remained the middle strata and the working class. The middle strata suffered taxation heavy in relation to that on the rich.[3] A policy of Social Reform would attract the working class; were it paid for largely by the rich the party would retain the support of the middle strata; could it be twisted against the landed gentry the party might be able to keep the Liberal industrialists in line. The circumstances of Edwardian Britain, its past development, and its existing wealth distribution and franchise, made just this issue possible, and preserved the Liberal party for its final achievement before its function was complete; a final achievement because now the working class had established its own party, and progressive political groupings founded on sectional interests are not illimitably elastic. Liberalism and Labour could march together against the Conservative foe. They could not coalesce. They sprang from different roots.

British democracy is generally held to rest on the Parliamentary system, but an important part of democracy depends on the possibility of people coming together in groups for the agitation of certain questions. Thus was slavery ended, thus the Corn

---

[1] Within the Methodist movement S. E. Keeble represented with considerable force and integrity Left Wing tendencies. See his *Industrial Daydreams*, 1896.

[2] " Sir Charles Dilke defied the Nonconformist Conscience and is a political outcast to-day. Parnell despised the Nonconformist Conscience and so destroyed himself and his party. Lord Rosebery ignored the Nonconformist Conscience for a racehorse, and all the world sees the result." *Methodist Times*, 15th October 1896. Quoted by M. Edwards, *Methodism and England: A study of Methodism in its social and political aspects during the period 1850–1932.*

[3] See article by H. Samuel, *Liberal Magazine, July* 1904.

Laws, by middle-class societies permitted to assemble and to press their cause. Similarly, after stern struggles, the working class formed its democratic groups: co-operative societies, trades councils, and most important of all, trade unions, in which the special interests of the working class, largely ignored by others, found expression. The total sales of the co-operative societies were not much more than £18,000,000 of co-operative-produced goods out of a total wage aggregate of perhaps £700,000,000.[1] The number of trade unionists was under 2,000,000, but the solidarity of the working class was growing, and with the new century a distinct political party with influential trade-union support had been formed.

It was not a Socialist party, although it contained some socialists, and some who called themselves socialists. It was not exclusively a working-class party, for it accepted middle-class elements, particularly from the Fabian Society. It was a Labour party, or, as it was then described, a Labour Representation Committee, designed to form " a distinct Labour Group in Parliament, who shall have their own whips, and agree upon their policy, which must embrace a readiness to co-operate with any party which, for the time being, may be engaged in promoting legislation in the direct interests of Labour, and may be equally ready to associate themselves with any party opposing measures having an opposite tendency." [2] It was based on some but not all of the trade unions, many of whose members were not yet convinced that the Liberal party would not adequately represent them in Parliament, and even more doubtful of the need for special representation at all. Only by accepting these facts could the party have been formed at this time, and Keir Hardie, perhaps the leading influence in its birth, was willing to pay the price of compromise and to keep Socialism from the party programme. The British Labour movement is still in mid-passage. Only when it has reached the further shore of a Socialist state can this decision be judged. Socialists

[1] P. Redfern, The Story of the C.W.S., 317. Clapham, op. cit., Vol. 3, 250, states that in the middle eighties £20,000,000 out of £480,000,000 wages was spent at the Co-ops. This figure includes of course goods not made by the C.W.S. He gives the 1911–3 figure as £80,000,000 out of £700,000,000 wages. Bowley, Wages and Income in the United Kingdom since 1860, 92, gives the wages total for 1906–10 as £753,000,000.

[2] Resolution moved by Keir Hardie at Labour Representation Conference, 27–28th February 1900, and carried. See report.

will probably consider that it was not the joining with non-Socialists that was the error, but the failure of the Socialists to preserve their own integrity. The dismal failure of the Social Democratic Federation over twenty years to win working-class support emphasized to Keir Hardie and his colleagues the necessity of bringing in the trade unions if the political Labour movement was to become effective; but perhaps if the S.D.F. had not been controlled by the dictatorial Hyndman, who had been educated at Trinity College, Cambridge, played cricket for Sussex, moved in London Society, and thought it good tactics for a working-class movement to accept election funds from the Conservatives, the failure might not have been so dismal.

British Socialism was opportunist. It rejected Marxism, and in particular " the class war " which " found its way into the general body of Socialist dogma quite simply. Marx saw that no proletarian movement could be created in Europe without some passion. . . . Those who still use it (the idea) are like those more backward religious communities, which express their theologies in the terms used before there was a science of geology. . . . The materialist conception of history is . . . in no way essential to the Socialist theory. . . . Socialism is a tendency, not a revealed dogma, and therefore it is modified in its forms of expression from generation to generation. . . . The Socialists of half a century ago lived when revolution was in the air in Europe and this coloured their statement of the Socialist position. The atmosphere has changed and so the colour has changed. . . . Like a dissolving view on a screen commercialism fades away and the image of Socialism comes out in clearer outline." [1]

Thus the considered opinion of J. Ramsay MacDonald, Secretary of the L.R.C.,[2] one of the Socialists whose task it was to permeate the Labour party with Socialism; Ramsay MacDonald, the first Labour Prime Minister. Philip Snowden, Chancellor of the Exchequer designate, had never read Marx.[3] For H. G. Wells " the advent of a strongly Socialist Government would mean no immediate revolutionary changes at all, . . . the constructive part

[1] J. Ramsay MacDonald, *The Socialist Movement*, 1911, xii, 99, 112, 146, 150, 195.

[2] Brocklehurst (I.L.P.) had suggested two secretaries. He was invited to serve, refused, and proposed MacDonald.

[3] P. Snowden, *Autobiography*.

of the Marxist programme was too slight. It has no psychology." [1]
The origin of Keir Hardie's Socialism was his strong religious
conviction,[2] and his experience in the working class, from
which, unlike MacDonald, he never divorced himself. These
kept him on a straight line to the end, but his influence waned
after the great achievement of the formation of the party, and
his lack of theory was never put seriously to the test of leadership.

Also hostile to Marxism among British Socialists at this time
were the members of the Fabian Society, whose descent was
from Bentham by way of John Stuart Mill.[3] One of their achievements, according to the Society's historian, was " breaking the
spell of Marxism "; [4] the view of an inevitable class war was
naturally unattractive to members of the middle class. They held
the opinion that Socialism was so obviously commonsensical that
propaganda would lead inevitably to its establishment without
the intervention of the working class.[5] On this basis a group of
first-class ability, most prominent among whom were Sidney and
Beatrice Webb, produced a remarkable body of sociological
material, not the least value of which was the standard of scientific
accuracy set to the Labour movement and indeed to all workers
in the field of social studies.

Such were the political tendencies of the Labour party, which
would compete with the Liberals for the votes of the working
class, and for power to carry out the Liberal policy of Social
Reform, but with this difference. The Liberals had no idea
where Social Reform would lead them. The British Socialists
believed that it would lead them to Socialism, and that, in the

[1] H. G. Wells, *New Worlds for Old*, 1908.
[2] " I myself have found in the Christianity of Christ the inspiration which
first of all drove me into the movement and has carried me on it yet." Quoted
by J. Clayton, *Rise and Decline of Socialism*, 73 n. Keir Hardie was addressing
the National Council of the Pleasant Sunday Afternoon and Brotherhood.
Thus too in his *From Serfdom to Socialism* he writes: " It would be an easy
task to show that Communism, the final goal of Socialism, is a form of Social
Economy very closely akin to the principles set forth in the Sermon on the
Mount," 36.
[3] " The Socialists are the Benthamites of this generation." S. Webb to
Fabian Society, 21st January 1894. Lecture, *Socialism true and false*, reprinted
in *Problems of Modern Industry*.
[4] Chapter heading, *The History of the Fabian Society*, E. R. Pease.
[5] See F. Engels to Sorge, 18th January 1893; also H. G. Wells, *Experiment
in Autobiography*, Vol. 1, 253.

words of Keir Hardie, " the world may wake up some morning to find that Socialism has come." [1]

But, when Edward began to reign, the L.R.C. was a sickly child. The election of 1900 had caught it only a few months after birth. The leaders of the historic parties had no sleepless nights, nor were the trade unions very proud of the brat that had been fathered on them. Only Keir Hardie and the unreliable Richard Bell had been elected of the thirteen candidates. The miners still fought in Liberal alliance, and John Burns at Battersea, the vain but terrific hero of the Dock Strike and the Trafalgar Square Riot, " with his voice of slightly modulated thunder and a nature as buoyant as a schoolboy's," [2] was ploughing the lonely furrow that led to the Liberal Cabinet of 1906.

More important in existing circumstances than the L.R.C. were the Irish Nationalists, whose solid strength of 80 members enabled them to hold the balance, whenever Tories and Liberals were near in numbers. The overwhelming victory of the Tories in the election of 1900, the " khaki " election of the Boer War, had for the moment robbed them of their maximum power, but it was still on them rather than on the new Labour party that the eyes of the political managers were fixed.

But fundamental in the electoral situation of Edwardian Britain was the contrast between the number of voters and the distribution of wealth. The electorate was now 6,700,000 males. These numbers are to be compared with the ten thousand incomes of over £13 a week, the nine hundred thousand incomes of between £3 and £13, and the remainder of under £3. Detailed statistical calculation would relate the figures with precision, but the broad picture is clear enough. Red herrings might for a while divert the attention of the electorate, but the inevitable pressure of the increased franchise would finally affect the distribution of wealth.

[1] Keir Hardie in *Nineteenth Century* after meeting of Second International in Amsterdam, 1904. Quoted by W. Stewart, *J. Keir Hardie: a Biography.*
[2] Keir Hardie, quoted by J. Clayton, *op. cit.*, 37.

CHAPTER VI

THE ECONOMIC TREND

Considerable changes were occurring in the economic position and organization of Britain. The structure of industry was being transformed. Starting with the Salt Union in 1888, which was said to control over 90% of the salt production of the United Kingdom, large-scale amalgamation had begun to replace free competition. The movement had started in the United States with the Rockefeller absorptions of the seventies, and once again Britain was following in the footsteps of America, from which she had adopted the limited liability company in the fifties. The textile section was particularly affected. Bleachers, Bradford Dyers, Calico Printers and Fine Cotton Spinners were formed in this period. Conditions approaching monopoly were reached by Wall Paper Manufacturers and Associated Portland Cement. The chain-store appeared, Joseph Lyons and International Tea and T. Lipton, among whose first shareholders, as Sir John Clapham has recorded, were Mr. Asquith, Lord Rothschild and the King's son-in-law, the Duke of Fife. The large business unit had arrived.[1]

Side by side and slightly in advance in point of time, Bank amalgamations proceeded with smooth efficiency.

But if competition was shrinking at home it was growing more intense abroad, and to Britain the first trading nation of the world, to Britain so largely dependent on imports of raw materials and foreign food, to Britain tenaciously clinging to a standard of life, which, however uneven, compared so favourably with that in any other part of the world, competition began to present menacing aspects.

At the opening of the century the British Tobacco companies came hurriedly together to meet a serious American threat to their market. The formation of the United States Steel Corporation by the Morgan interests, with an ancillary fleet of steamers bought

[1] J. H. Clapham, *op. cit.*, Vol. 3, 239.

from Britain, was so frightening to those in the seat of power that a subsidy was given to Cunard. German trade was ubiquitous, uncomfortably enterprising,[1] and unpleasantly concentrated on just those articles which Britain had previously monopolized; in the East the Japanese were beginning to threaten the British supremacy. From the Straits Settlements, Hong Kong and Australia (where in the State of Victoria one-third of the hand-kerchiefs were now made in Japan) warning of this new menace reached the Colonial Office in 1897.[2] It does not appear to have been taken into account when the Anglo-Japanese treaty was negotiated in 1901–2. The present perils were too urgent for eyes to range into the future.

For the British people had other problems than the distribution of their national income. Although they lived on an island, and, even after Blériot flew the Channel in 1909, still preserved much of their geographical security,[3] their rulers were now looking anxiously beyond the moat. Gone was the time when only a combination of France and Russia could frighten the Foreign Office. New Great Powers, countries with vast war potential, had appeared in the world. What was to be the policy of the British Government in the face of the new constellations of Germany and the United States?

Nor was it only a national and insular problem. Ever since 1870, when shortly after the outbreak of the Franco-Prussian war an urgent memorandum had reached London from New Zealand,[4] the problem of Imperial Defence had more and more exercised the British Government. Defence had been the final cause of Gladstone's retirement. Defence was to be the main problem of the new reign.

It was not only the threat of actual hostilities, but the threat of damage to the standard of life, that Britain faced. Those who attempt to separate politics and economics are arguing in a circle.

---

[1] When the Tariff Reform campaign was launched, a clockmaker in Bavaria produced a clock surmounted with a figure of Chamberlain making a speech, which emerged when the clock struck. Fitzroy, *op. cit.*, Vol 1, 170.

[2] Clapham, *op. cit.*, Vol. 3, 40.

[3] Sir Daniel Goddard, M.P., at T.U.C., Ipswich, September 1909, was prophetic: " He supposed there were some people who regarded the delegates as dangerous people, . . . as one of those modern aeroplanes hovering over some city and dropping murderous explosives on industrial places."

[4] *Cambridge History of British Empire*, Vol. 7, Part 2, 215.

By 1901 the population of U.S.A. was 79 millions and of Germany 57 millions. In an age when the large production unit was beginning to prove its superiority the figures were threatening. Both countries had overtaken the United Kingdom in the production of steel, and the United States now made three times as much as Britain and twice as much as Germany. It was significant that these results had been obtained from very different degrees of industrialization. Time was not on Britain's side. While only one-third of Americans now lived in urban areas, and half of Germans, the British figure was three-quarters. Her export trade, of which 60% was to foreign countries and 40% within the Empire, still touched new records with the summit of each trade cycle. In the export of manufactured goods she still led the world. But the rate of growth was less satisfactory. Between 1880–4 and 1900–4 British manufactures exported increased by only £18,000,000. The German increase in the period was £62,000,000 and the American £69,000,000; nor was it agreeable that while Britain exported 25% of her manufacturing output, the German proportion was 12 and the American only 4.

It is therefore not surprising that the editor of the Census of 1901, reflecting official opinion, preserved his most serious tone, not for the declining birth rate (that was a distant danger), not for the " standard of comfort," but for a decline in employment in the cotton industry, which provided one-quarter of the total exports.

The political significance of increasing competition did not pass unrecognized by respectable contemporary observers. Henry Cabot Lodge, writing to Theodore Roosevelt in March 1901, remarked: " We are putting a terrible pressure on Europe, and this situation may produce war at any time. The economic forces will not be the ostensible cause of the trouble but they will be the real cause, and no one can tell where the break will come." [1]

Balfour in March 1907 had a revealing conversation with Henry White, the American diplomat.

Balfour (somewhat lightly): We are probably fools not to find a reason for declaring war on Germany before she builds too many ships and takes away our trade.

[1] *Selections from the correspondence of Theodore Roosevelt and Henry Cabot Lodge, 1884–1918*, Vol. 1, 486–8.

White: You are a very high-minded man in private life. How can you possibly contemplate anything so politically immoral as provoking a war against a harmless nation which has as good a right to a navy as you have? If you wish to compete with German trade, work harder.

Balfour: That would mean lowering our standard of living. Perhaps it would be simpler to have a war.

White: I am shocked that you of all men should enunciate such principles.

Balfour (again lightly): Is it a question of right or wrong? Maybe it is just a question of keeping our supremacy.[1]

In September 1901 a leading article in *The Times*, which in July had declared Marxism to be " a spent intellectual force," informed its readers that " Germany is becoming a maritime power, not so much by choice, or as some people think by sheer ambition, but by the same compulsion as ourselves—by the irresistible compulsion of economic pressure." A memorandum prepared for the German Admiralty at the end of 1905 used similar language: " The duty of feeding and employing a steadily increasing population in such a manner as to raise the standard of living as far as possible throughout the community, and thereby to maintain and promote a healthy social development, can only be fulfilled by affording a properly extended protection to those important branches of economic activity which enable German capital and German labour to find profitable employment abroad, and especially in the countries beyond the seas." [2]

The triangular situation between Britain, Germany and the United States was a fundamental factor in the reign of Edward VII. Too much attention has been directed to the Anglo-German rivalry as an exclusive problem. The partnership in two Great wars has made it difficult for historians to stress the American threat to British supremacy. It is not only a question of historical truth. The misunderstanding of the past can destroy the present. Under a competitive economic system the friendships of Great Powers carry as their price the enmity of others. Great Britain was faced with a choice. The fact that on any analysis she chose

[1] A. Nevins, *Henry White: Thirty Years of American Diplomacy*, 256.
[2] E. L. Woodward, *Great Britain and the German Navy*, 118–9.

correctly does not alter the case. The interesting question is why the choice was made.

It has been often stated that American trade competition was as serious as German,[1] but this is not true of this period.[2] American competition neither covered so wide a range of articles, nor was it ubiquitous as was the German. American exports comprised many products such as timber, petroleum and agricultural machinery, which British business men did not market. It was in the territories nearest to the United States that American competition was most keen. In the Empire market, where foreign competition aroused particular wrath, the American was a far less serious competitor than the German.[3]

It was the goods " made in Germany " that were the bane of the British business man. Wherever he turned in the export market they pushed and hustled him; and the former monopoly position enjoyed by the British manufacturer made it difficult for him to adjust himself to conditions in which the customer had to be considered and his actual requirements taken in account. Small wonder that hostility to the German grew.

But if Britain was no longer " the workshop of the world," there were still powerful cards in her hand. In the changing circumstances the financial magnates became more important. They were able to promote British exports by capital investment. They could grant loans which would save governments from bankruptcy. Supported by the vast deposits of the British banking system, assisted according to the German industrialist Siemens by the possibility of issuing shares in London with a denomination as low as one pound, the Cassels and Revelstokes and Rothschilds took the centre of the stage. They enlisted the political support of the British investor. Sir Frank Mowat, a leading Civil Servant, declared that " the support and admiration of the vulgar rich of this country for Stock Exchange piracy . . . had made diplomacy

---

[1] E.g. E. Halévy, E. L. Woodward, W. J. Ashley.

[2] Cf. Henry Birchenough, *Some aspects of our Imperial Trade*, Paper read to Royal Colonial Society, 8th February 1898. *Proceedings*, Vol. 29, 105.

[3] In Cd. 8449 of 1897, *Trade of the British Empire and Foreign Competition*, there is a summary in which the principal countries competing are given (5, 6). Germany is mentioned 45 times, U.S.A. 12, and France 3. See also Sir Alfred Bateman, K.C.M.G., *Memorandum on the comparative statistics of population, industry and commerce in the United Kingdom and some leading foreign countries.* Cd. 1199, 1902.

impossible " at the time of the South African War.[1] The interest and commissions on foreign and colonial investment buttressed the standard of life, and all classes in Britain, though unevenly, benefited, accessories after the fact. How many ministers, how many members of parliament held gold shares during the Chinese labour controversy we do not know. A later age may consider the failure of the biographers of leading statesmen to reveal the sources of their heroes' wealth a significant reticence. (Can psychologists explain why Lord Lansdowne, disturbed at the fall of Delcassé, uses Stock Exchange metaphors in writing to his friends?) [2]

The link of finance with politics was extremely close. Lord Rothschild entertained statesmen of both the historic parties, but not of the Labour party. While Mr. Asquith dined with the King, his wife went off to the Leo Rothschilds for the week-end, and found there the Duke of Devonshire.[3] Lord Milner, giving a friend an example of a busy day during his leave from the Cape, started his engagement list with an hour with Rothschild in the City, and ended with a Royal audience at Windsor.[4] Balfour and Morley buried political opposition beneath the Rothschild table.[5] Haldane was " very intimate " with the family.[6] He was frequently offered Stock Exchange tips.[7] William Harcourt visited the Rothschild mansion at Tring and met there Cecil Rhodes and Lord Randolph Churchill. Rhodes went everywhere. Harcourt was " delighted with him, likes his hard sense and knowledge of affairs, and says even Jingoism is tolerable if it is done on the cheap." [8]   " How often," records Baron von Eckardstein, Counsellor of the German Embassy, who had married a daughter of Sir Blundell Maple, founder of the store and a prominent company promotor, " have I sat with Rhodes and Chamberlain at the round table at the Burlington, drinking old port, for which they both had a particular weakness. At these times we roughed out plan

[1] A. G. Gardiner, *Life of Sir William Harcourt*, Vol. 2, 514.
[2] Lord Newton, *Lord Lansdowne*, 341: " The Entente is quoted at a lower price. . . . The fall of Delcassé . . . has sent the Entente down any number of points in the market."
[3] *Autobiography of Margot Asquith*, Vol. 2, 84.
[4] *Milner Papers*, Vol. 2, 479.
[5] Morley, *Recollections*, Vol. 2, 133.
[6] R. B. Haldane, *An Autobiography*, 162.
[7] Sir F. Maurice, *Haldane, 1856–1915*, 117.
[8] Gardiner, *op. cit.*, Vol. 2, 199.

after plan for possible partitions of the world." [1] Bryce " favourably regarded Rhodes," [2] who was also an Oriel man. Edward VII, when Prince of Wales, " spoke most enthusiastically of him." He was " a fine fellow, a wonderful man." [3]

The purpose of these extracts is not to paint a picture in which a small group of capitalists are shown twisting the nation's rulers round their fingers. The influences in Edwardian England came not from capitalists but from capitalism. Cecil Spring Rice, later ambassador in Washington, describes the scene as it appeared to a sensitive and idealistic young man. " I feel more and more disgusted," he wrote in November 1903. " I can't help believing that our Government (with the consent of the people) is becoming more and more the Government of interested people, with the trail of finance over them all. . . . I don't think the opposition are any better; the most able, Asquith and Rosebery, are in fact exactly the same." [4] H. Feis well describes the position: " The habits and structure of British society contributed to foster a natural harmony of action. In the small circles of power, financial power was united with political power and held mainly the same ideas. Partners of the important issue houses sat in the House of Commons or among the Lords, where they were in easy touch with the Ministry. In clubs, country week-ends, shooting parties, Sir Ernest Cassel, Lord Rothschild or Lord Revelstoke could learn the official mind and reveal their own; and there was ample opportunity to discuss the wisdom or needs of the moment." [5]

Leading prelates were subjected to the same influences. When Dr. Davidson became the first Archbishop of Canterbury to visit the United States, J. P. Morgan appropriately enough represented the American Episcopal Church, and provided him with a special train for his use. " Nothing could exceed his kindness, and he laid emphasis in superlative terms upon the advantage to the Nation as well as to the Church, which would accrue from such a visit," wrote Dr. Davidson in a memorandum of June 1904. " He says: Ask whom you like on either side of the Atlantic who knows the condition of affairs, and he will tell you that no single

[1] Baron von Eckardstein, *Ten years at the Court of St. James's, 1895–1905*, 234.
[2] H. A. L. Fisher, *James Bryce*, Vol. 1, 305.
[3] F. Whyte, *W. T. Stead*, Vol. 2, 107.
[4] S. Gwyn, *Letters and Friendships of Cecil Spring Rice*, Vol. 1, 369.
[5] *Europe, the World's Banker*, 87.

act, which could be taken by England, would do more at this moment to cement friendship than a visit by the Archbishop in the way now suggested, and obviously he really cares about the matter from that point of view." [1]

Morgan dominated the American Episcopal Church. When he went to a Church Convention he was considerate enough to leave his mistress in the car outside until his work was done. His will contains a passage worth quoting as the religion of a capitalist in the Edwardian age: " I commit my soul into the hands of my Saviour, in the full confidence that, having redeemed it and washed it in his most precious blood, he will present it faultless before the throne of my Heavenly Father; and I entreat my children to maintain and defend at all hazard, and at any cost of personal sacrifice, the blessed doctrine of the complete atone-ment for sin through the blood of Jesus Christ, once offered and through that alone." [2]

Strange are the spiritual fruits of the ruling class, whose root was in the economic conditions of the period.

Morgan had important interests on both sides of the Atlantic, but London still remained the world's financial centre, and although, while the City was occupied with the loan problems of the Boer War, America had already for the first time lent money to European governments,[3] British supremacy in the financial field was not yet seriously threatened.

It was, as we have seen, otherwise in the field of industry. Significantly the British trade cycle now followed about six months after the American.[4] Trade competition, both from Germany and the United States, has been noted, menacing the standard of life of the British people, caught in a competitive economic system geared to a competitive world. It remains to note the dimensions of the problem of Defence, which more and more was occupying the attention of the rulers of the British Empire.

[1] G. K. Bell, *Life of Randall Davidson*, 442.
[2] J. K. Winkler, *Life of Pierpont Morgan, 1837–1913*, 16, 20, 21.
[3] Clapham, *op. cit.*, Vol. 3, 43.
[4] Ibid., 46. Symbolically the first Derby of the new reign was won by Mr. W. C. Whitney's Volodyovsky. Whitney was a rich corporation lawyer, who had played a prominent part in U. S. politics, particularly during the Cleveland era.

CHAPTER VII

THE DEFENCE OF THE REALM

The Achilles heel of Britain in matters of defence was food. When Peel repealed the Corn Laws he did more than any of the conscious architects of Anglo-American friendship to make war between the two nations impossible. Even at the time the repeal assisted a favourable settlement of the troublesome boundary question in Oregon,[1] but its great effect on the relations between the two Great Powers came with the arrival after the seventies of increasing quantities of American wheat in Britain. As a writer in the *Navy Annual* pointed out in 1898: " Another very serious feature of our dependence upon foreign breadstuffs lies in the large proportion of wheat and flour from the United States and from Russia . . . it is conceivable that we might at any moment be forced into war with one of these great wheat-exporting countries, and if so, we should in present circumstances be quite unable to obtain our normal supply of wheat. The growth of wheat the world over is limited by the normal demand, so that, if suddenly deprived owing to war of our large imports from Russia or the United States, the deficiencies could not be met. . . . War with the United States might deprive us of nearly 52% of our total import of breadstuffs. We have thus by allowing the decline of British agriculture put a tremendous power in the hands of possible foes." [2]

Less important at the time, but beginning to be discussed by progressive naval experts, notably by Sir John Fisher, was the question of oil fuel, of which the United States and Russia were again the main sources of known supply.[3]

[1] Greville, *Diary*, edition by P. H. Wilson, Vol. 2, 552.
[2] *Navy Annual*, 1898, 161. Cf. Report of Royal Commission on Supply of Food and Raw Material in time of War. Cd. 2643, 1905, 7. See also Brooks Adams, *America's Economic Supremacy*, 1900, 6. T. Brassey at Royal Colonial Society, *Proceedings*, Vol. 34, " Steps to Imperial Federation." " It is well to point out that under present conditions we are absolutely at her (America's) mercy."
[3] Cd. 8449, 1897, 363.

But what of the actual naval position, what of the outlook for the British fleet, on which the safety both of the British Isles and the far-flung Empire depended?

Anglo-German naval rivalry has naturally received the most attention. Forecast by writers as early as 1872,[1] and by such a prominent statesman as Sir Charles Dilke in 1890,[2] it arrived with the Naval Law of 1898, but the Anglo-German rivalry must not be considered in isolation. Britain moved on the world stage.

France and Russia had hitherto been the powers against whom she kept her ships in commission. Over their combined strength she maintained a comfortable margin. Now economic development was adding to the threat of a hostile France and Russia other navies, actual or potential, which would have to be brought into Admiralty calculations.

In the Eastern Hemisphere the victory of the Japanese over China in 1895 had " thrown all the Chinese fleet, which was not destroyed in the war, into their hands. The Japanese are already building two powerful battleships in England. . . . It is clear that with this new competitor in the field we cannot hope to hold much longer the prominent position we have hitherto done in the waters of Eastern Asia." Thus the *Navy Annual* in 1896.[3] And what of the United States? Her navy was still small, and to remain small until after the turn of the century, but her potentialities were obvious. " No other power—or combination of powers—could vie with the people of the United States, if it were their policy to employ their unrivalled and rapidly growing resources in the creation of a predominant navy. They are self-contained and their situation does not compel them to divert expenditure to the defence of land frontiers." [4]

Choices, inevitable choices, had to be made by British statesmen; none the less choices in that they may not have been fully conscious of them.

There were not wanting groups who favoured an agreement

[1] J. Mathews, *A Colonist on the Colonial Question*, 48. Quoted by J. E. Tyler, *The Struggle for Imperial Unity, 1868-1895*, 17.
[2] December 1890 address to Statistical Society, *Defence Expenditure of the Chief Naval and Military Powers*. " The German navy does not as yet exist. I say ' as yet,' for the Germans mean business."
[3] *Navy Annual*, 1896, 61.
[4] *Navy Annual*, 1903, xii.

with Germany, notably Chamberlain and the Duke of Devonshire.[1] Their attempts will be discussed later. Had they been successful a collision with the United States could scarcely have been avoided, for German colonial ambitions were turning to the Caribbean and to South America, and with a British alliance would have been the more exclusively directed thither as they were diverted from the territories of the British Empire.

Faced with a somewhat similar situation the Romans had called their legions home; now Britain was to enlist the Japanese against the Russians in the Far East, and to yield the Caribbean to the United States Navy, while she concentrated her released strength in home waters.

It was the logical issue of a difficult problem. For Britain it had the particular advantage of promising the preservation of the Empire, including that hostage to fortune on the American border, Canada. The United States was not the serious competitor at this time that Germany was for colonial territories. Better to be dependent on America for food than on Russia with the Germans in between, a position which they would have well known how to exploit. For America it gave the protection of the British Navy which Mahan was teaching them to value,[2] and the possibility of continued peaceful development within their own borders, in the Caribbean, and in the Far East, where in 1898 they had taken the Philippines from Spain, after President McKinley had sought the consent of God and, it seems, obtained it.[3]

Thus inevitably economic development, through trade competition and national struggle for existence, influenced the triangular relationship of the three Great Powers.

But, although the naval position was the predominant anxiety of the rulers of Great Britain, the war which had begun in South Africa in 1899 drew attention to the tasks which battleships could not perform. A significant address had been delivered by a high-ranking Austrian soldier in 1900, which is worth quoting: " When we speak therefore of the critical military condition of England

[1] Also Sir V. Chirol, the eminent publicist. See Memorandum by Holstein, 31st October 1901, G.D.D., Vol. 3, 148.
[2] Mahan to Roosevelt, December 1904. C. C. Taylor, *The Life of Admiral Mahan*, 146–7.
[3] C. and M. Beard, *The Rise of American Civilization*, Vol. 2, 375.

we do not refer to that of the army engaged in South Africa, but to the fact that by this employment England was all but denuded of troops. . . . When we contemplate the perturbations of the political world brought about seemingly by the imperialism of the Anglo-Saxon race; when we note that the war in South Africa revealed, as a sudden flash of lightning illuminates a dark night, the hatred of Great Britain by all but the Anglo-Saxon people, then England as a world power, supported solely by its fleet, stands out in its proper perspective." [1] How much longer could Britain preserve its traditional isolation behind the single defence of its Navy, against the trained armies of hostile Europe?

The decision had not yet been made when Edward VII began to reign. The foreign political situation we will defer considering at this stage. We will first turn to the Empire, to which in the circumstances of deepening competition increased attention was naturally being directed, and in particular to that part which Chamberlain had described as Britain's " undeveloped estates."

---

[1] Lieutenant Field-Marshal Gustavus Ritzenhofen, President of the Austro-Hungarian Military Supreme Court. Address at the Military Club, Vienna, 30th November 1900. Dunlop, *Development of the British Army*, 129, 130.

CHAPTER VIII

HISTORICAL CAUSATION

The British Empire raises such controversial issues, particularly of motive, that here is an appropriate place for a note on Historical Causation.

History is concerned with the narration of events and their genesis. The reader of history wishes to know not only what happened, but why. The historian, whether he is conscious of the fact or not, inevitably reaches a philosophy of history, which is the sum total of his judgments, the quintessence of his experience. He will have taken a view of the degree of free choice possessed by the individual in the making of history. He will have estimated the place of natural phenomena, of economic factors, of divine intervention. All this will appear in the result and needs no previous formulation.

It is, however, worth pointing out that modern psychology by its dissection of human motive has provided the historian with an invaluable distinction. The discovery of the human unconscious has certainly made history more difficult, but it has increased the possibility of accuracy. We know now not only that the reasons given by an individual for his actions may be incorrect (this after all was already recognized in the whole question of " reliability "—in the rejection of some evidence and the acceptance of other); now we know far more. We know that incorrectness of statement is not confined to the deliberate liar. The most upright and consciously truthful witness may be as unreliable as the rogue. He may be unconscious of his true motives.[1]

---

[1] An interesting parallel from Literature of unconscious action has been confirmed by T. S. Eliot. See *Essays on the eighteenth century presented to David Nichol Smith*. " The inspiration of Pope's Poetry," John Butt, 76 n. A reviewer of a reprint of Dowson's poems had pointed out a resemblance between Dowson's " Non sum qualis eram " and " The Hollow Men." Mr. Eliot, in a letter to *The Times Literary Supplement* of 10th January 1935, remarked: " The derivation had not occurred to my mind, but I believe it to be correct, because the lines have always run in my head, and because I regard Dowson as a poet whose technical innovations have been underestimated."

Thus the fact that the leaders of a political party or of a power group may be truthful in the popular sense does not guarantee that the reasons given by them for their actions can be accepted *ipso facto* as correct.

To that extent history has become more difficult.

But although statement needs deeper analysis, its value to the historian has not been destroyed. Statement may be often intended consciously or unconsciously to conceal the truth (as Talleyrand remarked, " La langue a été donné à l'homme pour déguiser ses pensées "), but few are in full control of themselves. Sooner or later the authentic note appears. It is in the recognition of this note that the work of the historian now consists; and he will be guided by the proof of relevant facts. Thus history, although now more difficult, can be more accurate.

The controversy that has raged over Sir Edward Grey provides an illustration. To those who knew him in Britain he was an upright and truthful man. To himself he was pacific and of the most honourable intentions. To the Germans he was the arch-planner of their encirclement behind smooth unctuous phrases. These judgments are not irreconcilable. The historian has no need to choose between them. The truth is that Grey was largely unconscious of his motives (that was what made him so admirable a representative of British interests). We shall not understand Anglo-German relations and much else if we fail to grasp the general truth of this distinction. Attempts have been made to dismiss as fantastic the historical philosophy that attributes war responsibility in these years primarily to Finance Capital. It has been pointed out by Professor Robbins in *The Economic Causes of War* that Cassel and Ballin were most persistent in the arrangement of *détentes*, that City opinion both in Berlin and London was horrified at the thought of war in 1914 and was weak-kneed in the face of political complications. " One is tempted to ask," he writes, " whether its authors have ever so much as seen an animal of the species banker," [1] the suggestion being that because financiers did not consciously wish war therefore the responsibility cannot lie there. The responsibility of Finance does not depend upon the conscious intentions of individual financiers (this pre-occupation with intentions is of course a " hangover " from the

[1] p. 53.

days when heroes and villains filled the pages of History; it is time that History came of age), but on the effects of the system, which they operated, on National decision and policy. The effects on Finance on National decision and policy are not to be confined to instances of conscious and deliberate pressure by individual financiers or groups (although these have occurred). History might be simpler and more easily understood by some if it were so. We can only remark that the world we live in is more complex, and we are only just beginning to understand it. Few are fully aware of their circumstances. One of the purposes of History is to increase consciousness.

As we consider the British Empire we are faced with a bewildering volume of statement regarding motive, which becomes intelligible only in terms of the above analysis.

CHAPTER IX

IMPERIALISM AND ITS ROOTS

Between the origin of Imperialism and its manifestations little resemblance reveals itself to the superficial gaze. Only an understanding of the mechanism of the historical process can show the links. The individual acts of bravery and of selfless persistence, which Empire building and Empire maintenance have often produced (and not only in Britons), are not to be confused with the motive power of the Imperial urge. Bravery and selflessness are to be found on both sides in all wars, but even if it were possible to arrive at their total and strike a balance, this would give little guidance to a searcher of the war-motive. There is no inconsistency, there is no slander on courageous and often disinterested individuals, in finding an ugly motive at the base of Imperialism. The capacity for self-deception in human beings is itself immense. Consciousness is rare, and in an unequal society the capacity for deception by others is greater still.

If we attempt to estimate the motives of the British people and the German in 1914, how shall we decide the issue? To the selfless August volunteers Little Belgium made an irresistible appeal. The Cabinet had its eyes on the Channel Ports. The earnest German Social Democrat following the letter of Marxism was swept into a Holy War against the Tsarist autocracy. The Army chiefs moved under a different banner. It is not therefore surprising that Imperialism, which is a branch of war, should show such a patchwork of individual motives, should have made its way by means of such a multiplicity of appeals.

The Imperialism which permeated the years of Edward's life, and was accepted by majority opinion before he ascended the throne, was rooted, as Imperial creeds always have been rooted, in the value of Empire.

The Colonial prophets of Early Victorianism found its value in an outlet for Britain's surplus population, and in a market for

Britain's surplus goods. Carlyle advocated " an effective system of emigration " and in his individual idiom declared the job of the colonists to be " raising new crops for us, purchasing new webs and hatchets from us " [1]—a division of labour—and profit—which seemed most satisfactory to the ruling class in Britain.

Imperialism is to be regarded not as an isolated phenomenon, but as a stage in historical development, the product of the Industrial Revolution.

" The predominant motive of British expansion," writes an Imperialist historian, " which actuated both individuals and the Government in every century was the desire to obtain markets, food products and raw materials. But in the nineteenth century new factors came into play and accentuated the urgency of both. These were the demands of the industrial revolution, the competition of new nations such as Germany and the United States, and the enormous growth of population in England and elsewhere, with the consequent demand for new food supplies and new markets." [2]

This was the golden age of British capital export. The foreign competition, which vexed the exporter of British goods, caused no sleepless nights in the City of London, from which the vast accumulations poured overseas to lands where the rate of interest was higher and Labour movements embryonic or illegal.

J. A. Hobson in his *Imperialism*, published early in the new reign, and received with approbation by Gladstonian Liberals, including Sir Henry Campbell-Bannerman, argued that the profits went to a small section of the population, and attempted to turn back the nation to Little Englandism.

Why was he unsuccessful?

Not only because Liberal members of Parliament shared in the Stock Exchange spoils; [3] not only because of the strong Liberal-Imperialist group, led by Lord Rosebery, the former Prime Minister and the husband of a Rothschild; not only because

---

[1] Quoted by C. M. MacInnes, *An Introduction to the Economic History of the British Empire*, 165. Cf. Sir Patrick Playfair, Annual Dinner, London Chamber of Commerce, 1912: " India must be in the main an agricultural country raising crops in great quantities and of great value."

[2] L. C. A. Knowles, *Economic Development of the British Overseas Empire*, Vol. 1, 102. Her Imperialism is stressed in the *Memoir*, Vol. 2, 21.

[3] *The Autobiography of Margot Asquith*, Vol. 2, 84.

E

Rhodes, whom Rosebery had made a Privy Councillor,[1] was a contributor to the Liberal party funds, a symbolic gesture (though as Edward Grey remarked, " he was not exactly what you would call a Liberal ");[2] but because Imperialism made its appeal to almost every section of the British people.[3]

In 1871 Andrew Halliday in *The Retention of India* drew a horrifying picture of the plight of the investing class if India were lost. " It would be well for this country to consider what would be the consequence of the loss of the Indian Empire. What would be the fate of those dependent for subsistence on the Indian revenues, and what would become of the vast sums invested in Indian securities, railways and other property? . . . a frightful amount of pauperism in this country among classes ill-adapted by nature to a state of penury." [4] Had this been all—and the weakness of Hobson's appeal was that he seemed to imply it— Imperialism would never have conquered public opinion. It was the dependence of the livelihood of the working class on that of their masters that determined the response of the masses to the call of Empire.

As early as 1884 Joseph Chamberlain sounded the note of popular appeal: " Is there any man in his senses who believes that the crowded population of these islands could exist for a single day if it were to cut adrift from us the great dependencies, which now look to us for protection and assistance, and which are the natural outlets for our trade?" [5] And again in 1888: " A great part of our population is dependent at the present moment upon the interchange of commodities with our colonial fellow-subjects." [6] And again in 1905: " Speaking generally, the great cure for this difficulty of employment is to find new

---

[1] *Annual Register*, 1902: Obituary of Rhodes.

[2] G. M. Trevelyan, *Grey of Fallodon*, 61.

[3] Only the Royal Family could enjoy one particular facet of possessiveness, as when Queen Victoria wrote to her uncle Leopold, King of the Belgians: " Albert is so much amused at my having got the island of Hong Kong, and we think Victoria might be called Princess of Hong Kong in addition to Princess Royal." 13th April 1841. Hong Kong was to become a more important port than London. Light on the island during the Edwardian period is thrown by an article in the *British Empire Series*, Vol. I, 1906, by Dr. James Cantlie, 516: " The jail does not present to the Chinaman the bogie it is to most Europeans. The coolie condemned to incessant labour and on a starvation diet finds, within the precincts of the jail, rest and food."

[4] Pp. 160, 161.   [5] Quoted by Langer, *Diplomacy of Imperialism*, Vol. I, 77.

[6] Speech at Devonshire Club, April 1888.

markets." [1] Rhodes significantly struck the same note: " The mechanic has woke up to the fact that unless he keeps the markets of the world he will be starved." [2]

Small wonder that the working class climbed on to the Imperialist waggon, and went on its way to the strains of " the little patch of red " instead of the Red Flag.

> " For of pluck he's brimming full is young John Bull,
> And he's happy when we let him have his head.
>   It's a feather in his cap
>   When he's helped to paint the map
> With another little patch of red."

There were of course two Empires; the more or less self-governing and the dependent; there was too the benefit from trade and the benefit from investment, profit and tribute; but in the final analysis the benefit of Empire was spread among all classes, although most unevenly spread. The working class was tied to the ruling class; their destinies were linked as the destiny of the dog is linked with that of his master.

For we can see now what the choice was: Imperialism or Socialism. George Wyndham, one of the most gifted of the Conservatives of the period, had a glimmering of this when he wrote to his leader, Mr. Balfour, in 1905: " I want to save the party for Imperialism, . . . for the avoidance of Class Conflicts." [3] Either the British working class accepted their unity with workers everywhere, and made their single aim the overthrow of their common masters, or else they identified themselves with them, sharing part of the spoils from the Imperialist venture, and occupying a status which, though inferior to that of their own masters,

---

[1] House of Commons, 23rd August 1905. Chamberlain was always downright and candid in the expression of his Imperialist creed. Thus in the Commons, 21st July 1904, he confessed: " After all we do hold our position by being the dominant races, and if we admit equality with these inferior races we shall lose the power which gives us our predominance."

[2] Quoted by Langer, *op. cit.*, Vol. 1, 80.

[3] J. W. Mackail and Guy Wyndham, *Life and Letters of George Wyndham*, Vol. 2, 501. Cf. Sir Raymond West, LL.D., K.C.I.E., Introduction to *British Empire Series*, Vol. 1, 1906, xviii: " In the midst of this pæan over conquered nature a querulous note of complaint arises that the natives of India have not obtained a due share in the governing power, in the highest places and rewards of the state. The murmur is not unnatural; it is but analogous to the socialist moan which forms the refrain of labour's psalm in Europe."

yet comprised superiority to the coloured workers overseas. This is the fact behind Winston Churchill's remarks to Wilfrid Blunt: " Winston sympathizes much with my ideas about the native question in India, and in general about the enslavement of the coloured by the white races. But he says he is an Imperialist, and his chief interest is in the condition and welfare of the poor in England." [1]

And so British capitalism maintained itself a little longer by shifting part of the pressure from the white worker to the coloured, and by driving a convenient wedge between two groups whose unity would have been so dangerous.

It is this situation which is reflected in the vast superstructure of Imperialist literature and Imperialist religion, in the whole conception of the divine mission of the Imperial race. The strength of identity of interest between the white and the coloured worker is to be gauged by the tremendous effort required to obscure it.

Priest, politician and poet were enlisted in the Imperialist chorus. Canon Hensley Henson in St. Margaret's Church, Westminster, declared that " to his thinking, this Imperial mission represented a divine vocation." [2] Lord Rosebery described the Empire as " Human and yet not wholly human—for the most heedless and the most cynical must see the finger of the Divine." [3] Lord Curzon thought it " a preordained dispensation, intended to be a source of strength and discipline to ourselves and of moral and material blessing to others." [4] " Let the Englishman and the Indian," he urged, " accept the consecration of a union that is so mysterious as to have in it something of the Divine." [5] A leading missionary wrote that " it is religion which has given the comparatively small United Kingdom its Imperial power and responsibilities. The English-speaking race or races . . . are conscious of a mission or destiny. . . . The spawning power and the adventurous instinct . . . are not directed by blind force." [6] The Roman Catholic Cardinal Vaughan oracularly told his clergy that " this

---

[1] W. S. Blunt, *op. cit.*, Vol. 2, 287.
[2] *The Times*, 9th June 1902.
[3] Inaugural address as Rector of Glasgow University, 16th November 1900
[4] Zetland, *Lord Cromer*, 16.
[5] Speech to Convocation of Calcutta University, 15th February 1902.
[6] Rev. George Smith, C.I.E. See the *British Empire Series*, Vol. 5, 542.

Empire has been raised up by the same Providence that called the Roman Empire into existence, and as God used the one towards the attainment of His Own Divine purpose of mercy, so does He seem to be using the other." [1] Rudyard Kipling's " white man's burden " represents the same idea in untheological terms. Finally in this connexion may be quoted a characteristic revelation of the Rhodes religion: " If there be a God and He cares anything about what I do, I think it is clear that He would like me to do what He is doing himself. And as He is manifestly fashioning the English-speaking race as the chosen instrument by which He will bring in a state of society based upon justice, liberty and peace, He must obviously wish me to do what I can to give as much scope and power to that race as possible. Hence if there be a God I think what He would like me to do is to paint as much of the map of Africa British red as possible." [2]

Kipling was a best seller by the beginning of the reign. " What did Kipling give exactly?" asked Dick Remington, the hero of H. G. Wells's political novel *The New Macchiavelli*. " He helped to broaden my geographical sense immensely, and he provided phrases for just that desire for discipline and devotion and organized effort the Socialism of our time failed to express." [3] Kipling, declared Richard Le Gallienne, conveyed the feeling that " we peaceable stay-at-homes are poor milk-and-water creatures and that there is nothing in the world worth doing save slicing and potting your fellow creatures." [4]

Also worth noting, an offshoot of the Imperialist movement, was the remarkable appearance of " a new sort of little boy—a most agreeable development of the slouching, cunning, cigarette-smoking, town-bred youngster—a small boy in a khaki hat with bare knees and athletic bearing, engaged in wholesome and in-vigorating games—the Boy Scout." [5]

In 1897 Baden-Powell, an army officer, had advocated Scouting as a method of training young soldiers. In 1899, while he was besieged in Mafeking, his *Aids to Scouting* was published, and very naturally excited considerable attention. It was recommended

[1] Circular letter to his clergy, 20th December 1899.
[2] *Review of Reviews*, April 1902.
[3] Quoted by Amy Cruse, *After the Victorians*, 121.
[4] Quoted by Malcolm Elwin, *Old Gods Falling*, 219.
[5] See H. G. Wells, *The New Macchiavelli*.

for use by boys, and a few years later was rewritten by its author. " The ulterior object," he declared, " is to develop among boys a power of sympathizing with others, a spirit of self-sacrifice and patriotism, and generally to prepare them for becoming good citizens." Whatever the motive of the founder, the significant fact was that the movement did not conflict with, but rather supported, the idea of the Imperial Mission. It was approved by all the best people, and by all the religious denominations, including the Roman Catholic Church.[1]

The Empire has so far been considered as though it were all of a piece; and certainly there is more truth in this conception than in many of the artificial distinctions attempted by lawyers, politicians and historians.

For was there in the last analysis any difference between the nascent struggle of the Indian Congress for Swaraj, and the importunate demand of Sir Wilfrid Laurier, the Canadian Premier, for a greater share in the treaty-making power?

The basic situation, concealed by the party shibboleths and distorted by the reflection of outworn ideologies, was one of the Imperial Government in London, and the interests which it represented, reacting to two problems which, as Mr. Balfour had astutely realized, were in fact one problem; the maintenance of the British standard of life in relation to that of the other powers, and the problem of Imperial Defence.

In their attitude to the problem the two historic parties reflected the influences of their origin, transmuted by the changing facts of the national existence. The Conservatives, representing the landed interest, sought to restore their greatness in the new Britains beyond the seas. From their younger sons the majority of the Empire builders and administrators came. It was significant that both Chamberlain and Milner thought the word " estate " appropriate.[2] At a meeting of the Royal Colonial Society an ex-Colonial administrator thus described the men who brought the Pax Britannica: " You will see a man who at home would be

---

[1] For Baden-Powell, see life by E. E. Reynolds, 1942. Reynolds notes the link with Sherlock Holmes, created by Conan Doyle in 1888. The rise of the detective story is worthy of research. Was there something psychologically satisfying in the statement and solution of problems to a nation moving into ever deeper perplexities and contradictions?

[2] 8th February 1902, *Milner Papers*, Vol. 2, 304.

a country gentleman, a J.P., perhaps riding to hounds." [1] In his will Rhodes sympathetically refers to the British landed gentry.

The Liberal party, sprung from the manufacturing interest, left Little England theories behind only when the Colonies began to be significant markets for British goods. In 1851 the total of Canadian exports and imports was less than £13,000,000; and of Australian, £8,000,000. Ten years later the totals were for Canada £22,000,000 and for Australia £49,000,000. The theory as is usual continued to flourish after its root had been removed, but a party based on the manufacturing interest had to transform itself, although the tradition of Liberalism, of freedom, lingered on to shape the Self-government given by Campbell-Bannerman's Government to South Africa.

But besides the landed interest and the manufacturing interest, there were two others able to exercise pressure on the organs of government; the financial interest and the Labour movement. At first the former gravitated to the Liberal party, which freed the powerful Jewish element from its disabilities. The importance of the Finance Houses at this period is sometimes underestimated. Professor Robbins criticizes J. A. Hobson for writing in his *Imperialism*: " Does anyone seriously suppose that a great war could be undertaken by any European State, or a great state loan subscribed, if the House of Rothschild and its connexions set their face against it?" [2] The truth is that at this time, before the modern organization of the money market with the great power of the Treasury Bill, the private houses did control the situation. Jacob Schiff, the American financier, played an important part in bringing Japan to consent to end the war with Russia in 1905, and to accept the Treaty of Portsmouth, by the threat of a cessation of loans. That war itself could not have been financed except through the private houses.[3] Finance first rose to power in France. As early as 1879, Disraeli, who had practical experience of the

[1] Sir W. T. Thistleton-Dyer, K.C.M.G., C.I.E. See *Proceedings*, Vol. 30, 158–9. Cf. Lord Milner: " Countrymen are the best settlers. They have formed the core of the Army and Navy as well as the Administrative service of the Empire." Preface to *The Nation and Empire*, xli.

[2] *The Economic Causes of War*, 58. J. H. Clapham, *op. cit.*, Vol. 3, 293, rightly points out that it was after 1902 that the use of the Treasury Bill was extended.

[3] *The Economist*, 19th Aug. 1905.

City, wrote: " In France finance, and even private finance, is politics." [1]

The maintenance of Free Trade was also a City interest, which inclined the finance magnates towards the Liberal party, influencing it accordingly, as when Mr. Gladstone approved the bombardment of Alexandria to the gratification of the British bondholders though at the cost of losing John Bright from his cabinet.

The benefit of Empire to Finance needs no stressing, but what of the Labour movement? Why did it follow the Imperialist call? The answer we suggest is that the working class, not prepared to accept the only alternative, Socialism, and the sharp cleavage with the past required to bring it to birth, inevitably reflected the same influences that moved their masters. They shared in the overflow of the spoils. They would expiate with their masters the guilt.

The Fabians supported Imperialism in the interests of Efficiency (Bernard Shaw called it " brains and political science ").[2] Sidney Webb thought that " Lord Rosebery is right about an Imperial Race." [3] Trade Unionists were preoccupied with the day-to-day struggle, although we shall see that they appreciated the issue of Chinese Labour. Anti-Imperialist speeches were not lacking in the Labour movement, but it was a dusty answer that was returned, while the Imperialists were hot with certainty. Isolated figures, notably Keir Hardie, perceived the identity of interest between the British workers and the worker overseas. It is interesting to contrast the reaction of Hardie to India with that of Ramsay MacDonald. They both paid a visit to India during the reign of Edward VII.

Keir Hardie was impressed by the $1\frac{1}{2}d.$ per head spent by the Government of India on Education, as against $1s.$ per head on the Army; that there were fewer children at school there than in the United Kingdom, though the population was nearly eight times as large; that two official parties were held to celebrate the King's birthday, one for the whites, the other for the natives; that there was a colour line on the railways; that public urinals were for European Gentlemen, Men, and Females. He con-

[1] Monypenny and Buckle, *Life*, Vol. 2, 1316.
[2] G. B. Shaw, *Fabianism and the Empire*, September 1900.
[3] M. Hamilton, *Sidney and Beatrice Webb*, 151.

sidered that conditions had grown worse under British rule. He declared that " everything in India is seditious which does not slavishly applaud every act of the Government." [1] Ramsay MacDonald adopted a different attitude. His book is not without criticism of the British rule, but he went out of his way to defend British capital, which had been so kindly lent at cheap rates to develop India. He expressed warm approval of the annual reports of the State of Gwalior, in which the Maharajah, in absolute power, issued censures on his officials for inefficiency. He thought that " for many a long year British sovereignty will be necessary for India." He looked forward to the time when " a Viceroy will go to India . . . steeped in Liberal traditions, and whose political mind will be made up of axioms of government which have sprung out of Liberal experience." He cheerfully concluded that " India will not rise all at once, and if we are wise the day when it goes so far as to threaten us with expulsion is so remote that we need hardly think of it at all." [2]

The basic Imperialist situation was beginning to grow more and more difficult. Nationalist movements were emerging in India and in Egypt which were to receive a special impetus in the reign of Edward VII. Political pressure from the self-governing colonies on the Imperial Government in London for a greater share in the direction of their destiny was increasing, and economic competition from this source was beginning to excite comment. Most menacing of all was the trade competition and military threat of other powers.

[1] J. Keir Hardie, *India: Impressions and Suggestions.*
[2] J. R. MacDonald, *The Awakening of India.*

73

CHAPTER X

AMERICA OR GERMANY?

Britain's dominant trade position, and her favourable geographical situation, had been reflected in the policy of " splendid isolation," tenaciously pursued by Lord Salisbury behind the invincible shield of the British Navy. Changing economic development made that policy inappropriate, although, as is usual, it retained power over men's minds after its roots had been removed.

Not only was there the increasing trade competition, the disturbance of British naval supremacy, and the dangerous dependence on foreign food, but Colonies had themselves ceased to be a British monopoly. " The other powers," declared Lord Rosebery in the eighties, " are beginning a career of colonial aggrandizement. We formerly did not have to trouble ourselves much with colonial questions, because we had a monopoly of colonies. That monopoly has ceased." [1] In the decade after the Franco-Prussian war, when Bismarck encouraged France to forget Alsace-Lorraine in Colonial expansion, and thus, he must have thought, inevitably embroil herself with England, Germany was not a competitor for Empire. German economic development had not yet reached boiling-point; but by the middle eighties Bismarck, against his judgment, was forced to obey economic urgency expressed through the Reichstag, writing to his minister in London in tart terms: " If Lord Granville (the British Foreign Secretary) finds that the English Parliament's friendly feeling towards us is incompatible with our pursuit of a Colonial policy, we should be curious to learn why the right to colonize, which England uses to the fullest extent, should be denied to us. . . . I foresee that when the Reichstag meets again we shall be called upon to answer questions concerning our overseas policy, and the attitude of England towards it in particular." And a little later: " I repeat, therefore, . . . that the Colonial question is already a matter of life and death for reasons of domestic policy. I hope that my last dispatches as well

---

[1] Speech at Leeds, 1888. Quoted by Langer, *op. cit.*, Vol. I, 77.

as the recent debates in the Reichstag may have caused you to realize the bearing of this question on our internal politics. Public opinion in Germany lays so great a stress on our Colonial policy that the Government's position in the country actually depends on its success." [1]

Thus the competitive economic system was driving the German and the British peoples into collision.

The hereditary enemy of Britain was France. From France she had won the world supremacy in the eighteenth century. France she had crushed in the Napoleonic war. France under Napoleon III was again a bogey, causing a rush to the Volunteers and the construction of a chain of forts covering London. Even after 1870 France continued to preoccupy British statesmen; but by the turn of the century Sir Robert Giffen was telling the British Association that " the foreign nations then with which the British Empire is likely to be concerned in the near future are Russia, Germany and the United States; and other powers, even France, must more and more occupy a second place, although France for the moment, partly in consequence of its relations with Russia, occupies a special place." [2]

There were two alliances in Europe, the alliance of France and Russia, now drawn closer, and the complex relationship of Germany, Austro-Hungary and Italy in the Triple Alliance. Surprise has been expressed at the revolution in British Foreign policy during the reign of Edward VII, when Britain came to terms with her hereditary foe, and later with Russia; but economic development had made France increasingly less a rival. She lacked coal in an age when coal was the basis of industrial power. She was not a competitor in the British export markets to any serious extent; most of her exports were non-competitive; those that were mostly went to her own Empire. It is significant that when the entente was concluded public reference was made to the lack of trade competition between the two countries.[3]

France was also becoming increasingly dependent on Britain,

---

[1] 25th January 1885.   [2] 12th September 1901.
[3] As Sir E. Sassoon, when French Deputies visited England in July 1903, remarked: " The one Entente which is really stable is that based on material interests." Stephen H. Roberts, *History of French Colonial Policy*, Vol. 2, 634, well expresses an important point: " To France, not sea-girt, of small area and of increasing population like U.K., Colonial enterprise was a hazard, not a necessity." Cf. Clapham, *Economic Development of France and Germany*, 251.

both for her import of raw materials and, as tariffs rose generally at the end of the nineteenth century, for her own export trade.[1] The ties linking the countries were increasing as the facts keeping them apart diminished.

We must not exaggerate the importance of Fashoda, when it appeared that colonial war between France and England might occur. The Colonial interest existed in France, but it was not the power that it was across the Channel, where one-third of the total production was dependent on the export market and nearly one-third of the exports were to British possessions. France, moreover, had an empire. She lacked an increasing population. The pressure towards a greater acquisition was not so strong as to overcome other interests, and in particular the interest of the *révanche* against Germany to recover Alsace and Lorraine. " I have lost two children," said Paul Deroulède to the Colonial party, " and you offer me twenty domestics." [2]

With Germany the fact of trade competition was more important than the fact of mutual commercial interest. Everywhere the German business man trod on the heels or on the toes of the British. German economic development was following closely in the British pattern, with the same products seeking outlets abroad, which the exigencies of the profit system could not make available in the home market.[3] And yet there were those in

[1] Jean Finot, editor of *Revue des Révues*, was reported by *The Times*, 15th November 1902, as writing: " France is so far bound up with her fate that the disappearance of England's economic power would cause her incalculable mischief. Our total exports in 1901 were only 4,155,000,000 francs, of which England took 1,264,000,000 francs, or more than 30%." English purchases in France were growing, viz. 1896, 1,032,000,000 francs; 1899, 1,238,000,000; 1901, 1,264,000,000. Anglo-German trade, although important, was not dominant to this extent for either country.

[2] G. P. Gooch, *Franco-German Relations, 1871–1914*, 21.

[3] For an interesting instance of a not uncommon British attitude to Germany see *The British Empire Series*, article by R. W. Murray, *The Railways of Great Britain*. " We may possibly feel some antipathy to a German because he *is* a German, but when he has been beaten in a game of Lawn Tennis and comes up to his opponent cheerfully and congratulates him, then we say, ' Here is a sportsman who plays the game.' "

Alfred Austin, the Poet Laureate, was openly hostile to Germany. See address at Toynbee Hall (*The Times*, 7th November 1901): " What in respect of political morality was Germany's record? Most of them he imagined sympathized at the time with the desire of the German people, as they did more warmly still with the desire of the Italian people, for national unity. But in bringing about the wars of 1859–70 means were unquestionably resorted to which they could not conceive Alfred the Great or any modern British minister employing."

Britain who favoured a deal with Germany, notably Joseph Chamberlain, whose family business had monopoly arrangements with German firms.[1] If he could make a business arrangement with the Germans, why couldn't the nation? Three attempts he made to come to terms, the last at the beginning of the reign. Only after these failures did he change his direction and cease to be philo-German, and reach the point of regarding " a good and complete understanding with America as the corner-stone of English policy " (" odd from him," as Cecil Spring Rice remarked).[2]

The ties drawing Britain to America and America to Britain at this period also reflected economic development. Reference has already been made to the smaller dimension of American trade competition with British exports. Also to be noted are the links of mutual trade, which lead in a competitive world to international friendship. Of American foreign trade almost a third was with Great Britain, who took nearly half her exports, the German total being one-fifth. With the British Empire as a whole the United States did one-half of all her foreign trade, three-fifths of her exports going to countries flying the Union Jack. Strong indeed were the links between Britain and America. Disgruntled groups might nurse enmities. In March 1898 Arnold Bennett recorded in his journal a conversation between his employer on *Women* and Dunn, editor of the *Morning Post*: " We ought to have fought the U.S.A. a year or two ago, when they wanted a war. We should have thrashed them easily and that would have cleared the air of the war cloud." [3] As American steel manufactures began to pour in increasing quantities across the Atlantic towards the end of the nineteenth century, hostility significantly grew in interested quarters. Christopher Furness, a member of a well-known steel family, wrote of *The American Invasion*. But the decision had been taken. The course had been set. The " grizzly terror " of Germany, as Henry Adams described it,[4] had thrown the two English-speaking nations together; and it is not the growth of Anglo-American friendship that is so interesting to the historian, as the terms on which Britain had to

[1] Lord George Hamilton, *Parliamentary Reminiscences and Reflections, 1886–1906*, 25.
[2] S. Gwynn, *op. cit.*, Vol. 1, 462.   [3] Arnold Bennett, *Journals*, Vol 1, 73.
[4] *Education of Henry Adams.*

obtain it, terms which showed clearly that Britain's former world leadership was passing to the great Western Republic.

In 1895 President Cleveland challenged England by his intervention in the Anglo-Venezuelan dispute, using language that in other circumstances would have been answered by war. There was something of a panic in the cabinet (some ministers suggesting that Mrs. Maybrick, a convicted murderess of American birth, should be released to appease opinion in the United States);[1] for the challenge came at a most inconvenient time. That Christmas Jameson rode and failed. On 3rd January 1896 the Kaiser publicly congratulated Kruger in his notorious telegram. On 4th January Chamberlain wrote to Salisbury: " It does not matter which of our numerous foes we defy, but we ought to defy someone," an attitude of mind that recalls Secretary of State Seward's advice to Lincoln, on the eve of the American Civil War, to unite the country in a foreign war. Was there ever a doubt which way Britain would turn? Was this the moment of decision? Chamberlain was at this time and for some years after philo-German. Lord Salisbury's life has not yet been written beyond 1892. When he died the preservation of friendship with America was cited as his most enduring title to fame.[2] As Professor Langer has remarked: " The reaction of the English people to the Kruger telegram will always remain something of a mystery."[3]   In the event it was Germany that was defied. A furious newspaper campaign bearing all the signs of official inspiration was launched, and from the Kruger telegram Anglo-German relations never recovered.

But if 1895–6 was not the turning-point, if indeed it is not possible to say that on such and such a day a decision was taken to come to terms with the United States rather than with Germany, the history of the period is incomprehensible without a realization that Britain had in fact a choice to make.

---

[1] Lord Newton, *Retrospection*, 112.
[2] But see *H. H. A., Letters of the Earl of Oxford and Asquith to a friend, First Series*, 1915–22, 25, 26.   According to Sir Ronald Lindsay, one of our ambassadors in Washington, " at the height of the dispute Lord Salisbury wrote a very tart and provocative dispatch, which by mistake was put into the Foreign Office bag for Pekin instead of that for Washington.   It was perhaps what is called a providential blunder, for it allowed time for the atmosphere to cool."
[3] *The Diplomacy of Imperialism*, Vol. 1, 243.

An Anglo-German alliance would inevitably have meant an ultimate conflict with the United States. Germany had colonial ambitions in South America. When Denmark was considering the sale of the Virgin Islands in the Caribbean to the United States it was German pressure in Copenhagen which was believed to have prevented ratification of the agreement.[1] Reports that Germany aimed at absorbing Holland, which were later to receive semi-official authority in Professor von Halle's *Volks und See-wirthschaft* dedicated to the Minister for the Navy, haunted American as well as British statesmen; for what of the Dutch colonies? In July 1902 the Dutch press feared that a pretext might be sought by Great Britain for seizing upon some of Holland's possessions in the East Indies and elsewhere.[2] In Samoa the three powers confronted each other.

But if Britain had a choice to make, had not the United States too? Why should not they come to terms with Germany and divide the British Empire between them?

The basis for American imperialism was as yet small. By the end of the nineteenth century the United States exported only 4% of her manufactures; Germany 12%, and Britain 25%. Germany too was the greater potential threat. The talk of English decadence which came from foreign lips was never applied to Germany. Britain had clearly passed her peak. America had taken her measure. But Germany, a Germany who might turn her hegemony of the continent into an economic and political bloc which would rival the wealth and power of the new world, there was the enemy. Britain too had a hostage in American hands, Canada. " Let the fight come if it must," wrote Theodore Roosevelt in December 1895, " I don't care whether our sea-coast cities are bombarded or not; we would take Canada." [3]

But although the advantages to Britain of a friendly America were so obvious, the benefit to the United States was also of account. The surrender of Britain in 1896 led to British support of Washington in the Spanish-American war, with the victories of Santiago and Manila Bay received as almost British victories

---

[1] A. Nevins, *Henry White*, 206. See for German manœuvres for a British alliance against U.S.A., Earl of Midleton, *Records and Reactions, 1856–1939*, 175.
[2] *The Times*, 14th July 1902.
[3] *Selected Correspondence*, Vol. I, 200. 20th December 1895, T. Roosevelt to Cabot Lodge.

by the London press, and the annexation of the Philippines encouraged by the British Government.[1] In the next year it was Britain who was at war; in South Africa, where the friendly American attitude was valuable not only because of the facilities for purchasing war materials and in particular horses from the United States,[2] but because so easily the struggle of the Boers for independence might have raised awkward memories of the great American struggle against Britain a hundred years before. Britain was isolated at this hour. Only America remained her friend at this time of danger when whispers of continental combinations began to be heard. The Irish-Americans were naturally vociferous against British Imperialism, and made many attempts to raise an Irish brigade; but the American Government prevented all these efforts; only an Irish ambulance unit was recruited, which as soon as it reached South Africa proceeded to fight against Britain.[3] Congress petitions for intervention or mediation looked formidable, but the American Government had little difficulty in preventing any action, and in the election of 1900 pro-Boer senators were mostly defeated.[4]

It must not, however, be thought that the rapprochement between Britain and America was an equal partnership. As Tyler Dennett, the biographer of Secretary of State John Hay, remarks: " The conflict in South Africa provided a favourable opportunity for dealing with England, . . . to give England another push towards the Atlantic Ocean. . . . The partnership of beneficence policy involved a division and a reapportionment of naval responsibility, in which Great Britain . . . would leave the Caribbean to the United States." [5]

Two outstanding questions were left over to the reign of Edward VII; the question of the Isthmus, where Britain had treaty rights and the United States wished to build an American-controlled canal; and the boundary between Canada and the territory of Alaska, which Russia had sold to America in 1867.

Russia was an important factor in the British international situation. Her expansionist policy menaced Britain in vital parts,

---

[1] J. Hay to Day, 28th July 1898. Quoted by L. M. Gelber, *The Rise of Anglo-American Friendship*, 31.
[2] J. H. Ferguson, *American Diplomacy and the Boer War*, 49, 50.
[3] Ibid., 67.   [4] Ibid., 212.
[5] Tyler Dennett, *John Hay: From Poetry to Politics*, 271.

the Eastern Mediterranean and the Suez Canal, Persia and the Indian frontier. In the Far East her advance into Northern China threatened Britain's very important market for the cotton industry, which was to such a considerable extent dependent on foreign outlet for its products, and provided one-quarter of Britain's total exports.

But if Russia had long been a menace, the rise of Japan as a power in the Far East had both added to the danger of the British position and provided the means of dissolving it. Should the Russians and Japanese join in alliance, their combined fleets would destroy the British supremacy in those waters. If they could be persuaded to draw each other's teeth, then the British position would be preserved for the time being; only of course for the time being. But Britain now must consider short views and temporary expedients as she tacked and veered to escape the rocks on which her Empire might suffer shipwreck.

CHAPTER XI

GOVERNMENT AND OPPOSITIONS

The first Government of Edward VII had been returned at the
General Election of 1900, which produced a Conservative majority
substantial enough to diminish the importance of the Irish
Nationalists, who were not in a position to hold the balance of
power.[1]

At its head was Lord Salisbury, that " glorious Bohemian," [2]
with the beard of his Elizabethan ancestor and the acid-stained
clothes of a chemist; still shrewd in the evening of his days,
clear-sighted in respect of all facts within his vision, but not
seeing very far, perhaps because he did not very much like the
look of the distant scene.

Its leading figure was Joseph Chamberlain, now seventy, but
with an energy which never let him rest. He had entered Parliament rather late in life, and appropriately made his maiden
speech just a week before Disraeli left the Commons. He came
with a solid reputation for municipal administration, a solid fortune acquired in the manufacture of screws, and with the advantage of a safe seat. He was already a well-known political figure,
a leading light among the Radicals of the period. King Edward
remembered him when as Prince of Wales he had visited Birmingham during Chamberlain's mayoralty. He was " a terrific socialist
then, quite the kind of man whom, if you mentioned his name at
a dinner table, it was like as if you talked of Tom Mann or someone like that." [3] He was indeed a terror to the Conservatives in
these early days. Disraeli was stung by his attacks: " Coarse
commonplace abuse, such as you might expect from the cad of
an omnibus " [4] though " he wears his monocle like a gentle-

[1] 334 Conservatives and 68 Liberal Unionists were returned (402 out of
670); 186 Liberals (and others classed with the Opposition, e.g. Keir Hardie);
and 82 Irish Nationalists.
[2] Balfour's phrase. Esher, *op. cit.*, Vol. 2, 55.
[3] F. Whyte, *Life of W. T. Stead*, Vol. 2, 109.
[4] Monypenny and Buckle, *Life of Disraeli*, Vol. 2, 820.

man."[1] He was formidable in debate, with a power of lucid and logical exposition rarely rivalled, and a command of cool insolence that infuriated his opponents and did not always win the approval of his friends.   There was something in the tall, smooth-faced figure, with the " lean long head and the adventurous nose,"[2] the monocle and the flamboyant orchid, which repelled as much as it attracted. Lord Salisbury agreed with a writer in an evening newspaper that he was " as touchy as a schoolgirl, and as implacable as Juno." " The personal element," he added, " is very strong."[3] He had an unforgiving temperament and refused to subscribe to a memorial for Mr. Gladstone, from whom he had separated on the Home Rule issue. Beatrice Webb, who had the chance of marrying him,[4] noted in her diary that he was " an enthusiast and a despot."[5] Bulow, the German Chancellor, who met him when he was sixty-three years old, commented on his youthful appearance, which he found the " more remarkable since he was unlike most of his compatriots in that he had no interest in sports or games, playing neither golf nor lawn tennis, never hunting or yachting or even going for walks. Not only that, but he was in the habit of smoking very long and very strong Havana cigars."[6]

But if he did not take walks he was fond of dancing and something of a phenomenon on the ballroom floor in Washington, whence not long since he had brought home his third wife. " He is nice enough," commented an American belle, " but he doesn't know how to dance. He takes such a short step that you think he must have practised on a postage stamp."[7]

He was loyal to his friends; in the case of Cecil Rhodes more loyal than to his Privy Councillor's oath. He did all that he could for Charles Dilke, when social catastrophe ruined that statesman's career.   Although ambitious for the achievement of political causes, which the demands of his temperament made him transform into crusades, he was not personally ambitious for office. Had he remained with Gladstone there was no rival for the Liberal succession.   After he had joined the Conservatives he never

[1] Arthur Mee, *Joseph Chamberlain*, 63.
[2] George Meredith's phrase. *Annual Register*, 1906, 9.
[3] Blanche C. Dugdale, *Arthur James Balfour*, Vol. 1, 101.
[4] M. I. Cole, *Beatrice Webb*.   [5] *My Apprenticeship*, 124.
[6] Bulow, *op. cit.*, Vol. 1, 312.   [7] Mee, *op. cit.*, 130.

intrigued against the ruling house of Cecil for the Premiership.

But what was the root of his Imperialism?

First it must be noted that it was limited in its emphasis. He paid small attention to India,[1] and it was indeed the economic position of India which did so much to wreck his Protection proposals. The split with Gladstone came on Home Rule. Was Ireland then the origin of his Imperialism? His friend Charles Dilke, ever since his voyage round the Empire as a young man, had expressed Imperialist sentiments. Did Dilke then sow the seed? Or must we attribute the main influence to commerce, " that greatest of all political interests," [2] to the awakening of Chamberlain and his Birmingham industrialist friends to the material rewards of Empire? In 1882 Chamberlain was one of the initial subscribers for shares in the Royal Niger Company, in which he made up his allotment to 1500 £2 fully paid shares.[3] He told an after-dinner audience that the completion of the Natal railway to Johannesburg would yield " dividends to make the mouth of an English director water." [4]

There was indeed a materialistic tinge in Chamberlain's political religion, which led Cecil Spring Rice to write sadly to a friend: " What do you think of Chamberlain? I should like to have someone lay stress on another aspect of patriotism, which friend Wordsworth describes so well; I mean the desire not only that your country should be great, but that it should be as a condition of greatness—good." [5] He seemed to glory in the violence with which his policy was attended.[6] He miscalculated the military hazards of the Boer War. His attempts at master-strokes of foreign policy were prejudiced by his substitution of business methods for diplomatic, and doomed to failure by their roots being rather in his own temperament than in the facts of the situation. But when all is said the man remains. He was, as Lord Esher remarked, " such a devil of a fellow." He was so " unlike

[1] See Zetland, *Curzon*, Vol. 3, 24. Cf. Lord George Hamilton, speech at Ealing, 22nd October 1903.
[2] J. Chamberlain, speech at Birmingham Chamber of Commerce Banquet, 1896.
[3] House of Commons debate, 6th July 1899.
[4] *British Empire Series*, Vol. 2, 96.
[5] S. Gwynn, *op. cit.*, Vol. 1, 235.
[6] See speech at Annual Dinner of Royal Colonial Society, 31st March 1897.

the ordinary politician or official." [1] He possessed such astonishing industry, although compared with Gladstone's Home Rule battles at 77 and 83, Chamberlain's Tariff Reform crusade at 67 appears somewhat feverish and neurotic. His seven years at the Colonial Office opened the funds of British trustees to the self-governing Colonies, laid the foundations of a Colonial Medical Service, introduced the Imperial penny postage, and sought to build up in the Colonial territories those reserves of raw materials essential to supremacy in the world of his day.

As liaison with Chamberlain, who remained to the end of his Cabinet career Colonial Secretary but much else besides, was the Prime Minister's nephew, Arthur Balfour. It was a curious combination: the crude Birmingham industrialist and the noble-born, dilettante philosopher, who found politics an amusing exercise for his dialectical nonchalance. But the two were not antipathetic. It was difficult to dislike Balfour, while the vigour of Chamberlain possessed an attraction for the more easy-going scion of the dominant house of Cecil. But there was another tie. Balfour had stood loyally by Chamberlain in the dark days at the beginning of the Boer War, when a section of the Conservative party might have welcomed a scapegoat. Such treatment appealed to Chamberlain and he never forgot it. [2]

Until his appointment as Irish Secretary in the eighties Balfour was considered a " silk-skinned sybarite, whose rest a crumpled rose leaf would disturb." [3] He was thought to have inherited some of the political cynicism of his uncle. He was an amateur philosopher, and one of the " Souls " who gathered round the fascinating Margot Tennant, later Mr. Asquith's second wife. Dialectics were his special forte, and when he was Prime Minister the King found him " rather more argumentative on paper than he liked." [4] He was widely read, and once informed an audience of working men that the work of Karl Marx was infinitely superior to that of Henry George. [5] Campbell-Bannerman called him " *l'enfant gâté*," in comparison with Chamberlain, " *l'enfant terrible*."

[1] Esher, *op. cit.*, Vol. I, 244.
[2] Esher, *op. cit.*, Vol. I, 340.
[3] Irish press. Quoted by E. T. Raymond, *Mr. Balfour*, 39.
[4] S. Lee, *op. cit.*
[5] E. R. Pease, *History of Fabian Society*, 45.

His conduct as Irish Secretary revealed a new Balfour. He met opposition with ruthless action, and employed the Coercion Act with excruciating efficiency.

There was always something detached in Balfour's attitude to the political scene. His defeat by the Manchester electors in 1906 seems to have been the only event that moved him to anger,[1] although when the Duke of Devonshire resigned in 1903 he felt so cross that he wrote to him from the New Club before he had even had his bath. His official biographer describes him as a " solitary at heart." [2] He was not a successful platform speaker, but in the House of Commons he displayed a superlative knowledge of that particular game called parliamentarianism. His health was not robust, but he enjoyed both lawn tennis and golf, and had shocked Mr. Gladstone by the spectacle of the Leader of the House riding a bicycle.[3] He was a frequent victim of influenza. Whether he had political convictions beyond the conviction that men of his class should govern Britain is doubtful. It seems probable that it was not only the aim of keeping his party together that led him to play down the Tariff Reform controversy. His mind was not a mind of black and white, but of fine shades. When he was making a speech he felt " a kind of subconscious mental doubt whether I am exaggerating and overstating my argument." [4] He was liked by most leading statesmen, although Campbell-Bannerman was a notable exception.[5] Mr. Balfour had of course no knowledge of the working man and little sympathy. He had been heard asking: " What is a trade union?" [6] When he was defeated at the 1906 election it was appropriate that he should petulantly remark: " I am certainly not going to go about the country explaining that I am honest and industrious like a second footman out of a place." [7] For Balfour belonged to the powerful Conservative group who considered that theirs was the government by divine right.

[1] Lord Newton, *Retrospection*, 146.
[2] Blanche C. Dugdale, *op. cit.*, Vol. 2, 19.
[3] A. J. Balfour, *Chapters of Autobiography*, 76.
[4] Fitzroy, *op. cit.*, Vol. 1, 401. Cf. Dugdale, *op. cit.*, Vol. 2, 40.
[5] Cf. Fitzroy, *op. cit.*, Vol. 1, 261. In Sir William Harcourt's opinion, " Balfour is one of the rare men who make public life tolerable and even respectable."
[6] Lucy B. Masterman, *C. F. G. Masterman*, 61.
[7] Dugdale, *op. cit.*, Vol. 2, 49.

The Chancellor of the Exchequer was Sir Michael Hicks-Beach, " Black Michael," whose " piratical manners " made elderly civil servants quail, although Balfour thought that in fact he had the " courage of a governess." [1] The Duke of Devonshire, whom the *National Review* described as " a statesman in the last stage of political ossification," [2] was Lord President of the Council, and a leading figure. The position occupied by this nobleman in English political life is not easily appreciated by a later generation. His character was considered a national asset. When Lord Salisbury was fixing the date of a Cabinet meeting he was careful to inquire of the Duke whether that was a " sacred day," meaning a race-day.[3] He was an inveterate bridge player. He was remarkable for a slow-working mind, which only endeared him to the public, although finally it was to cause him acute personal discomfort. He was the leading figure with Chamberlain in the Liberal Unionist group, which had left Gladstone on Home Rule, and was now fully integrated into the Conservative party. A great landowner, he had important financial interests. He was Chairman of the Barrow Hæmatite Steel Company, which made armour for British battleships. He was particularly concerned with British trade in China. His second wife was a German, and he seconded Chamberlain in all his efforts to bring about an Anglo-German alliance.

At the Foreign Office was Lord Lansdowne, to whom at Eton Balfour had been fag. As War Secretary at the outbreak of the Boer War he had been the target of violent criticism as the full measure of British military ineptitude became revealed. The *National Review* considered his promotion " a first-rate joke of Lord Salisbury's—one of the most cynical acts of our time." [4] The *Daily Mail*, the new popular paper, written so the Prime Minister declared " by office boys for office boys," was equally hostile. " It is a thoroughly bad precedent that a minister who had failed in one office should be rewarded by promotion to a higher and even more important office." [5] It is probable that Salisbury's choice was influenced partly by the need to give the old Liberal Unionists to whom Lansdowne belonged powerful

[1] A. Chamberlain, *Politics from the inside*, 183.   [2] December 1900.
[3] Lord Askwith, *Lord James of Hereford*, 256.
[4] December 1900.   [5] 1st November 1900.

representation in the new Government resulting from the Chamberlain victory at the polls, and partly by the belief that Lansdowne would listen to the permanent officials at the Foreign Office, and would not pursue a reckless policy. He proved a capable agent in bringing about the new orientation towards France, with whom he was sympathetically linked by the possession of a French mother.

At the Admiralty was Lord Selborne, allied to the house of Cecil by marriage. At the India Office was Lord George Hamilton. Secretary of State for Scotland was Lord Balfour of Burleigh, Deputy-Governor of the Bank of Scotland. Another bank director was Home Secretary, C. T. Ritchie, who was to have his political moment a few years ahead. To the Irish Office had been appointed George Wyndham, the most talented and cultured of the younger Conservatives, in whom some thought they saw a future Prime Minister. Seemingly for all time Lord Halsbury sat on the woolsack. Such were the leading figures in the first government of Edward VII, which followed the Conservative custom, which the Liberals eschewed, of permitting ministers to retain directorships. Ten Cabinet ministers held 15 directorships, and sixteen ministers not in the Cabinet held 26.[1]

The election, which had produced a comfortable Conservative majority, had been Chamberlain's election, the celebrated Khaki election of 1900 when the Boer War appeared, or was made to appear, over, and the stage was set for a vote of thanks to the men who had saved British honour (and British investments in the Transvaal Gold Mines); and a vote of censure on the Liberals, hopelessly divided on the war issue.

Chamberlain's tactics were simple and successful. A vote for a Liberal candidate was a vote for Kruger. Once the gage had been thrown down few Conservative candidates scorned to profit by it. Mr. Balfour used a poster which ran: " Our brave soldiers in South Africa expect that every voter this day will do his duty. To vote for a Liberal is to vote for the Boer." [2] Winston Churchill, fighting his last election as a Conservative for some years, ex-

---

[1] Balfour in the House of Commons, 19th February 1903, said that public life would become poorer not purer if ministers were prevented from holding directorships. A few months later the Financial Secretary to the Treasury resigned because of comments by Mr. Justice Buckley regarding the Telescriptor Syndicate of which he was a director.
[2] *Liberal Magazine*, November 1900.

pressed the same idea in cruder language: "Be it known that every vote given to the Radicals means 2 pats on the back for Kruger and 2 smacks in the face for our country."[1] It is surprising that the Liberal defeat was not even greater than it was.

At the 1895 election the Conservatives polled 1,780,000 votes and obtained 390 seats, and the Liberals 1,657,000 to obtain 177 seats. In 1900 the Conservative poll was 1,676,020 with 380 seats, and the Liberal 1,520,000 with 186 seats. The figures require the qualification of many unopposed Conservative returns, but there can be little doubt that only Chamberlain's astute tactics saved the day and postponed the end of the long period of Conservative rule until the avalanche of 1906.

It certainly cannot be said that there was any intense enthusiasm for the Conservative administration which had presented itself to the electorate after five years of office and one of war. The disasters in South Africa were too obviously in part due to miscalculations, and in particular to the somnolent inactivity since the Crimean War of the War Office, for the voters to feel any deep gratitude; but the Conservatives had one invaluable asset. As always in time of war they were united.

Arrayed against them was not one Liberal party, but a series of loosely connected groups.

There were the out-and-out supporters of the war, the group professing Liberal-Imperialism; "Chamberlain wine with a Rosebery label," Morley called it.[2] Led (if that is not too strong a word for the intermittent fulminations of that sulky Achilles) by the ex-Prime Minister, Lord Rosebery, the group was full of generals, Asquith, Edward Grey, Haldane, but without much support from the rank and file. There were the official Liberals, to whose uneasy leadership Sir Henry Campbell-Bannerman had succeeded at the beginning of 1899, when the feud between Sir William Harcourt and Lord Rosebery had been recognized to be interminable. With him was Lord Spencer, whom some fancied as the next Liberal Prime Minister (if there ever was going to be a next Liberal Prime Minister), Augustine Birrell, the witty man of letters, who was now presiding over the party publication department, and in a slightly detached position Morley, the biographer of Gladstone, and Sir William Harcourt,

[1] Ibid.   [2] Speech at Forfar, January 1900.

the former Chancellor of the Exchequer, now in semi-retirement.

They accepted to a greater or less degree the necessity of pursuing the war to a successful conclusion, but rejected the Chamberlain Imperialist policy, which they held had alone made war inevitable.

Finally there was the Radical group of the Liberal party, among whom Lloyd George was beginning to make his name. They condemned the war root and branch, and openly supported the Boers as a nation fighting for independence and therefore worthy of the sympathy of true Liberals.

CHAPTER XII

A POLITICIAN MANQUÉ

An important figure in a state with an Established Church was the Archbishop of Canterbury. At the accession the post was occupied by the aged Dr. Temple, but everyone knew that his days were few, and it was understood by those in the inner circle of politics that his successor was already chosen, the favourite chaplain of Queen Victoria, Randall Davidson, Bishop of Winchester. Dr. Temple survived to crown the King, although there was great anxiety whether he would have sufficient strength to perform the prescribed ceremonial. Soon afterwards he died, and Randall Davidson reigned in his stead.

The new Archbishop, who was to preside over the Church of England for twenty-six years, is rightly numbered among the politicians. He was " a cheerful-looking . . . man with very little of the prelate and nothing of the ascetic about him." [1] He had for long been closely associated with the Court, and when staying with Queen Victoria on the Riviera, felt " freshened up " on hearing that she wished to see him after luncheon.[2] The Duke of Argyll said that he was one of the very few preachers who prevented him from falling asleep.[3] It was, however, another influence that the acute Canon Scott Holland thought more dangerous to the new Archbishop than the Court. " Bishop Davidson's point of danger," he wrote, " is not the Court. . . . Rather is it to be sought in the Athenæum. There dwell the sirens who are apt to beguile and bewitch him. They have ceased to be mermaids with harps and have adopted the disguise of elderly and excellent gentlemen of reputation, who lead you aside into corners and in impressive whispers inform you what will not do and what the intelligent British public will not stand. The Bishop has a deep veneration for the judgment and the wisdom of important laity of this type." [4]

[1] G. K. A. Bell, *Randall Davidson, Archbishop of Canterbury*, 337.
[2] Ibid., 311.   [3] Ibid., 388.   [4] Ibid., 406.

Dr. Davidson was ever careful not to embarrass the Government. He was exceedingly circumspect on the Chinese Labour issue.[1] He always inquired of the Foreign Office before associating the Church with any action that might be unacceptable there.[2] When the Unemployed Problem became acute he refused to receive a deputation introduced by a clergyman, on the ground that economic problems were so difficult, and that "a man who like myself has to work for 16 or 17 hours a day in discharging his more immediate responsibilities cannot hope to be able to give these studies so much time as others can." But after writing this letter during a committee meeting he did not scruple to show it to Lord St. Aldwyn, formerly, as Sir Michael Hicks-Beach, Conservative Chancellor of the Exchequer, and was no doubt gratified by the minute of assent: "Most excellent. Don't alter a word. A."[3]

[1] House of Lords, 6th March 1904. "I feel that if indeed the necessity be real it is one of the most regrettable necessities that has ever arisen in the history of our Colonial Government."
[2] Bell, *op. cit.*, 481, 548.
[3] Ibid., 488.

CHAPTER XIII

BRITONS, BOERS, KAFFIRS, AND CHINESE

Most urgent of the problems facing the Government was the war in South Africa, which the Conservatives had assured the country, during the election, was now over.[1] Lord Roberts had handed the command of the forces in the field to General Kitchener, and had returned home. But once again Chamberlain had miscalculated. He had never expected that Kruger would fight. He had thought he was bluffing; and now he was unable to understand how the Boers, their organized forces smashed, their political leaders in flight, could continue the struggle to the exasperation of Britons and the unconcealed merriment of the majority of people abroad.

The foreign attitude to the war had come as a rude shock to the British public, who found it difficult to understand why peoples in other lands did not automatically accept the generous motives which had been provided for the action taken.

In all countries save one (the United States) the difficulties of the British Army were hailed with hilarious and sometimes rude jests. Nemesis seemed to have overtaken proud Albion. The Vatican *Osservatore Romano* expressed the hope that Protestantism was about to collapse,[2] though Cardinal Bourne was quick to associate himself with the fortunes of British arms.[3] The Russian Government suggested intervention, and only the deeper enmities

[1] The *Liberal Magazine*, February 1901, gives the following examples:
" The war now happily drawing to a close." Mr. Balfour, Manchester.
" Under the skilful leadership of Lord Roberts all difficulties have been overcome." Mr. Chamberlain, Birmingham.
" It is for the electors to say whether that settlement (the peace settlement) should be in the hands of those who have carried this war to a successful termination." Mr. Ritchie, Croydon.
" The war is over. I do not think that the people of this country have yet quite realized how great a war, how difficult a war, it has been." Mr. Chamberlain, Coventry.
[2] *Osservatore Romano*, 26th September 1899. Quoted by W. T. Stead, *Through Thirty Years*, 156.
[3] E. Oldmeadow, *Francis Cardinal Bourne*, Vol. 1, 169.

of the proposed participants, Germany, France and Russia, averted the danger. As it was, compensations in Samoa were demanded by Germany and received, while the Kaiser early in 1900 had written a curious letter of advice to his uncle, then Prince of Wales, suggesting that England should accept defeat by the Boers in the same spirit as they had defeat in the Test Match with Australia in the previous summer.[1]

Only the United States remained neutral in deed and for the most part in word, for the small noisy section across the Atlantic, who found in the struggle of the Boers against the might of Britain an echo of their own great fight two hundred years before, were unimportant in the conditions already noted.[2]

It was a galling situation. Some part of the howl of execration must be attributed to the belligerent oratory of Chamberlain and the blunt utterances of Lord Salisbury.

" We sometimes wonder," remarked Lord Rosebery, " why we are unpopular abroad. It is, I think, because we are too much engrossed with our own virtues, and forget that what would annoy ourselves in others equally annoys others in ourselves. We, in the past few years, have passed censure on some of the nations in Europe in a way which must give them cause for reflection and for no enthusiastic affection for us. We have called one of the most ancient nations in the world a ' dying nation,' we have compared another great Empire of the world to the devil, we have hinted that another great Empire of the world is less in space than one of our Colonies." [3]   But, even had British politicians soft-pedalled, the privileged position of the country would have excited envy, and, in the hour of distress, enjoyment.

[1] S. Lee, *op. cit.*, Vol. 1, 810.

[2] Senator Hoar, who opposed the war, said: " I suppose that the attitude of the United States in general towards Great Britain is an attitude of warm cordial friendship, and that we, when we think her in the wrong, . . . have the same feelings which patriotic Englishmen have towards their own Government when they think her in the wrong, and the same feelings which patriotic Americans have towards their own Government when they think her in the wrong." Hoar was more representative of responsible opinion than Senator Pettigrew, who said: " During the reign of Queen Victoria England has been engaged in forty wars and in every one she was the aggressor. . . . I want nothing to do with that nation of robbers and murderers." *Congressional Record*, Vol. 33, 1252, 4116.

[3] Edinburgh, 1st December 1899. The references are to Spain (Lord Salisbury, Guildhall, 9th November 1898), Russia (Chamberlain, Birmingham, 13th May 1898), Germany (Chamberlain, Whitehall Rooms, London, 21st January 1896).

The British public became restive. Lord Salisbury complained, in a tone that suggested that the Boers had not " played cricket," that their " guns were generally introduced in boilers and locomotives, and the munitions of war were introduced in piano-cases and tubes." [1] The Bishop of Sierra Leone declared that the only solution was a national day of prayer. While on leave at Braemar he wrote to *The Times* to " sound the bugle and call the people once again to prayer. We cannot forget Septuagesima Sunday of last year, which was set apart for prayer at the beginning of the present war in South Africa, and how it was immediately followed by the relief of Kimberley, the defeat and capture of Cronje and his army, the relief of Ladysmith and the capture and occupation of Bloemfontein. Can it be that we have ceased to pray seeing that we are not yet able to bring the war to an end? We have faith in the justice of our cause; then let us to the Lord our God, who wanteth to be gracious, yet will be inquired of, as in the days of old, to do it for us." [2] But the Government put their trust in new military measures, in the building of block-houses, the herding of Boer women and children into concentration camps, which soon raised a parliamentary storm, and began to bring together all the Liberals save the Liberal-Imperialists.

John Morley had been one of the first to protest against the war: " You may carry fire and sword into the midst of peace and industry," he had cried, " it will be wrong. A war of the strongest government in the world with untold wealth and inexhaustible reserves against this little republic will bring you no glory; it will be wrong. You may make thousands of women widows and thousands of children fatherless; it will be wrong. It may add a new province to your empire; it will still be wrong. You may give buoyancy to the African Stock and Share market; it will still be wrong." [3] His voice had been silenced amid the beating

---

[1] 30th January 1900.

[2] *The Times*, 24th September 1901.

[3] Manchester, 15th September 1899. William Watson wrote indignant verses on the new methods:

" Fulfil your mission; spoil and burn;
Fling forth the helpless—babes as well,
And let the children's children learn
To hate you with the hate of hell."

of the drums,[1] but now revelations of the conditions in the concentration camps revived the pricking of the Nonconformist Conscience, as Miss Hobhouse at Bloemfontein on 22nd January 1901 pulled back the curtain.

" I call this camp system a wholesale cruelty," she declared. " It can never be wiped out of the memories of the people. It presses hardest on the children. They droop in the terrible heat and with the insufficient, unsuitable food." [2]

Mr. Winston Churchill might declare in his maiden speech in February 1901 that the Government were justified in using any methods of warfare supported by modern European and American precedents. Mr. Chamberlain might attribute the appalling mortality to an epidemic of measles; but that section of the community which preserved its humanity was shocked. The callous phrases used by Kitchener in his dispatches, " Total bag . . . so many Boers killed, so many cattle and rounds of ammunition taken," [3] also helped to dispel the myth of a glorious war. In June Campbell-Bannerman used the phrase " methods of barbarism," [4] and was supported by the Liberal rank and file, although the Liberal-Imperialists held aloof. A new note of bitterness appeared in party politics, for Ministers were quick to retort that only the existence of pro-Boer views among the political opposition encouraged the rebels to continue the struggle. " Apostles of Im-

[1] Herbert Samuel in his *Liberalism*, 1902, has an interesting passage on the popularity of War in the Edwardian age, which is worth quoting: " If warfare continues it is largely because even in an age of enlightenment wars are popular. The fighting is welcomed for its own sake. There is still surviving much of the old barbaric delight ' in the merry days of battle.' Any war, unless it be flagrantly unjust or the capaign unsuccessful, is sure to evoke intense enthusiasm, and any government which engages in military operations is more likely to be admired than condemned. If we are candid we are bound to confess that this spirit is not different from that which led all Rome on a feast-day to flock to the Colosseum, and sit crowding to see the gladiatorial shows; it is the thrilling joy of watching a game in which men's lives are at stake."

[2] General Smuts, speaking at the funeral of Emily Hobhouse, made clear her contribution: " We stood alone in the world, almost friendless among the peoples, the smallest nation ranged against the mightiest Empire on earth. And then one small hand, the hand of a woman, was stretched out to us. At that dark hour when our race seemed doomed to extinction, she appeared as an angel, as a heaven-sent messenger, and strangest of all she was an Englishwoman. In the future of South Africa the whole meaning and significance of the Anglo-Boer war was permanently affected by this Englishwoman. And she became the greatest symbol of reconciliation between the closely-kin people who should never have been enemies."

[3] J. A. Spender, *Life of Sir Henry Campbell-Bannerman*, Vol. 2, 4.
[4] National Reform Union Dinner, 14th June 1901.

perial disintegration " was Balfour's phrase for Campbell-Bannerman and his group.

In October Lord Milner, whose inflexible diplomacy as High Commissioner had contributed to the outbreak of hostilities, pessimistically suggested that in a formal sense the war might never be over.[1] As late as April 1902, within three months of the Peace of Vereeniging, Dr. Kuyper, the Dutch Prime Minister, told a journalist that the Boers could continue their resistance for ten years longer.[2] But Kitchener's methodical efficiency was doing its work. He had trained in the field an army capable of the task set it by the peculiar conditions. The time had passed when he needed to forbid " the carrying about with them, by his mobile column, of furniture, kitchen ranges, pianos and harmoniums." [3] A new attitude had entered the British Army, and the lessons of the Boer War were not without their influence on a later battlefield.

But although it was a long war it was a small one. From first to last less than 500,000 British and Colonial troops were involved. Only 20,000 lives were lost by the victors, and the greater number of these were by illness. It was the repeated defeats of the forces of the great British Empire that inflated the significance of the struggle, for few indeed were the homes visited by the angel of death. Peace might have been obtained earlier but for Lord Milner's stubborn character. To secure it before the Coronation was considered imperative. In the event it was Campbell-Bannerman's much criticized phrase " methods of barbarism " that induced the Boers to sign the treaty. The expectation that the Liberals would form the next government, and would treat South Africa generously, persuaded the delegates.[4] The terms were reasonable enough. Money was promised to the Boers to rebuild their farms. Self-government would be granted in due course. The Afrikaans tongue was to be permitted in the law courts and in the schools. Only the yielding of sovereignty to the British Crown was required of the defeated Boer.

And if the question is asked why was the war fought there can be only one answer. The recourse to arms occurred because an

[1] Speech at Durban, 28th October 1901.
[2] *The Times*, 9th April 1902.
[3] *Annual Register*, 1902, 199.
[4] J. A. Spender, *op. cit.*, Vol. 2, 40. Lord Shaw, *Letters to Isabel*, 202, 203 n.

irresistible force, the British Government, came into collision with an immovable object, obstinate Oom Paul Kruger. But what compulsion led the British Government towards the struggle? Why was it impossible for them to withdraw as Gladstone withdrew in 1881? Not because Mr. Chamberlain was an Imperialist and Mr. Gladstone a Little-Englander, but because of the discovery of gold in the Boer republics in the late eighties.

If it is desired to know the real as opposed to the ostensible motives of a war, it is necessary to look not at the professions of the victors but at the fruits of their victory.

Money flowed through the London Stock Exchange into Kaffirs, no small part sticking to the fingers of the promoters of the crop of companies that were formed on the Witwatersrand. Influential sections of Society became involved, and when Kruger stood in the way of the reaping of their profits Kruger was swept aside. The expectations of the speculators are reflected in the prices of leading Kaffir shares before and after the outbreak of war. On 3rd October 1899, Consolidated Goldfields were £27½. On 20th October £38½. In the same period East Rand rose from £4. 7s. 8d. to £7¼, and Modderfontein from £7½ to £10½. Even at the end of the year, after the Black Week of the British Army, all these shares were still standing above the level at the outbreak of the war.[1] It is unusual for shares to rise at the beginning of a war; what then were the hopes of the speculators, who as the Mining Correspondent of *The Economist* remarked were, many of them, " quite respectable and churchgoers "?

The first gold-mines in South Africa were comparatively shallow, but the later flotations of the great Kaffir boom had been concentrated on deep-level propositions, whose working would inevitably be more expensive—unless economies could be made. But in what direction was it anticipated that these should be sought? A pretty problem was set the mining magnates. It is not very surprising that their first action, after the recovery of the properties by the shedding of British blood, was a substantial reduction in the wages of the Kaffir workers.

But of course, as the Mining Correspondent of *The Economist* argued, this reduction from 50s. or 60s. a month to 30s. was really a kindness to the Kaffir who " got no real advantage from

[1] F. W. Hirst, *Liberalism and the Empire*, 57.

the higher figure. A few shillings each month were spent on clothes, coloured handkerchiefs, hand-mirrors, sardines, sugar or butcher's meat, but at least half of the whole, the Unearned Increment, so to speak, was spent on foul poisonous liquor, which only did harm to the native himself, the company, the industry and the State." [1]

The Kaffir, however, who did not like going underground any-how,[2] had different views, and since alternative employment was open to him in reconstruction work under the Government, there began to be talk of special measures being necessary to meet the situation. For, as the mining magnates hastened to point out, if the mines were not profitably worked, it would alas! be quite impossible for them to contribute to the cost of the war. Compulsion was considered, but this would not solve the shortage due to competitive forms of employment, and given a sufficient supply the poll-tax method of compelling work from unwilling Kaffirs, which had been so successfully employed by Cecil Rhodes, and was approved by such men as Sir Edward Grey,[3] was adequate. Only two solutions of the dilemma were possible: the attraction of white unskilled workers from Europe, or the introduction of the Chinese coolie.

It was a vital decision affecting the development of South Africa, and the tracing of the debate, up to the passing of the Ordinance in 1904 permitting the importation of the Chinese under indentures, provides a classic example of economic pressure.

The employment of the Chinese immigrant was no new proposition. There had been resolutions in South Africa in its favour as far back as 1874, but opposition by the white worker was strong. Cecil Rhodes was attracted by the idea, and in September 1900, while the war still had nearly two years to run, the Trade Union Congress at Huddersfield had passed by a large majority a resolution condemning " the proposal of Mr. Cecil Rhodes to import Chinese Labour into South Africa with a view to enriching himself and the Chartered Company at the expense and to the

[1] *The Economist*, 9th February 1901.
[2] *The Economist*, 10th August 1901. " Black men, being governed by superstitions about bogeys, spooks and the like, will not if free work underground." Dr. J. S. Haldane, F.R.S., in a letter to *The Westminster Gazette*, 25th May 1904, stated that the mortality rate for natives in the Transvaal mines was over eleven times greater than for miners in England.
[3] Felton, 4th February 1903.

detriment of British subjects both here and in South Africa." Four years were to pass before a British Government " ever tender to the South African financiers " [1] took the fateful plunge. The opposition in South Africa was strong. The workers were hostile. The Vicar of a Johannesburg church was indeed " attracted by the possibility of evangelistic work among these people under very favourable conditions " and " hoped to get many of them sent back to their country good practising Christians." [2] The Witwatersrand Free Church Council was to approve Chinese Labour by 30 votes to 1. The Bishop of Pretoria gave his support.[3] But the clergy followed public opinion: they did not lead it; and in the days immediately after the war public opinion had not yet been manufactured by the mine-owners. Lord Milner, an early convert to the proposal, realized that it would be extremely difficult to get the thing through.[4]

For expert opinion was not wholly favourable. Mr. Creswell, the engineer of the Village Main Reef, supported the employment of white immigrants. His directors overruled him. " I have consulted the Consolidated Goldfields people, and one of the members of the Board of the Village Main Reef has consulted Messrs. Wernher Beit and Co.," wrote his chairman on 3rd July 1902, " and the feeling seems to be one of fear that if a large number of white men are employed on the Rand the same troubles will arise as are now prevalent in the Australian Colonies, i.e. that the combination of the labouring classes will become so strong as to be able to more or less dictate, not only on questions of wages, but also on political questions by the power of their votes when a representative government is established." [5] Keir Hardie's article in the *Labour Leader* on the Boer War seemed fanciful and exaggerated at the time; who would now criticize it on that score?

" The war," he wrote, " is a capitalist war. The British merchant hopes to secure markets for his goods, the investor an outlet for his capital, the speculator more fools out of whom to make money, and the mining companies cheaper labour and increased dividends. We are told it is to spread freedom and to extend the

---

[1] *The Economist*, 28th May 1904, " The demands of the Rand Magnates."
[2] J. A. Spender, *op. cit.*, Vol. 2, 146 n.
[3] Duke of Marlborough, Under-Secretary for Colonies, 18th March 1904.
[4] *Milner Papers*, Vol. 2, 481.
[5] *The Economist*, 24th October 1903.

rights and liberties of the common people. When we find a Conservative Government expending the blood and treasure of the nation to extend the rights and liberties of the common people we may well pause and begin to think." [1]

Once the decision had been taken by the mining magnates the obtaining of their wishes was only a matter of preserving the forms. In the autumn of 1902 Chamberlain left England in one of the newest cruisers to visit South Africa, travelling through the country in regal state with " marquees luxuriously furnished with cut flowers in profusion . . . at the end of each day's journey . . . tables which would have done credit to any banquet, at least in South Africa . . . fresh fish from the cold-storage vans carried seventy-five miles on ice . . . and close on 1000 mules . . . to convey the party." [2] The Labour problem was one, perhaps the most important, reason for his tour, which Mr. Balfour described as a " happy intuition." In January 1903 *The Economist* expressed anxiety: " Thousands of miles from the centre of Government and from his colleagues in the Cabinet we have the Colonial Secretary settling the finances of this country with a group of capitalists. . . . The proposal that the difficulty (of Labour) should be met by the importation of Chinese Labour has produced strenuous protests from quarters usually favourable to the ministry. We sincerely trust that no bargain has been arrived at on this labour question, and that in return for their contribution (to the cost of the war) the mining companies have not been encouraged to believe that they will be accorded special privileges at the hands of the government." [3]

But Mr. Chamberlain was too astute to back directly Chinese Labour importation. When Lord Milner expressed his conversion to the introduction, the Colonial Secretary recorded in a minute that " such action would be extremely unpopular, and would raise a storm at home. . . . The feeling at present all over South Africa is against such a policy and as long as it continues it is not likely that the Home Government would give its assent." [4]

[1] William Stewart, *J. Keir Hardie*, 159.
[2] *The Times.* Quoted by *Annual Register*, 1902.
[3] *The Economist*, 17th January 1903. " The Rand and the Cost of the War."
[4] *Milner Papers*, Vol. 2, 314. For Milner's own view see letter to Bishop Hamilton Baynes, 28th March 1904: " As for slavery, there is no more slavery in this than in a hundred forms of service based upon free contract—certainly not as much as in ordinary enlistment in the Army." 487.

The Liberal party, always excepting the Liberal-Imperialists, girded itself for battle. Sir William Harcourt wrote passionately to *The Times*: "There are questions of vital importance not to be decided by Park Lane, nor even by Downing Street. There are things more precious than gold, and amongst them is the reputation of the British race both at home and beyond the seas. There is much to be said and much to be done before such an injustice to a defenceless people, who have passed under our dominion, can be accomplished. I say nothing of the danger of such a policy—though it is perilous enough—I enter my protest against its profound immorality and its lasting disgrace. In the evil days of American slavery it was thought to cloak the ugly word slave by the euphemism of ' persons held to labour.' No one will be deceived by the delusive phrase of ' indirect compulsion,' which in plain terms is neither more nor less than forced labour." [1]

The veteran statesman repeated his charges in debate, and Chamberlain in his reply was bland and smug: " As to Indian or Chinese Labour, no proposal had been made to him on the subject, nor so far as he knew was any proposal likely to be made. There was a strong feeling in South Africa against the introduction of Asiatic labour. . . . But," he added, " if, however, the view which they now entertained were to change, this country would be powerless to interfere, for it was the policy of the Government to treat the Transvaal as if it were a self-governing colony." [2]

This of course was a clear indication to the mine-owners that if they could secure a majority vote in the Transvaal Legislative Council the Government would issue the necessary ordinance.

The situation brooked no delay. Kaffir shares had fallen sharply, and six months after the end of the war they were lower than when peace had been signed. In October the Mining Correspondent of *The Economist*, while arguing for the attraction of European immigrants, although " of course if he came there he would have his Unions and perhaps give trouble now and then . . . his vote could not be relied on by the mine-owners; but eventually his presence would bring more prosperity to the country than would the presence of a horde of Asiatics working on indentures," had

[1] *Life of Sir W. Harcourt*, Vol. 2, 552.
[2] House of Commons, 19th March 1903.

illogically added: " I think the Transvaal is not ready for the immediate entrance of a big band of men, who would be mostly foreigners. The Chamber of Mines should meet at once and dispatch orders for the shipment of an army of Chinese coolies," and had ended with a threat: " If the Government refuses to allow this it must be prepared to see a huge slump all over South Africa and deep discontent among mine shareholders." [1]

In November there was a fresh break in Kaffir shares. " There is no doubt," wrote *The Economist*, " that the sponsors of the gold-mining industry in South Africa are putting as pessimistic a complexion upon them as they can well do. In the market such tactics are simply regarded as a little window-dressing entertainment preparatory to the Colonial Secretary's inspection on the spot. and that the New Comet has had to close down during the last few days in consequence of lacking labour is mentioned with a twinkle of one eyelid." [2] " To gamble in Kaffirs," it was added, " is like speculation in Yankees, and the public must recognize that the insiders play with loaded dice." [3] A member of the Stock Exchange, who had suffered losses in the market, committed suicide,[4] and a Dr. Meysey Thomson wrote to *The Economist* in plaintive terms: " Labour at reasonable rates is an absolute necessity. If it cannot be obtained the gold will remain in the earth, South Africa will languish, and we shall obtain no return for the sacrifice we have made, either in seeing South Africa happy and prosperous or in receiving back in hard cash any of the money we have spent there." [5]

The Economist was not easily enlisted in the campaign, though it gave free rein to its dashing Mining Correspondent, who wrote in March 1903: " It is a plain economic issue. A matter of £. s. d. If the people in England and elsewhere who own Transvaal mining shares to the aggregate of two hundred million pounds want to get their money back with interest they will have to tackle this labour question in the right spirit. . . . (The Chinaman) on the Rand with a full belly, with no cares, with money accumulating

---

[1] *The Economist*, 11th October 1902.

[2] *The Economist*, 15th November 1902. The New Comet Mine was the first to recommence production as a direct result of the importation of Chinese abour. *Milner Papers*, Vol. 2, 485.

[3] *The Economist*, 13th December 1902.

[4] *The Economist*, 22nd November 1902.

[5] *The Economist*, 22nd November 1902.

to his credit, will be as happy as a King." [1] The Editor pointed out that the question of whether the introduction of a lower and cheaper description of labour was necessary to make the mines pay " depends upon whether the earning capacity of the mines is to be calculated upon their original capitalization, their present capitalization, or the valuation of the capital in the market." [2]

It is important to realize that not profits but super-profits were at stake, profits large enough to show a return on the inflated prices at which many Kaffir shares had been issued or to which they had been subsequently hoisted.

The pressure continued. In May 1903 *The Economist* recorded that " whichever way the Asiatic question may be settled it remains very certain that the mines are not going to be permitted to starve for lack of labour." [3] The Mining Correspondent, more confident now, thus summed up the position a month later : " On the one side are the mine directors and shareholders who say this : ' Our ore is not rich ore; to work it at a profit we require cheap black labour, such as has existed since the commencement of the goldfields. We find that the local supply of black labour is not equal to the demand, and we therefore propose to seek elsewhere for a supply.' On the other side are the white labourers and the shopkeeper. The white labourer is afraid that cheap labour from outside will reduce the present scale of wages, and the shopkeeper is afraid that miners who come from a distant country will return to that country with their wages rather than spend them on the spot. . . . The victory will be with Capital. When I speak of Capital I do not necessarily refer to the few dozen capitalists (whose name is anathema to so many people), but to the great body of shareholders, many of whom I understand are quite respectable and churchgoers. . . . This is not the time to sell shares." [4]

But to obtain the coveted Ordinance a majority in the Transvaal Legislative Council was necessary. " Wholesale bribery " was used,[5] and on 30th December 1903 the proposal was approved

---

[1] *The Economist*, 21st March 1903.
[2] " The original capital of the City and Suburban was £85,000, which has been increased to £1,360,000, the shareholders receiving four £4 shares £1 paid for each original share. Present value £2,252,000."
[3] *The Economist*, 23rd May 1903.
[4] *The Economist*, 13th June 1903.
[5] *Annual Register*, 1903, 387. Wyberg, Commissioner of Mines, resigned because of influence by financial interests, 404.

by 22 votes to 4, the official, nominated members voting in the majority.

The centre of interest now shifted to London. Would public opinion be too strong, and prevent the mining shareholders reaping their profits? Chamberlain had left the Colonial Office, where that Test Match cricketer, Mr. Alfred Lyttleton, presided in his stead. Mr. Seddon, the Prime Minister of New Zealand, sent a special protest, and asked for a referendum on the issue. There were warnings of the disorders experienced in other places where cheap Chinese labour under indentures had been introduced. The Liberal party thundered against the Ordinance. The Labour movement, which had gone on record against the proposal over three years before, held a monster demonstration in Hyde Park.[1] Sections of the Church were still dismayed at the moral issues involved. The leadership of the Archbishop of Canterbury consisted in his remarking that " if indeed the necessity be real it is one of the most regrettable necessities that has ever arisen in the history of our Colonial Government." [2] The Ordinance was duly issued, and on 25th May 1904 the first shipload of Chinese, who were to save the speculators from ruin, left Hong Kong, reaching Cape Town on 18th June.

There were no women with them; [3] nor was this surprising, since it is doubtful whether they understood the indentures they signed,[4] and in any case not even two Chinese could live cheaper than one on the wages offered on the Witwatersrand.

The Ordinance laid it down that only unskilled labour for

[1] 26th March 1904.　　　　[2] House of Lords, 4th March 1904.
[3] Violet R. Markham, supporting Chinese Labour in *The New Era in South Africa*, 1904, stated: " Family life will not be interrupted, for wives and families are to accompany the coolies " (138); also that " he is free to return home at any time on paying his return fare and a proportion of his outward fare " (140). For another defence of Chinese Labour see Frank Johnson at Royal Colonial Society, 12th November 1901 (*Proceedings*, Vol. 33, " Rhodesia, its present and future "). " Unskilled Chinese Labour will effect a reduction of at least 3s. per ton in the average working cost of the mines and (what is of greater importance) will ensure the regularity of output and profits and thus by establishing confidence admit the inflow of Capital. . . . We should not import black British subjects who would claim equal rights with us directly they came inside our territory. We could not agree to their starting stores and ousting the white man. We think it proper to keep them in their proper place."
[4] Rev. Arnold Foster wrote to *The Chinese Times* that the advertisements made no mention that the labourer was to be compulsorily repatriated, that they would live in compounds, that they would be forbidden to trade or hold property, that they were allowed to bring wife and children, that the work would be underground.

mineral exploitation must be imported. A licence cost £100, and the importer was under the obligation of returning the labourer to his country at the end of the period. The indentures lasted for three years, renewable for a further two. The rights in a coolie could be transferred, but not at a profit. No property could be acquired by the labourer. A minimum wage of 1s. for a day of 10 hours was prescribed. Sundays, as the local clergy joyfully observed, were to be days of leisure for the Chinaman, who also was granted six further days a year for Chinese festivals.

They were to live in compounds, which Earl Grey told the House of Lords would be " more like a garden city than anything else." [1] Later a mining magnate declared at a banquet that the Chinese were " living like mandarins on the Rand." [2] But of the 1055 who left Hong Kong in the first shipload six died on the voyage, and soon beri-beri was reported to be rife. The promised disorders followed. By September 1905 out of 46,895, 2543 had been convicted, and, by an amending Ordinance, Superintendents and Inspectors were given criminal jurisdiction with power to impose penalties such as six months labour, 25 lashes and collective fines. But the Kaffir market revived. Ruin, which had come close to the Stock Exchange speculator, was averted; and, sustained by the strong arms of the coolie, prices moved upwards.

" Chinese Slavery " the Liberals called the system, a term which Mr. Winston Churchill later admitted was a " terminological inexactitude "; but if precision was wanting, the importation under restrictive indentures of foreign workers was a strange consequence of a war to which the British Government had summoned all parts of the Empire in the name of Freedom.

The gibe was often made by Conservative supporters, that when the Liberals came into office they would maintain the system. But when Sir Henry Campbell-Bannerman succeeded Mr. Balfour in December 1905 he at once tackled the problem. Further importations were stopped, although he was compelled by the advice of the Law Officers to maintain the existing indentures, a postponement which he was careful to explain to the country before the ensuing General Election.

[1] 18th March 1904.
[2] Mr. Lionel Phillips, Annual Banquet, 1904, of the Chemical, Metallurgical and Mining Society.

But the position remained difficult. The Transvaal Parliament was dependent on the mine-owners. How could it be made free, and the decision reversed by a democratic vote? The way was found when a loan guaranteed by the British Government was granted to General Botha's administration. The Colonial Secretary was frank: " The effect of the British guarantee has been to make the Transvaal Government independent of the influence and control of those great mining corporations. We wanted to show them that there were other credit resources in the world besides those dependent upon the favour of the Witwatersrand connexion." [1]

On 14th June 1907 the Transvaal Parliament brought Chinese Labour to an end and on 28th February 1910 the last batch of the imported coolies left the country. During the General Election of 1906 Lord Harris, Test Match cricketer and Mining Director, had declared in a speech at Dulwich that " if white men were employed at the rate of pay to which white men are entitled many of the mines would not be worked at all." The truth of this statement was never put to the proof. When the Chinese left, Kaffir labour was adequate to fill the gap. It is however important to realize that the gap had narrowed. As Sir Abe Bailey, one of the most prominent and successful of South African mining promoters, pointed out: " Owing to the improvement in machine hand-drills fewer natives are now required underground." [2]

Science had successfully solved the problem set it by Capitalism. It is interesting to note that small progress was made during this period in reducing the accident rate.[3]

[1] Winston Churchill, House of Commons, 20th June 1906.
[2] *Liberal Monthly*, November 1907, 645.
[3] See Annual Reports of the Government Mining Engineer, Transvaal Mines Department. The Report for 1909 gives the following annual averages of fatal accidents per 1000 workers: 1896, 4·89; 1897, 4·30; 1898, 4·31; 1901–2, 3·33; 1902–3, 4·04; 1903–4, 4·75; 1904–5, 4·53; 1905–6, 5·55; 1906–7, 4·71; 1907–8, 4·18; 1908–9, 5·29.

CHAPTER XIV

COUNTING THE COST

But, if the South African War was a small war, it was not a cheap one. Its direct cost to the Exchequer of about £200,000,000 was more than a quarter of the cost of the war against Napoleon, which had lasted eight times as long;[1] while the last foreign war in which British arms had been engaged, the Crimean, had cost only a third of the present total, and had left no greater mark on the national finances than the continuance of the Income Tax, which Gladstone had intended otherwise to remove.

How serious would the Exchequer find the exasperating prolongation of the Boer resistance?

The check in the eighties to the growth of British trade, the menace of foreign competition, the rise of new Great Powers, were all reflected in the tone of anxiety which, for some years past, had marked the Budget speeches of the Chancellor of the Exchequer. In his first Budget (1887) Goschen, a City man as well as a politician, declared that the revenue was no longer " elastic." A search began to be made for new forms of taxation, for it was generally accepted (to the comfort of the income-tax payer) that that tax was a war tax, as indeed it had been in its origin, a stand-by to be screwed up only to meet a great emergency.

Also in the United States the Income Tax had become a political symbol. It had been declared unconstitutional by the Supreme Court in 1895, when Mr. Justice Field summed up the issue in challenging words: " The present assault upon capital is but the beginning. It will be but the stepping-stone to others, larger and more sweeping, till our political conditions will become a war of the poor against the rich; a war growing in intensity and bitterness." [2] The Income Tax had been an issue in the memorable election of 1899, when Bryan, the Great Commoner

---

[1] See B. Mallett, *British Budgets*, 1887-8 to 1912-3. On his careful analysis I have drawn widely.

[2] *Pollock v. Farmers Loan and Trust Co.*

of America, went down before the wealth and intimidation of the Republican campaign.

In his second Budget Goschen proposed a tax on pleasure-horses and on racehorses, and, although this was later abandoned, its introduction shows how difficult the situation was for the Chancellor in a Conservative administration. Goschen, in the uncomfortable position of an ex-Liberal, could only point out that reform of the Death Duties was overdue, as also of the Income Tax. He did not dare to move in the matter, even if he wished to do so. The situation became increasingly serious. In 1889 a large naval construction programme had been introduced. But once again alcohol came to the rescue; alcohol, which in an earlier age had enabled the country to drink its way out of the Alabama claims. More tea too was being drunk by the working class and more tobacco smoked.[1] Goschen, enabled by the confidence with which he was regarded by the City to make a substantial saving in the National Debt charge, completed his six years at the Exchequer without mishap. There was indeed something unreal in the customary statements that the sources of revenue were exhausted, and the present ones no longer elastic. More precisely the position was, as a responsible Liberal member of parliament remarked in connexion with the Budget of 1899, that they had " a Government which dare not tax the poor, and will not tax the rich." [2]

To tax the poor was to run the risk of defeat at the polls by the increased electorate; to tax the rich has not been a habit of the Conservative party. How then could the dilemma be resolved?

In the event the solution for the time being was found in the interruption of Conservative rule in 1892, and the passing into law of Harcourt's revised death duties. But still expenditure rose, both from natural increases and from larger armaments. The country entered the Boer War under Conservative government with the assistance of the new duties, whose yield exceeded their

[1] Cigarette smoking was brought to Britain by the soldiers who fought in the Crimea. Ruskin criticized the habit for " enabling a man to do nothing without being ashamed of himself." Tobacco consumption, which in 1851 was 16·3 oz. per head, had risen to 30·2 oz. by 1901. It was still considerably lower than in Germany. The *New Dictionary of Statistics*, 1911, gives the German annual average consumption for 1904–6 as over 56 oz.

[2] Fletcher Moulton, afterwards Lord Moulton.

author's most sanguine expectations, but without a solution of the perennial dilemma.

The difference between Direct and Indirect taxation and its social and political implications had for some time been eagerly discussed, and although Hicks-Beach was able to point out that the proportions which in 1841 had been 27% Direct and 73% Indirect had now changed to 51·6% Direct and 48·4% Indirect, the new Electorate was not satisfied. Graduation, which is the relation of tax to the amount of income, and Differentiation, the relation of tax to the character of income, began to be urged. How then would Sir Michael Hicks-Beach finance the South African War?

In view of the Conservative dilemma it is not perhaps surprising that the proportion of the war expenditure raised by taxation was substantially lower than that provided from that source in either the Napoleonic or Crimean wars. Nearly 70% was covered by loans, the performance of Great Britain being imitated and excelled by Japan, when a few years later she fought the Russians.

The Income Tax was increased from 8d. to 1s. 3d.; Tobacco, Beer, Spirits, Sugar, Tea, all contributed. A proposed increase from 1d. to 2d. on cheques was abandoned under City pressure, but a coal export tax was maintained in spite of representations by the coal-owners and a threatened strike by the mine-workers.

The raising of loans was assisted by the exceptionally high price of Consols. For part of his second loan Hicks-Beach went to Wall Street, since the English market thought his terms not sufficiently attractive.

Only the Corn Tax, the last of the taxes imposed, requires comment. Was this only a war tax? What were the real motives of the Chancellor in introducing it? He must have realized the storm which a tax on food would inevitably raise. He cannot have forgotten the Anti-Corn-Law League, and the fatal split in the Tory party in the days of Peel and Disraeli.

It would be interesting to know when Hicks-Beach made his decision. Sir Robert Giffen had written a series of letters to *The Times* three months before the Corn Tax Budget of 1902. In these he suggested a drastic broadening of the basis of taxation. In addition to 1s. on corn he advised 1d. per gallon on petroleum, 1s. on timber, 3d. more on tea, ½d. more on sugar. Was this a kite? Was the ground being prepared so that when Hicks-Beach proposed only 1s. on corn the tax would be received with relief for its insignificance?

For it was an insignificant imposition in itself. It is true that some bakers immediately increased the price of bread by $\frac{1}{2}d.$ per quartern loaf, but although naturally the opposition linked this increase with the new duty it is probable that the decision had been made before the Budget was introduced. It was rather as a portent that the new tax was important, and in this respect the Giffen letters with their larger programme were significant.

But these letters were not the first reference to a Corn Tax in the pages of the influential *Times* at this period. In March 1901, a year before Hicks-Beach took the plunge, the City Page contained an article " from a correspondent " on " The Reform of Taxation," in which " a moderate duty on sugar with moderate duties on imported corn and agricultural produce " were proposed. Pressure was even then being exercised on the leaders of the Conservative party by their supporters.

Whence did this pressure come?

The party still included unrepentant Protectionists. The question was declared an open one, and the prophecy of Disraeli that Protection would come again, and come at the request of the working classes, had not been forgotten. Henry Chaplin, Sir Howard Vincent and James Lowther still hoped to convert their Tory colleagues to their views. But there was another figure, more powerful, more formidable than they, who may have played a part; Joseph Chamberlain, whose interest in the coherence of the British Empire was already turning his thoughts to Protective duties, and to the dangerous territory of food taxation.

The Chancellor publicly declared that only the need of revenue induced him to impose the duty. He was a free trader. He was also at heart a timid man, although his manner was rude. He cannot have been unaware that Mr. Chamberlain would, to say the least, not be opposed to its introduction; nor can he have forgotten that in July 1902 the Colonial Conference, on which Chamberlain built high hopes, was to be held in London. Sir Wilfrid Laurier, the Canadian Premier, remarked that with this Budget England introduced a policy of protection.[1]

[1] *The Times*, 23rd April 1902.

But there was another group interested in the duty, those who were concerned with the problem of Britain's food supplies in time of war. Any improvement in the yield of native agriculture would assist the nation in that contingency. Might not a corn tax be a form of insurance? The Duke of Devonshire, in spite of his free trade traditions, was perhaps influenced by this argument.[1]

The genesis of the tax therefore was probably complex, with the need for revenue other than from a further rise in the Income Tax playing the chief conscious part in the mind of Hicks-Beach, but the need to conciliate Chamberlain exerting a perhaps unconscious pressure on the ageing Free Trade Chancellor.[2] He was of course able to put up a good debating case for the new duty. When protection had been swept away in the forties the old registration duty of 1s. a quarter on foreign corn had been retained. Mr. Gladstone had failed to remove it, and it was only when Lowe in 1869 found himself with a surplus, which he did not know where to apply, that the duty had gone. But as Liberals, strongly supported by Harcourt, at once realized, there was a difference between a Protective duty prolonged after the introduction of Free Trade, and one inserted into an established Free Trade system, the difference between the last snows of summer and the thin end of the wedge.

For it was a protective duty. The Milling industry reaped a substantial benefit from this so-called revenue tax. Three million more sacks of flour were ground during 1902–3, and a deputation of Millers, introduced by Henry Chaplin, made furious representations when the duty was removed in 1903 by Mr. Ritchie, Hicks-Beach's successor. It was this removal that precipitated Chamberlain's Tariff Reform campaign in May 1903, an event which will occupy a later part of this narrative.

In the Budget debates of 1902 the young Winston Churchill made a memorable speech. He asked what would happen if the free trade issue were openly raised by some responsible person of

---

[1] He was Chairman of the Royal Commission on Food Supplies in Time of War.

[2] According to W. S. Hewins (see *Apologia of an Imperialist*) Hicks-Beach would have preferred a tax on manufactured goods, but the data were not available. It is interesting to speculate whether this would have affected the course of events so unfavourably for his party, but such speculations are of course unhistorical.

eminence and authority in the country. They would stand once more on the old battlefields. He wondered how the advent of such a tremendous issue would affect the existing disposition of the political parties. The issue was raised. Mr. Balfour, mindful of the disastrous split in the Tory party under Peel, preserved unity, and Winston Churchill made the first of his party changes in time to be included in the Liberal ministry of 1906.

The influence of the corn tax on the fortunes of the Conservative party was swallowed up in the greater influence of the ensuing Chamberlain campaign, but it produced an immediate reaction in the loss of a by-election largely fought on the issue, while a flood of leaflets from Conservative Headquarters show how powerful the ghost of the Anti-Corn-Law League was realized to be.

Most important, it provided the common ground for the various Liberal groups to come together.

" Dear Food " and " Chinese Labour " were to haunt the Conservatives at the Election of 1906, and to contribute to the overwhelming Liberal victory. It was natural that they should. Less natural at first sight is the storm raised by the Education Act of 1902, of which Joseph Chamberlain was to write to the Duke of Devonshire: " The political future seems to me—an optimist by profession—most gloomy. . . . Our best friends are leaving us by scores and hundreds, and they will not come back." [1]

[1] B. Holland, *Life of Duke of Devonshire.*

CHAPTER XV

CHURCHMEN, NONCONFORMISTS, AND SCHOOLCHILDREN

Although it is possible to trace many factors in the development of the British Educational system (the counterpart of the extension of the franchise—" we must educate our masters "—the urge from below, the compulsion from above; the perennial interest of the Church in Religious Education; the secular passion of a handful of University teachers), it is impossible to reach any other conclusion than that the decisive factor was the economic, the growth of trade competition from Germany and the United States.

" Our public education system as adopted in 1870 was the outcome of agitation on the part of two classes—the intellectual class, who saw that we were very nearly the worst educated nation in Christendom, and the commercial class, which saw that our markets were threatened by competitors unless we took up in earnest the task of providing our children with the key of knowledge." Thus *The Economist* in 1901.[1] Aware of the connexion between economics and politics we can go further. Bismarck was the midwife of our educational system. Düppel and Konnigratz gave the necessary shock, and drew attention to the formidable fruit of Prussian instruction. Trade competition in the seventies underlined the relative backwardness of Britain in the schooling of its children. In 1901 *The Times* used the King Alfred Millenary celebrations in a Trafalgar Day plea for " an invincible Navy and an instructed Nation." [2] The lengthy debates of 1902 (for Education is one of those subjects on which we are all experts, particularly members of parliament) teem with references to the American and the German accomplishment. Michael Sadler in one of his

---

[1] 13th April 1901. See also Lloyd George: " Menacing rivals stand in our industrial path, and education is the best means of keeping abreast or of getting ahead of them. The ship of state is making its way through the midst of rocks, and what is the Government's proposal? To put the chaplain on the bridge." Quoted by W. Watkin-Davies, *Lloyd George, 1863–1914.*

[2] 21st October 1901. Leading Article.

educational reports, quoted in the debates, stated that " the very existence of the Empire depends on sea-power and school-power." [1] Educationalists and Imperialists at the beginning of the century were agreed that a further advance was necessary, and it fell to the Conservative government to be the agent for a measure which a mixture of motives drew from it.

It is clear from Mr. Balfour's later admissions of surprise at the expensive development that the Act produced, and from the absence of any party educational policy (one was borrowed from Mr. Sidney Webb), that educational advance was not the compelling motive of the Government in 1902.

The Act of 1870 establishing the School Boards had not been concerned with secondary education, which had been the subject of a Royal Commission set up under the chairmanship of Mr. Bryce, the author of *The American Commonwealth*, in 1894. The Bryce Commission issued its report in the following year, advising a central authority for secondary education, which should take over the small existing provision; and that in each county and county borough a local authority for secondary education, supervised but not controlled from the centre, should be established. These bodies were to be independent, with the power of determining the amount of the rate.

In its broad principles the Report represented informed educational opinion, but the position of the School Boards in connexion with extended secondary education was a matter of controversy.

Sidney Webb,[2] the educational expert of the Fabians, strongly opposed the control of secondary education by the School Boards on the ground of their educational unfitness; but these Boards had had time to grow into a vested interest, and when Lord Salisbury's government introduced a bill in 1896 giving the County Councils direct control of secondary education, and at the same time repealing the Cowper-Temple clause of 1870 (which forbade denominational teaching in a school provided out of public funds), the opposition was so vehement that the bill was withdrawn. The religious issue was explosive. Any government reopened it at its peril.

---

[1] Speech by Mr. Emmot (Oldham), *Hansard*, CVII, 753.
[2] See B. Webb *Our Partnership*, 252-5, for his support of Act of 1902.

And yet without the raising of the issue further educational advance was scarcely possible, for the voluntary schools were falling behind the schools provided from the rates. The Church was finding the pace too great. Although Mr. Balfour informed the Commons that what the voluntary schools had done in the way of raising money was "perfectly marvellous,"[1] the marvellous was not enough, even though the Minister responsible for Education had done all that he could by administrative means to ease the burden.[2] The premises and equipment of the Church schools were inferior, and their teaching staffs less well qualified, so that while in the Board Schools 51% of the teachers were certificated, in the Church schools the proportion was only 38%.[3] From pulpit and platform and in the more discreet contacts with government the cry of help for the Church schools rose ever more strongly. In December 1901 the Bishop of Rochester wrote significantly to Mr. Balfour: " I think I can claim that the battle has been gallantly fought; the Bishops have everywhere put their whole influence into the task of heartening the clergy to keep on; the clergy have worked themselves in many places to the bone about it; subscriptions have very slightly fallen (in my diocese, not fallen) and all through spirit has been kept up by the belief that change was coming and that this government would give relief."[4] The Roman Catholic Church considered the situation so serious that a united front with the Church of England was publicly advised. " Let me point out to you," declared Cardinal Vaughan, " that the next session of Parliament may settle for ever the position of Christianity in this country. . . . Let us join hands then in the campaign that is before us with all who are like-minded; with members of the Church of England."[5] Already in the election of 1900 the Catholic vote had been marshalled against the Liberals on this issue. A letter of the Roman Catholic Bishop of Nottingham in *The Catholic Times* was thought by the Liberals to have lost them Stockton, where it was issued as a leaflet. " If the result of the Election should be that the Liberal party is returned to power," wrote the Bishop, " we shall be sub-

[1] House of Commons, 24th March 1902.
[2] G. A. N. Lowndes, *The Silent Social Revolution*, 71, 75.
[3] Ibid., 71.
[4] B. M. Allen, *Sir R. Morant*, 163.
[5] Speech at Newcastle-on-Tyne, 1st September 1901.

jected to the government of men who are pledged to promote a system of public education opposed to the teaching of the Catholic faith and to the very existence of the Catholic schools. . . . Hand over your schools to be made Board Schools, or shut them up. Such would be their cruel mandate. They know full well that without our fair share in the state-aid we cannot comply with the exorbitant State requirements. We pay already what we cannot afford that they may fatten on the rates at our expense. That does not suffice. They must screw up the payments till we are ruined and they are left masters of the field. Fellow Catholics, let us stand up and defend ourselves against such selfish, cold-blooded calculating tyranny. It would be a tyranny such as was exercised by Julian the Apostate against the early Christians. It would be a savage persecution falling short only of the horrors of the Elizabethan persecution of our ancestors. Let us organize ourselves, and not only vote but work with all our might to keep out of Parliament every supporter of these dastardly would-be persecutors until they repent; let us not give any support to men who call themselves Liberals, but maintain a policy both illiberal and unjust."[1]

The pressure from the Churches was intensified. In the Church schools only 11s. 5d. (including a 5s. special aid) was available per pupil against 25s. 6d. for the child in the Board School.[2] It was not therefore surprising that the campaign against the Boards quickened. They had always met violent criticism. It is not easy to decide how far the attacks were justified.

It is true that not always the most suitable candidates were elected to the Boards, an event not unknown in the House of Commons. G. A. N. Lowndes in *The Silent Social Revolution* tells of " the cab-stall proprietor whose knowledge of education was nil, but who was elected to the local school board by the cumulative vote of the local cabbies because he sold good coffee; of farmers who put up the fees to children as soon as they reached the age of exemption in order to force them out into the fields; of the candidate who was disallowed election expenses of £60 spent on oyster patties; and, strangest of all to modern notions, of the notice posted in a school to the effect that double fees would

---

[1] *The Catholic Times,* 28th September 1900.
[2] Lowndes, *op. cit.,* 71.

be charged in future in respect of any children whose parents had joined the labourers' union."[1] The Dean of St. Paul's thought that " School Boards have been a great misfortune all over the country; they have lowered the tone of morality and have increased the amount of crime." He regarded the " paying of the School Board rate as helping the promotion of vice rather than the increase of virtue."[2] It is significant that when the bill to sweep them away was discussed in Parliament few defended the School Boards, although, had the Liberals not been preoccupied with the religious issue, more might have been heard in their defence. It would perhaps be true to say that the Boards exhibited all the vices of which democracy is accused, and not all the virtues.[3]

But the issue was not straightforward: Board Schools against Church Schools. It was confused by the determination of the Churches to retain their schools, and the impossibility of applying the secular solution in the existing balance of British politics; and one must add of British finances staggering after the Boer War. When Mr. Balfour remarked that to replace all the voluntary schools would cost £26,000,000 no one dared to suggest that the sum could be raised;[4] and the other solution of aid to the voluntary schools became inevitable.

In 1870 there had been 8000 voluntary schools. In 1902 the number had risen to 14,000; and in these schools 3,000,000 of the nation's children were educated against 2,600,000 in the 5700 Board Schools.[5] The Church of England in political communion with the Church of Rome was a formidable pressure group, and although a section of the Liberal party still adhered to the secular solution, which Joseph Chamberlain in his younger days had championed, the compromise of 1870 had in fact ruled this out in favour of undenominational teaching. The battle was fought on less definite ground. The Nonconformist Conscience was exercised by the fate of the Nonconformist child in an area where

[1] Lowndes, *op. cit.*, 69.
[2] Quoted by J. Bryce in House of Commons, 5th May 1902.
[3] R. L. Archer, *Secondary Education in the Nineteenth Century*, has a good word to say for the larger Board.
[4] It is interesting to note that the cost of Conscription (favourably regarded by the Royal Commission on the Militia and the Volunteers) was calculated as similar in amount. Cd. 2061, of 1904.
[5] R. L. Archer, *op. cit.*

the only school was a Church school, a situation particularly prevalent in rural Wales.[1]

The Nonconformist case was reasonable once the special position of the Established Church was denied. The Free Church leaders had not been consulted by the Government when the bill was framed,[2] which as they declared " made permanent what was decaying and sure to die." They " knew that the present system could not last as the Church of England could not raise the subscriptions, and they were content to wait a while for a national system," but " all the worst vices of the old system are now secured and perpetuated." [3] The alliance of the Anglicans with the Catholics they found particularly sinister. It was noted that the Anglicans had recently adopted the Catholic view that religous education was not a matter of an hour's religious instruction but comprised the saturation of all the teaching. They had seen Ritualism grow in the Church of England, and had noted the formidable secessions to the Church of Rome, which showed no signs of abating, and indeed were soon to include the son of a former Archbishop of Canterbury. Why does the Church of England make these additional claims, they asked? And replied: Because she is proceeding faster and faster on the road to Rome. Thus it was that the Nonconformists failed to respond to the eloquent speech of Lord Hugh Cecil, pleading for a closing of the ranks of Christendom for " the great contest ahead of us in which we shall have to fight shoulder to shoulder." [4] Comforted by statistics which showed 3,103,285 children in Nonconformist Sunday Schools against 2,329,813 in those of the Church of England,[5] the Nonconformists' leaders felt that time was on their side, and that the Established Church was to be compared with one of those " dying nations " to which Lord Salisbury rudely referred.

In a few areas, notably in Wales, sectarian bitterness continued with all its pristine vehemence. A certain Canon Penning-

[1] Even in England there were many villages with only Anglican Schools, e.g. 117 in Notts, 313 in Lincolnshire, 549 in Yorkshire. *Report of First National Council of the Evangelical Free Churches, 10–12th March 1896.*

[2] *The British Weekly Catechism of the Education Bill,* Rev. W. Robertson Nicoll. Supplement, 2nd October 1902. Q. 21.

[3] Ibid., Q. 33.

[4] *Hansard,* CVII, 847.

[5] Lowndes, *op. cit.,* 72.

ton, a Diocesan Inspector, was often to be quoted during the tumult raised by the Education Act of 1902. He had written to *The Guardian* in August 1897: " Our syllabus is arranged so as to give distinctive denominational instruction. I always saw that it was given and always asked the children of Nonconformists questions bearing upon it. Thus in fact we trained the children of Nonconformists to be children of the Church." [1] But the overtime on which this letter was worked suggests that although there was a grievance, perhaps it was not quite so real as young Mr. Lloyd George astutely made it appear.

But before the Conservative Government could come to the rescue of the Church schools, before the problem of secondary school education could be solved along the lines of the Bryce report, the vested interest of the School Boards had to be destroyed; for the Boards had been extending their work into the secondary field, and the longer they had to establish themselves there the more difficult it would be to dislodge them.

It was now that a young Civil Servant played the part of a *Deus ex Machina*. Robert Morant [1] had been educated at Oxford, and had very nearly entered the Church. A man of restless energy, autocratic temperament and intellectual passion, who spared others no more than he spared himself, puritanical, severe, he began his career as tutor in the household of the King of Siam, entering the Education Office of his democratic homeland on his return. An address given by him at Manchester in 1899 reveals something of the nature of the man: " How frequently do I wonder now that I am back in England again, whether you in England are not almost losing the appreciation of this great factor for life and influence for good—I mean discipline. It misgives me at times whether individual liberty amongst you in England has not almost been exaggerated into a craze, so that the value of discipline, of leadership and of rule (when it is disinterested in aim and just in operation) needs some re-appreciation and insistence nowadays amongst you." Morant was friendly with Dr. Garnett, Secretary of the London Technical Committee. He also met many of the leading members of the Fabian Society at Toynbee Hall, and when, in his midnight reading on the Educational system, which he seems to have believed that it was his duty in

[1] See B. M. Allen, *Sir R. Morant.*

life to reform, he discovered that it was *ultra vires* for the School Boards to carry on secondary education, he did not scruple to supply this knowledge to Dr. Garnett for use in a court of law.

In December 1900 judgment was given in what is known as the Cockerton case, establishing the illegality of the practice of the Boards, and in April 1901 the judgment was upheld in the Court of Appeal.

The School Boards now appeared before public opinion as bodies guilty of illegal practices, and their whole position in meeting attack on the general issue was substantially weakened.

A one-clause bill in May 1901 legalized the status quo for a year, and in the following spring the Bill, which afterwards became the Act of 1902, was laid before Parliament.

Meanwhile the Church had not been slothful. A joint conference of the Convocations of Canterbury and York was held in July 1901, where a unanimously passed resolution urged: " 1. That all schools be financed as far as the cost of maintenance, exclusive of repairs in the structure, of voluntary schools is concerned, out of public funds, whether Imperial or Local, and that it be no condition of participation in these funds by voluntary schools, whether any form of religious instruction be or be not taught in the schools. 2. That the funds needed for capital expenditure on the school buildings as well as for the necessary extensions and structural alterations be provided by the body to which the school belongs, but that the managers be not liable for any other expenditure. 3. That the government of every school and especially the appointment and dismissal of the teachers be left in the hands of the present committees of management with the addition of certain members appointed by, or under rules made by, the local authority; such additional members not to exceed one-third of the whole number. 4. That wherever a reasonable number of parents desire that religious instruction in accordance with their own belief should be given to their children, opportunity for such instruction should be secured to them by statute in all elementary schools, provided that this can be done without expense to the managers."

Dr. Temple, now in the last year of his Primacy, spoke cautiously at this time about the Government attitude: " He thought that on the whole the Government were well disposed towards the Church and the Church Schools; but it was not a very brave Government, and they were a little timid about fighting battles." The timidity was not surprising; the leading member of the Cabinet was Joseph Chamberlain, a Unitarian, who in his salad days, before obtaining office, had been the foremost supporter of the secular solution. What would be his attitude to the proposals of the Church. Morant's biographer, B. M. Allen, tells how the young Civil Servant visited Chamberlain in December 1901 to explain the Bill.[1] He suggests that the politician was convinced by Morant's persuasiveness; but is history made like this? Was Chamberlain's support ever seriously in doubt? Was it not merely a question of making his adhesion to the measure as easy as possible? He had crossed the Rubicon. The Boer War as well as Ireland was now between him and his former Liberal colleagues. Short of retirement from politics he had no alternative but to support Mr. Balfour's solution, reserving the right of saying " I told you so " when the Liberal Nonconformist voters, whom he had brought over when he left Gladstone, returned to their former allegiance.

For Nonconformity, led in this battle by the redoubtable Dr. Clifford, whom some thought the foremost platform orator of the day, was still a powerful political force; and the return of the Nonconformists to the fold was to make the decisive Liberal victory of 1906 possible, and to sweep over a hundred Nonconformists into the House of Commons.

The Bill, floated on a sea of verbiage with patches of eloquence, passed slowly into law. The first and second reading took five days. Forty-eight days were spent in Committee, and seven on the Report stage; six more in the House of Lords. Perhaps for the last time Greek was quoted in the Commons when Mr. Bryce, noting that London was excepted from the Bill for treatment in the following year, remarked that for the London Board was reserved the fate of Ulysses, whom Polyphemus decided to eat last.[2]

Nearly three thousand School Boards were swept away, and direct access to Whitehall of over fourteen thousand bodies of management of voluntary schools was abolished. Now the Board of Education dealt with 328 Local Education Authorities, a tremendous advantage for purposes of administration and for bring-

---

[1] See B. M. Allen, *Sir R. Morant*, 167. [2] *Hansard*, CVII, 730.

ing about uniform educational standards. The voluntary schools, as Lowndes remarks, no longer had to subsist on a mixture of " grants, endowments, ping-pong tournaments, whist drives and jumble sales." [1] They were placed on the rates, retaining only the burden of the structure and its upkeep, although to the detriment of several generations of children this " burden " also was too great for the faithful to bear. So far as the management of these schools was concerned one-third of the new committee was to be nominated by the Local Authority. Popular control was rejected by the Government. As Mr. Balfour explained when an amendment was moved: " To give popular control would be to violate our principles and our pledges and to betray those who sent us to this House and would be monstrously and utterly unjust."

Only one important departure from the original intentions of the Government was approved: by the Kenyon-Slaney amendment, which provided that religious instruction in a school not provided by the Local Education Authority must be in accordance with the terms of the original trust deed. Thus if the feared drift to Ritualism continued in the Church of England it would not be reflected in the schools. It is an indication of the political temperature that the gallant Conservative member who moved this amendment received letters of extreme violence and even indecency from clergymen. In one of these the amendment was described as the " greatest betrayal since the Crucifixion," the writer stating that he would have preferred that the Colonel should have seduced the writer's wife rather than come to Parliament with such a proposal. [2]

It was a substantial victory for the Church. Already in January 1902 Dr. Temple had noted that " there were signs that the Government would listen to anything that was said because in a very great degree their own political position depended upon it, and it would be rather awkward for them to face the Church if only its members were united on this subject." [3] Dr. Temple's successor, Randall Davidson, played a part second only to that of Morant in advising Balfour in his conduct of the bill. In

---

[1] Lowndes, *op. cit.*, 57.
[2] Sir A. Fitzroy, *Memoirs*, Vol. I, 112.
[3] Quoted in House of Commons. *Hansard*, CVII, 730–1.

September 1902 Dr. Bourne, the Roman Catholic Bishop of South-wark, announced that " the Government were doing everything in their power to meet the needs of the Catholic position, and he thought they ought to give them every possible support." [1] When the Act was finally passed Cardinal Vaughan wrote to Morant in grateful terms: " Now that your ship has entered port after so much stress of weather I must write one line of con-gratulation and of most hearty thanks for all you have done for us —for the tact and determination by which you have brought about the impossible on more than one occasion, and for a Bill that is destined to save Christianity in England while it is being wrecked by Education in so many other lands." [2]

One question puzzles the historian. Why at a time when or-ganized religion was losing ground was it possible for the Church to improve its position educationally as compared with 1870? The answer is surely to be found in two developments which did not face the educationalists of Forster's day: in 1869 was held the great Œcumenical Council, which restated Papal infallibility and set a new course, expressed in a strengthening of Catholic in-fluence throughout the Christian world; in 1870 Isaac Butt founded the Irish Home Rule party, which confused British politics for half a century and to some extent played the part acted in other countries by Catholic political parties. The Parliament of 1868–74 was the last two-party Parliament. At the election of 1874, 58 Irish Nationalists were returned, and in the Parliament of 1900–6, 82 Nationalists sat with 380 Conser-vatives and 178 Liberals. Nor was this all: in many English constituencies the Irish and Catholic vote was not a negligible factor.

But what of the Labour Movement? What interest did the working classes take in Education? The privilege of the Public Schools was not yet a major target, although Mr. Smyth, a work-ing man, had shocked the Cross Commission in 1889 by telling them that " it would be next to expecting a boy out of the London Board Schools to take wings as to expect him to advance by his own efforts to the University." [3] There were other priorities. First the knowledge from experience that the children often came

[1] *British Weekly Catechism*, Q. 55.   [2] B. M. Allen, *op. cit.* 197.
[3] Lowndes, *op. cit.*, 102.

to school in a state unfit to profit by such education that was available. Charles Booth had referred to the " puny, pale-faced, scantily clothed and badly shod " children; and had stated that " these small and feeble folk may be found sitting limp and chill on the school benches in all the poorer parts of London. They swell the bills of mortality as want and sickness thin them off, or survive to be the needy and enfeebled adults whose burden of helplessness the next generation will have to bear." If the Labour Movement took small part in the controversies surrounding the Act of 1902 it was because to them the discussions had a certain air of unreality about them. It was a sound sense of proportion which led them to link meals for school children with unemployment as the main problem of the time.

There were also within the Movement other important educational developments. In 1899 Ruskin Hall had been founded at Oxford with the aid of American money as " a protest against the exclusive tradition of our great Universities." Workers who went there were not " encouraged to become barristers, schoolmasters or journalists " but were " expected to use their education for the benefit of their fellow-workers." On the first governing body Trade Union representatives sat with University lecturers of Labour sympathies. The new foundation was significant, but Albert Mansbridge, a clerk in the co-operative movement, realizing that the small college could not hope to touch more than an infinitesimal part of the working class, had been thinking along different lines. Thirty years earlier the University Extension Movement had been started to bring the Universities to the people. University lecturers descended on widely separated areas, and collected audiences by advertisement for courses which were often but a repetition of those which they had recently given within the University. Little or no attempt was made to discover the wishes and needs of the people, and it is no disparagement of the time and labour given by the peripatetic lecturers to describe their effort as a form of intellectual slumming. Moreover before long the Movement, as Halévy justly notes, had been " captured by the middle class." Mansbridge and his colleagues were determined that the new attempt should not suffer the same fate.

The Workers' Educational Association, founded in 1903, was

a democratic movement based on an alliance between the Universities, the Co-operatives and the Trade Unions. By forging this triple link and by the widest possible introduction of democratic method within the classroom it was hoped to preserve the purity of its inspiration. The highest hopes of the founders were perhaps not realized. The numbers affected in relation to the total working-class population do not appear large. In 1910 there was a membership of 5800. But when the numbers are related to the number of University students at any time their significance appears in a truer perspective. Economic and political subjects formed the usual curriculum, and those who passed through W.E.A. classes were a leaven in the mass of Trade Unionists. The Classes provided the nearest approach to a poor man's university that had yet been achieved. Nor were the members of the branches of the W.E.A. concerned only with their own education. From the beginning a strong social purpose knit them together, the reform and extension of the whole educational system.

Nor were the Trade Unions without an educational policy of their own. The unanimous resolution passed at the Swansea Congress in September 1901 (i.e. before the introduction of Balfour's Education Bill) put forward a six-point programme: 1. Local Education Authorities specially elected for the purpose. 2. A school-leaving age of fifteen. 3. Free Education. 4. Scholarships. 5. Training colleges for teachers. 6. Labour representation on the Board of Education. The following Congress, held in London, found the Act " decidedly reactionary "; its weak points were noted: " No provisions are made for any improvement in the way of elementary education; . . . under our present system an attempt is made to feed the brain while the body is starved."

The great achievement of the Act of 1902 is often held to have been the introduction of Secondary Education into the Public system. Halévy describes the Act as " a social revolution of the first magnitude." It is however unfair to previous workers in the field to ignore the 53 secondary schools taken over by the Local Education Authorities in 1902 when we acclaim the 329 new schools set up in the following decade.

The Bill passed into law. Two by-elections went against the

Government; but the Nonconformists realized that meetings and elections could not stop the inevitable. Wise Freechurchmen even foresaw that " a huge Liberal majority at the next election would be unable to transfer the Church schools to the public." [1] Recourse was had to the traditional Noncomformist tactics. *The Methodist Weekly* declared in December 1902 that " Hampden was not more justified in refusing to pay Ship Money than will be the Non-conformists in refusing to pay the education rate." [2] Even Lord Rosebery went so far as to tell a group of Nonconformist delegates: " I am not going to utter my approval beforehand of any methods you may choose to adopt. I am not myself in favour of the refusal of the payment of rates; but then I am not in your position. I confess that if the Nonconformists of England submit tamely to the enactments of this Bill, I will not say that they would be weakened religiously, but I will say this—that in my judgment politically they will have ceased to exist." [3]

Mr. G. M. Trevelyan, writing in the *Liberal Monthly*, thus recorded his objection to the Bill: " Denominational teaching of religion in schools maintained by the ratepayer if you like: but no denominational management and no denominational tests for teachers." [4] For the outlook for the non-Anglican teacher was bleak, particularly at a time when the pupil teacher was still frequent and the vast majority of the teachers' training colleges were under the control of the Established Church. And in all the tumult the child was less and less mentioned. One feels that his voice was too faint to be heard above the clamour. Dr. Clifford coined the phrase " Rome on the Rates," and attracted such audiences that Mr. Balfour declared that he did not like his style. " And I do not like Mr. Balfour's works," retorted Dr. Clifford. Prominent on the Government side was Balfour, who succeeded his uncle as Prime Minister during the passage of the Bill. Indeed the Act was to a large extent Balfour's act, for Chamberlain was not the only Cabinet colleague who had misgivings about the expediency of the enactment. But the author of *In Defence of Philosophic Doubt* rode deliberately to battle for the Anglican and Catholic Churches, displaying an energy and combativeness which

[1] *British Weekly Catechism*, Q. 62.
[2] Quoted by M. Edwards, *Methodism and England*, 125.
[3] 8th December 1902, *Annual Register*, 1902, 232.
[4] *Liberal Magazine*, November 1902.

he reserved for rare occasions. He answered (his friends thought he demolished) Dr. Clifford in a clever pamphlet. It was certainly a dialectical victory; but of greater future significance was the election for the Executive Committee of the National Liberal Federation in February 1903. Dr. Clifford was returned at the head of the poll.

CHAPTER XVI

THE UNITY IN FOREIGN POLICY

Education and Chinese Labour split Public Opinion more or less on party-political lines. In Foreign Affairs unity was preserved, so that when Sir Edward Grey succeeded Lord Lansdowne in 1905 nobody noticed any change. There is no evidence that the Conservative party had they been successful at the polls in 1906 would have followed a different policy from the Liberals.

It has been suggested that the unity was specious, that only the ignorance in which Public Opinion and even fellow Cabinet ministers were kept by the Foreign Secretary preserved agreement. Of the ignorance there is no doubt. The concealment of the Anglo-French military conversations from the Cabinet for several years has often been discussed and Grey blamed for the subterfuge, although perhaps Campbell-Bannerman as Prime Minister must bear the final responsibility. The Anglo-German conversations of 1901 seem never to have been disclosed to the full Cabinet. Foreign Affairs was considered a subject for the experts, who would apply the rules deduced from experience and formulated in tradition with a precise skill similar to that with which the Governor of the Bank of England operated the Gold Standard. It is however surely doubtful whether ignorance was the true cause of the unity of Foreign Policy during this period.

For Foreign Policy is the reflection in external relations of the domestic position in a country. When there is basic unity at home there will be unity in relations abroad. It was characteristic of the Edwardian period that beneath the sharp Liberal-Conservative cleavage basic unity existed. Fierce though the party conflict was, it was a conflict between Reformers and Conservers, both of whom accepted the existence and persistence of the prevalent social, economic and political system. This Liberal-Conservative unity in Foreign Policy foreshadowed indeed Liberal disintegration. It was an indication that the identity of Liberalism was merging ever more closely with that of Conservatism.

I

The reign of Edward VII was to see the end of Isolation as a Foreign Policy, and its supersession by a policy of alliance. It was to see the inexorable result of Britain's changing world position. Pre-eminently strong must be the nation which can afford Isolation, and with the rise of other Great Powers, Britain could no longer support a policy which had been indeed " splendid " while it had been practical. The change, as we have seen, had begun to set in during the seventies, although it needed the Boer War to convince the British public that the time when they could afford to walk alone was gone beyond recall.

It may seem strange that the country chosen to be the first of the British allies should have been the yellow people of Japan; but it must be noted that only the traditions of American politics prevented a formal alliance with the United States being sought, while the treaty with Japan was the first of the new links only because the predisposing factors were here greatest and the opposing factors the least. Professor William Langer indeed suggests that the Anglo-Japanese alliance was an accident, a *pis aller*; that what the British Government desired was a tie-up with Russia; that only the fear of a Russo-Japanese rapprochement led them to accept the Japanese advances.[1] This is to exaggerate into a major motive on the British side the diplomatic pressure employed by the Japanese in the course of the negotiations as they struggled to land the British fish. In fact the Anglo-Japanese alliance was the culmination of a series of events which over a long period of years had been bringing the two countries together.

It was an American squadron under Commodore Perry that had opened Japan to the formidable blessings of western civilization in 1853–4, but British traders were soon in the Japanese market, and as early as 1857 British shipyards were building war-ships for Japan. By 1892 the *Annual Register* was noting that British trade held the foremost place, amounting to more than half the imports and more than a quarter of the exports. In 1894, shortly before the outbreak of the Sino-Japanese war, Lord Rosebery made a new commercial treaty with Japan, and abolished extra-territoriality. At the conclusion of the war, when other European powers exerted pressure to rob victorious Japan of her

---

[1] *Diplomacy of Imperialism*, Vol. 2.

gains (Germany even threatening war), Britain ostentatiously held aloof. In 1896, when war between Britain and the United States was not beyond the bounds of possibility, the British Government received an offer from Japan to release to them two warships then building in British shipyards.[1] Chamberlain was an early convert to an agreement with Japan, although it was probably Salisbury who played the principal part in bringing about the alliance of 1902.

It was of course directed against Russia. According to Hatzfeld, the German ambassador in London (a reliable witness), Salisbury had hopes as early as 1899 of a Russo-Japanese conflict, although he thought that it would be a couple of years before the Japanese fleet (built in Britain) would be ready.[2] As Balfour later wrote to the King: " The interest of this country is now as always *Peace*. But a war between Japan and Russia, in which Japan did not suffer serious defeat, would not be an unmixed curse." [3]

Russia, stretching down towards China, threatened the valuable Chinese market, in which Chamberlain's friend and cabinet colleague, the Duke of Devonshire, was keenly interested; and although there were powerful groups in Britain who favoured an agreement with Russia, the price which would have to be paid to a Russia with China at her feet was too great for British statesmen to contemplate: the Chinese market? India? Persia? the Dardanelles? A war between Russia and Japan, thought Balfour, would have this advantage: Russia " would be much easier to deal with both in Asia and in Europe than at present." And so he was " completely sceptical about the Yellow Peril; . . . and thought that Japan was never likely to have a navy sufficient to meet the fleets of the Christian world." [4] Balfour, the nephew of the Prime Minister, and Leader of the House of Commons, supported the treaty.

Important financial interests were of the same opinion. Rothschild remained at this time opposed to the Tsarist régime, which persecuted the Jews. Bearsted, the oil magnate, was to be one of the financial backers of Japan when the time came for the " Britain of the Orient " to challenge Russia on the battlefield.[5]

[1] J. L. Garvin, *Life of Joseph Chamberlain*, Vol. 3, 96.
[2] Bulow, *op. cit.*, 1897–1903, 308.   [3] Dugdale, *op. cit.*, Vol. 1.   [4] Ibid.
[5] Lord Birkenhead, *Contemporary Personalities*, 303. See also B. D., Vol. 2, 227, 265. Lansdowne to Sir C. Macdonald, 30th December 1903.

At first the negotiations were tied up with the last attempt for an Anglo-German alliance in 1901. Early in January Eckardstein, the Secretary of the Germany Embassy, was invited by the Duchess of Devonshire to meet Chamberlain, and the first discussions took place. A few weeks later the Kaiser was at Windsor for the Queen's funeral. He seems to have done his best to frighten his uncle with stories of an American-Russian rapprochement. He made speeches of friendship to prepare the ground for a political agreement. When he left, *The Times* published some sentimental verses.[1] At the end of February Eckardstein, who had been in Berlin, returned to London, and in March suggested to Count Hayashi, the Japanese ambassador, that there should be a triple agreement between Germany, Britain and Japan. There followed the direct approach by Hayashi to Lansdowne, and finally in January 1902 the Anglo-Japanese agreement was signed.

Professor Langer states that there had been no audible demand in the press for the agreement;[2] but a series of articles published in *The Times* between 29th January and 21st March 1901 can only have helped to prepare the ground, even though they may not have been consciously intended to do so. The articles were written from Tokio, and were always sympathetic to the Japanese and sometimes enthusiastic. Thus on 29th January the Japanese were contrasted with the Russians: " for fierce and sanguinary as the temperament of the Japanese may at times show itself to be, violence to women and children and cruelty to children are things against which their nature revolts. Towards children especially they display a tenderness which is surpassed in no other country . . . the discipline of the Japanese troops in China has been admirable, and their behaviour towards the defenceless population humane and even generous." The Russian soldiers on the other hand introduced " a veritable reign of terror."

In April *The Economist* hinted that in the event of a Russo-Japanese war " some power—America or England for instance " might help Japan.[3]

In November *The Times* recorded that satisfactory legislation had been introduced regarding the titles of foreign landholders

---

[1] 6th February 1901.
[2] *Diplomacy of Imperialism*, Vol. 2, 779. Cf. Tyler Dennett, *John Hay*, 303.
[3] 27th April 1901.

in Japan, and in an article on the industrial exhibition at Osaka drew attention to the opportunities of the Japanese market. The fact is that the preparation for the agreement had been made over a long period, and not only through the medium of the more serious publications. The British public had been given a picture of a land of peach blossom and dainty Geishas, where the traditions of Samurai somewhat resembled the good form of the public school code. Had the alliance with Russia (which, according to Professor Langer, the British Government really sought at this time) been attempted, a far greater press preparation would have been necessary.

When the treaty was announced in February 1902 it was received with enthusiasm, particularly by the upper classes, as was expressed by the unusual burst of applause that greeted the Foreign Secretary when he entered the House of Lords on the day after the treaty was announced. In the Commons Campbell-Bannerman referred to " a certain strong sympathy with the Japanese " [1] and although *The Economist* felt that the price paid for the treaty was too great, *The Times* was dithyrambic: " the gallantry, the efficiency, and the humanity displayed by the naval and military forces of Japan during the recent operations in Northern China, justify the assurance that should the necessity ever arise the King's soldiers and sailors will find their Japanese allies comrades with whom they will be proud to fight shoulder to shoulder." [2] In October a five million sterling loan was successfully floated in London by Barings and the Hong Kong-Shanghai Bank.

The terms of the treaty were simple and clear. Special British rights in China, special Japanese rights in Korea, were recognized. In the event of either power being involved in war with more than one other power the alliance would come into operation. Thus Japan was protected from French assistance to Russia in the event of a Russo-Japanese clash, or from intervention against her by any other power. It had been the wish of the British Government to extend the area covered by the treaty to take in India, but the Japanese could not be persuaded to accept the

[1] House of Commons, 13th February 1902. Sir W. Harcourt, however, was critical of the treaty as " staking upon the dice the peace and the future of your Indian Empire."
[2] 12th February 1902.

liability, and the proposal was dropped to be raised again and successfully when the treaty was renewed in 1905. As it was, Britain was assured of Japanese assistance should she be involved in war in the Far East with the Dual or the Triple Alliance.

It has been generally held that the treaty was directed against Russia by Britain without any *arrière pensée*. The need to distinguish conscious and unconscious motivation has already been stressed. Whatever the conscious motive of the British Government it is clear that one of the most important advantages of the treaty was the release of British naval power from the Far East for concentration in Home waters. Sir John Fisher indeed later remarked that he had never been in favour of the treaty,[1] but Sir John Fisher did not represent predominant naval opinion at this time, and his remarks were made to Isvolsky after the Anglo-Russian rapprochement. It would be interesting to know what was the advice tendered to the Foreign Office by the Board of Admiralty.[2]

If in Russia the significance of the treaty was understood, and in France Delcassé, the foreign minister, increased his efforts to bring about an Anglo-French agreement, the treaty had a good press abroad. In the United States it was approved as being likely to check Russian expansion, which was considered the main menace to American trade and financial interests in China.[3] In Germany it was approved as being likely to lead to war between Russia and Great Britain, a consummation devoutly wished by the Wilhelmstrasse and most confidently expected, a salient example of that German diplomatic miscalculation which so often surprises as one surveys the period of King Edward VII.

And if one asks why was it that German diplomacy was so much at fault, why was it that events turned out so differently from what was confidently expected in Berlin, is the answer to be found more in a personal ineptitude than in the facts of the

---

[1] R. H. Bacon, *Lord Fisher*, Vol. 2, 80.
[2] The close links between The British and Japanese navies leave little doubt of its nature.
[3] I do not know why G. P. Gooch in his study *Before the War*, Vol. 1, 22, should say, " The disapproval of the United States was unconcealed." It was the overwhelming victories of Japan in 1904 and the reports of the American military observers which produced hostility to the treaty. As late as May 1905 Roosevelt was approving the treaty. Tyler Dennett, *Roosevelt and the Russo-Japanese War*, 115, 116.

case? Were the German advisers a poor blind breed, or was the pattern of history woven inexorably to German disadvantage so that no skill at the Wilhelmstrasse could have prevailed?

It is clear that the strength and flexibility of the British Empire was under-estimated, both its material resources and its capacity to appeal to the moral consciousness of the world. " We were already sated like a lion surrounded with the carcasses of its prey," wrote Wilfrid Blunt, " while Germany was alert and hungry. Well might we want peace. Almost as well might Germany prepare for war." It is a great moral advantage to be in favour of the *status quo*.

It was to be the fate of Germany to enter war in 1914 in most unfavourable circumstances. Caught between France and Russia, with Britain, linked to a friendly United States by her fleet, in the balance against her, the odds were tremendous. Could an Anglo-German alliance have been achieved had the German diplomats been wiser? The last attempt was made in 1901. Why did it fail?

German public opinion was more hostile towards Britain than British against Germany at this time, which in itself would have made it difficult for the German Government to draw closer. To the German business man and industrialist Britain was the great competitor whom they were always meeting. To the British *vis-à-vis* Germany was one of several competitors, although the most dangerous and ubiquitous. Ancient rivalries with France still persisted, but with the economic basis steadily being removed. Russia threatened the vital Lancashire market in China. Not easily would British public opinion have accepted an Anglo-German alliance, but even greater resistance would have been experienced in Germany, where a Britain standing in the path of German expansion, a Britain which had contemptuously rejected German requests for colonies, a Britain clearly ceasing to be predominant on the world stage, came more and more to occupy the position of the inevitable enemy.

Only if another foe threatening both more than they did each other were to appear, would Germany and Britain be persuaded to sink their differences in the face of the greater menace. Always remembering the distinction between conscious and unconscious motives we can say that Chamberlain, who tried again and again for an Anglo-German alliance, stood for an agreement with Germany which could only have been directed against the United States, the potential threat to both powers. But Germany, not yet supreme in Europe, could not contemplate/ that contest, and Britain declining rather than America rising, Britain so near and so similar in economic development, appeared as that " Enemy No. 1 " which in a competitive world Great Powers are destined to have.

German public opinion had resented the tone with which Britain had received their rise to power. " Whenever I talk with Englishmen about my fatherland," wrote Heine in 1846, " I notice with deep humiliation that the hate which they feel for the French is more honourable to the latter than the impertinent affection which they bestow upon us Germans, and for which we must thank our shortcoming in worldly power or our intelligence. They love us because of our maritime weakness which prevents any fear of commercial rivalry. They love us because of our political *naïveté*, which they hope to exploit in the old way." [1] As late as 1860 *The Times* employed this tone: " The vagaries of German policy are such that we cannot pretend to follow them. It is useless to look for profundity where in all likelihood there is only pedantry, or for a tangible object in what may be only a desire to carry out some dreamy historical notion. Were the ways of Germans like our ways—were they governed by practical statesmen instead of martinets and sophists—we should fancy that they had some far-seen end in view when they thus propose to create political complication in Europe. But knowing what they are we only see in their conduct another instance of that weakness and perversity which has brought on them so many misfortunes." [2] The outbreak of the Franco-Prussian war led to some favourable comments (largely based upon the age-old antipathy for the French). Carlyle wrote to *The Times*: " That noble, patient, deep, pious and solid Germany should at length be welded into a nation and become queen of the continent instead of vapouring, vainglorious, gesticulating, quarrelsome, restless and over-sensitive France seems to me the hopefullest public fact that has occurred in my time." But Carlyle was not representative of the ruling

[1] Quoted by R. J. Sontag, *Germany and England: Background of Conflict, 1848–98*, 51. [2] Ibid., 31.

class, and as early as 1864 Lord Salisbury had described Bismarck as the heir of Frederick the Great, the heir " of his unblushing perfidy, of his cynical contempt for pledges given and treaties signed." [1] The attacks and counter-attacks in the earlier period were not perhaps frequent, but they were formidable. The Germans began to talk of British decadence. Thus the *Kolnische Zeitung*, in 1885, wrote: " England is going the same inexorable way that Phœnicia went against the Greeks, the Carthaginians against the Romans, the later Venetians and the Dutch in their contest with the national strength of modern peoples. It seems to be a law of world history that the commercial spirit and the manly fighting spirit cannot long be united in one people, and that unscrupulous diplomacy is substituted, diplomacy which can postpone the national decline for a time, but only for a time. Defy England, and England will astound the world by her cowardice." [2] On the other side of the North Sea may be noted the notorious *Saturday Review* article of 1895: " We English have always made war hitherto upon our rivals in trade and commerce, and our chief rival in trade and commerce to-day is not France but Germany."

Attempts have been made to prove that it was not economic competition but the decision of Germany to build a large fleet which brought the two countries into conflict.[3] Certainly the building of the fleet was the final expression of the German rivalry, but relations had been far from satisfactory before the fleet became a menace, while the very building was in itself but an expression of the economic conflict.

For difficult though it has been for Britons to appreciate that the possession of a navy is not their unique right, that the rest of the world does not readily accept the conception of a British fleet policing the globe in a completely non-aggressive fashion, it is essential if the period is to be understood, and its final tragedy realized, that the facts should be apprehended.

Heine, as noted above, had referred to Germany's maritime weakness. When Tirpitz in 1894 was making the case for the building of the High Seas Fleet he used significant words: " A state which has oceanic or—an equivalent term—world interests

[1] Ibid., 218.   [2] Ibid., 198.
[3] Notably by E. L. Woodward. Vide his *Great Britain and the German Navy*.

must be able to uphold them and make its power felt beyond its own territorial waters. National world commerce, world industry and to a certain extent fishing on the high seas, world intercourse and colonies, are impossible without a fleet capable of taking the offensive. The conflicts of interests between nations, the lack of confidence felt by capital and the business world, will either destroy these expressions of the vitality of a state or prevent them from taking form if they are not supported by national power on the seas and therefore beyond our own waters." [1] When ex-President Roosevelt met Lansdowne and Haldane in 1910 he was asked: " Why do the Germans build a fleet?" " Because," he answered, " every great power that respects itself cannot afford to be dependent for its existence on the goodwill or momentary kindly disposition of this or that power or group of powers whether they will attack it or leave it alone."[2] During the Boer War German ships were stopped and searched. The risk would never have been taken by London had the Kaiser possessed a fleet.

The tragedy of the period is not that Britain was wrong in taking the precautions she did, not that the orientation to the United States was less sensible than an alliance with Germany, but that the ruling class accepted the conflict as inevitable, that they were unable to envisage an economic system which would permit the ordinary folk of each nation to co-operate instead of to dispute for the markets of the world.

It was not easy to enlist German public opinion behind the Big Navy policy. The German Navy League was founded in 1898, largely with the aid of funds supplied by Krupp, and in the same year the first Navy Law was passed by the Reichstag with a vote of 212 to 139. It was not, however, until the Law of 1900 that the German Navy seriously entered into British calculations, although there had not been wanting isolated figures who had been foretelling German naval competition for some years past.

The Law of 1900 was fiercely attacked by the German Social Democrats, who held 19 large meetings in Berlin alone. Their leader, Bebel, was a consistent opponent of the policy up to his death on the eve of the Great War; but although the German

---

[1] Quoted by E. L. Woodward.
[2] Dugdale, *op. cit.*, Vol. 3, 414, 415.

Social Democrats were the largest Parliamentary Labour group in Europe they could not influence German policy, fixed by the Bismarckian system of personal government. Indeed it is true to say that the absence of first-class statesmen in German ruling circles in the time of William II was the result of Bismarck's political ideas. When autocratic government fails to provide a first-class autocrat parlous indeed is the position of the state.

The last German Kaiser was a man of considerable ability and fascination. W. T. Stead was reminded of General Gordon: " If you can imagine General Gordon born a Hohenzollern. Sir John Gorst finds him somewhat like Randolph Churchill. Mr. Balfour sees in him many points of resemblance to the first Napoleon. There is also a trace of Tim Healy in him. But I do not think he will last." [1] He was to last for twenty years, a vain, rather pathetic but dangerous figure lacking in stability and managed at the critical moments by his advisers.

But when the fact of ineptitude in high places in Germany has been acknowledged it still remains to be said that the German position was one of very great difficulty. The way of prudence, as Bismarck had seen, was to consolidate the continental position, and not to go into competition with Britain for African swamps and Asiatic trading ports. But the economic pressure, even in his lifetime, was too strong. Germany was developing at a terrific speed. She was not to be granted time to become supreme on the continent before she challenged Britain for the greater leadership.

Nor must the powerful position of Russia at this period be forgotten. An alliance with Britain meant a conflict with Russia, against whom the British navy would be of no assistance and the British Army a contemptible token. The shadow of Russia fell across the Anglo-German talks; for, argued the Germans, what would happen if Britain, unstable, parliamentary Britain, withdrew from the alliance at the moment of crisis and left Germany to face Russia alone? Then why not gain Russian support? The multiple Austro-Hungarian Empire, with its Slav subjects and German ruler, made that impossible. Difficult indeed was the German position. In the end they had no policy but the policy

[1] F. Whyte, *W. T. Stead*, Vol. 2, 30.

of Mr. Micawber, being so sure that something good must turn up, that time was on their side, that Britain was declining and must come to heel; instead of which Britain paid the price of survival—an alliance with France and with Russia, and the ultimate sacrifice of a million Empire lives.

CHAPTER XVII

CHAMBERLAIN AND GERMANY

The interesting question regarding the final attempt for an Anglo-German alliance in 1901 is why it was made at that particular time.

It is true that the German press hostility shown during the Boer War had revealed the less splendid side of British isolation, but this had been appreciated by Chamberlain and his friends for some years past. Was there then any particular event which may have led to the Duchess of Devonshire's urgent invitation to Eckardstein to come to Chatsworth for a talk with Chamberlain and with her husband?

The situation in China looked more and more menacing, and China, and the Lancashire trade there, was a special interest of the Duke. An agreement had been made between Britain and Germany in October 1900, but the security apparently offered by this evaporated when Germany explained that Manchuria was not included. The Russian bear was as dangerous as ever, and at the turn of the year strong rumours were current of a political and economic rapprochement between Russia and the United States, with a large loan from Wall Street as part of the deal. Perhaps this was the final event that precipitated the approach to Germany.

Eckardstein was informed that the time for " splendid isolation " was over; that England desired to settle all outstanding questions, especially Morocco and the Far East, in co-operation with the Triple Alliance or the Dual Alliance; that, unlike some of their colleagues, Devonshire and Chamberlain would prefer the former; and that failing agreement with the Triple Alliance they would turn to France and Russia.

There is still some mystery regarding the initiation of the official negotiations between the two Foreign Offices; the probability is that the anglophil Eckardstein, in his anxiety for an alliance, exceeded his instructions, so that Lansdowne thought that the approach had come from Germany, and Bulow that at long last the British were walking into his parlour.

A week after the Eckardstein-Chamberlain talks there occurred the death of the Queen and the visit of the Kaiser to England. He had been warned by Bulow to be very cautious, and seems to have confined himself to friendly after-dinner speeches and hints to his uncle of an American-Russian rapprochement. When he returned to Germany he left behind good personal feelings but denials in the press that his visit had had any political significance.

Thus *The Economist* wrote: " The Kaiser has come and gone like the brilliant meteor he so much resembles . . . the more of such visits the better . . . we should be glad therefore to welcome any European sovereign and still more the President of the United States. . . . We wish to be on good terms with Germany; but we wish also to be on good terms with France. To imagine that a great change will be made now is to be singularly blind to the motive forces which really determine public policy." [1]

In March talks between the two governments were under way, and Bulow, in reply to an inquiry, had suggested that England should join the Triple Alliance; that the *casus fœderis* should be an attack by *two* Powers; and that the treaty should be made public.[2] Very soon Lansdowne was expressing scepticism regarding the project: " In principle the idea is good enough. But when each side comes, if it ever does, to formulate its terms, we shall break down; and I know Lord Salisbury regards the scheme with, to say the least, suspicion." [3]

There was in fact no basis for an agreement. As Sir T. H. Sanderson wrote in a memorandum for Lansdowne in May 1901: " However the Convention may be worded it seems to me that it will practically amount to a guarantee to Germany of the provinces conquered from France, and that is the way in which the French will look at it. I do not see exactly what Germany will guarantee to us." [4] Lord Salisbury pointed out that " the liability of having to defend the German and Austrian frontiers against

---

[1] 9th February 1901.
[2] Bulow to Hatzfeldt, 24th March 1901. *G. P.*, XVII, 48.
[3] *B. D.*, Vol. 2, 63.   [4] Ibid., Vol. 2, 66.

Russia is heavier than that of having to defend the British Isles against France." [1]

The negotiations were bogged, and in June Chamberlain was telling Alfred Rothschild that he was quite disheartened: " If they are so short-sighted . . . as not to be able to see that the whole new world system depends upon it then there is nothing to be done for them." [2] What, one may well ask, was Chamberlain's " new world system "? What indeed but a British-German bloc —with or without the U.S.A.? We do not know. It is true that Chamberlain's earlier schemes had envisaged a pan-teutonic triple alliance, but American observers at this time did not consider him as a friend of their country, and although Lansdowne was careful to include in the draft Anglo-German Convention a clause excluding a conflict with the United States, it is obvious that such an agreement would have placed the American Government in a position of difficulty. As time went on the pressure of Germany towards South America (where as Chamberlain had remarked there were " districts with great future possibilities ") must surely have been hard for Britain to resist.

In August the Kaiser attempted to revive the negotiations, warning the British ambassador " against putting our faith in America, who was our most formidable commercial rival and would certainly throw us over as soon as it suited her interest to do so." [3] But the attempt failed, and in October Chamberlain cleared the decks for the new course towards the Dual Alliance by his Edinburgh speech, in which, answering criticisms of the conduct of the Boer War, he made sharp counter-accusations, referring to the methods used by foreign forces, notably the Germans in the Franco-Prussian war. Feeling ran high, particularly in the Reich, where Evangelical clergy of the Rhine province protested against the " wanton audacity " of the Colonial Secretary in comparing their fathers and brothers with the " craven bands of mercenaries who placed Boer women and old men in front of their ranks in battle in order to protect themselves from the bullets of the Boers." [4] A member of the Reichstag described Chamberlain as " the most accursed scoundrel on God's earth " and declared that Germany's " veteran soldiers must be protected

[1] Ibid., Vol. 2, 68.   [2] Eckardstein, *op. cit.*, 221.
[3] B. D., Vol. 2, 260.   [4] *Annual Register*, 1901, 286.

against comparison with gangs of robbers and packs of thieves, for that the greater part of the British army is composed of such elements is evident." [1] An appeal for better relations with England, signed by Professor Mommsen and others, produced little effect, but indicated that the alignment of the whole nation for war was not complete. In England Chamberlain's speech met with some criticism and it was significant that opinion was much calmer than in Germany.

And if it is asked why the attempt failed, the answer surely is that there was no basis for an agreement. An agreement offered insufficient advantages to either, for agreements between Great Powers under a competitive system bear as their price conflict with some other power. Two Foreign Office memoranda of November 1901 are interesting as expressing the official British view. The first by Mr. Bertie in which he wrote: " In considering offers of alliance from Germany it is necessary to remember the history of Prussia as regards alliances, and the conduct of the Bismarck government in making a treaty with Russia concerning and behind the back of Austria, the ally of Germany.

" She does what she can to keep open sores between France and England. The interests of England and Germany are not everywhere identical. In some parts of the world they are irreconcilable. . . . In our present position we hold the balance of power between the Triple and Dual Alliance. There is but little chance of a combination between them against us. . . . Treaty or no treaty, if ever there were danger of our destruction, or even defeat, by Russia and France, Germany would be bound, in order to avoid a like fate for herself, to come to our assistance." The Foreign Secretary was less convinced of the advantages of Isolation: " I think, however," he wrote, " that we may push too far the argument that because we have in the past survived in spite of our isolation, we need have no misgivings as to the effect of that isolation in the future. In approaching the Japanese we have indeed virtually admitted that we do not wish to stand alone." The objections to an agreement with Germany he summarized thus: " The difficulty of defining the *casus fœderis*; the alienation of France and Russia; Colonies; hanging on to the skirts of the Triple Alliance; the risk of entangling ourselves in

[1] Herr Liebermann von Sonnenberg, *Annual Register*, 1902, 298.

a policy which might be hostile to America (with our knowledge of the German Emperor's views in regard to the United States, this, to my mind, a formidable obstacle); the difficulty of carrying Parliament."

The attempt had failed. In December the Prince of Wales, later King George V, in the presence of Lord Salisbury, Lord Rosebery and Mr. Chamberlain at the Guildhall, was significantly introducing compliments to France into his celebrated " Wake Up " speech, describing the Suez Canal as " a monument to the genius and courage of a gifted son of the great friendly nation across the Channel " and speaking of the people of Mauritius as " gifted with the charming characteristics of Old France." The stage was being set for an Anglo-French agreement; but this scene was to be played under a new Prime Minister. In June 1902, for reasons which are not absolutely clear, Lord Salisbury resigned without waiting for the postponed coronation, and a new administration under his nephew, Arthur Balfour, was formed.

CHAPTER XVIII

FROM SALISBURY TO BALFOUR

The wildest comments on Lord Salisbury's resignation were made in the foreign press. In Berlin it was suggested that it had been accelerated " by the fear lest if there were any delay Mr. Chamberlain's popularity should in the meantime assume such proportions that it would not be possible for His Majesty to select any other successor to the late Prime Minister." [1] It was noted that Mr. Chamberlain had been temporarily removed from the political scene by a serious cab accident just four days before Salisbury withdrew. R. C. K. Ensor in his *England 1870–1914* seems to suggest that there was a doubt about the succession, that Chamberlain might otherwise have been a candidate.[2] The evidence is strongly against anything of the sort. Lord Esher notes in his journal, 15th July 1902: " He (Chamberlain) saw Arthur Balfour, however, and expressed his complete loyalty to him. He was so touched by Arthur's loyalty to *him* all through the most difficult moments of the South African war that he determined —at any cost—that Arthur should succeed Lord Salisbury and that he would serve under him." Similarly J. S. Sandars, Balfour's private secretary, while noting that Chamberlain had been approached by some Conservatives who wished him to be Prime Minister, states that Chamberlain replied: " I am not a candidate for that office. . . . I say again what I have said before. I shall be quite willing to serve under Balfour—but mark I would not serve under anyone." [3] As early as April 1899 Sir Henry Lucy declares that Chamberlain said to him: " Never at any time, in any circumstances, do I intend to be Prime Minister of the Unionist party. I am ready to serve under Arthur Balfour or anyone else who may be preferred to the post."

But because Chamberlain did not aspire to the supreme office

[1] *The Times*, 15th July 1902.   [2] P. 354.
[3] Dugdale, *op. cit.*, Vol. 1, 337.

does not mean that he did not aspire to the supreme power. Of equal importance to the resignation of Lord Salisbury was the withdrawal of Sir Michael Hicks-Beach. " A determined opponent of the efforts of the protectionists is leaving the cabinet," was the comment of the *Vossische Zeitung*.[1] The New York correspondent of *The Times* wrote: " Sir Michael Hicks-Beach's resignation surprises nobody. . . . It is considered here that Balfour, having to choose between Mr. Chamberlain and Sir M. Hicks-Beach, chose Mr. Chamberlain inevitably. But what American financiers ask is what now becomes of those declarations of inflexible Free Trade which the Chancellor of the Exchequer was allowed to make in the name of the late Government." [2]

The Times in a leading article remarked that " the Chancellor-ship of the Exchequer will not be so easily filled. There is no financier in the Unionist party whose endowments mark him out as particularly well fitted for the post." [3] As successors, Lord George Hamilton, Brodrick, Hanbury, Ritchie and Austen Chamberlain were all mentioned. Three days later the favourites were stated to be Ritchie and J. W. Lowther. The following day Lowther was thought the more likely. Three weeks later the post was still unfilled and " the latest lobby rumour is that Mr. Ritchie will succeed Sir M. Hicks-Beach." Two days later, on the eve of the Coronation, Ritchie, formerly President of the Board of Trade, was appointed. It was considered a safe but not a brilliant choice. " Mr. Ritchie has shown himself an excellent adminis-trator and a good man of business in all the offices he has held." [4]

It was to be a fateful choice. The hesitation of Balfour has not been explained. Was there a preliminary trial of strength between Free Traders and Protectionists? Was the appointment of *Austen* Chamberlain ever seriously considered? What were Joseph Chamberlain's views?

The last administration of Lord Salisbury had brought the Boer War to a victorious, if not glorious, conclusion. It had produced the Education Bill under the pressure of the Cockerton judgment. It had provided in the Anglo-Japanese treaty a serious breach in the Salisbury policy of " splendid isolation." It had

[1] *The Times*, 16th July 1902.   [2] Ibid., 15th July, 1902.
[3] Ibid., 18th July 1902.   [4] Ibid., 9th August 1902.

run into trade recession and declining employment, the classical method of meeting a slump being put into operation.

At the beginning of 1901 *The Times* had remarked: " We are entering upon the twentieth century upon the down grade after a prolonged period of business activity, high wages, high profits and overflowing revenue." [1]   A railway strike at Taff Vale in South Wales had aroused great bitterness among the employers because of its effectiveness, and among the workers because the company had attempted to employ professional blacklegs. Fog signals were used to warn pickets of the approach of trains carrying the strike-breakers. The rails were greased on gradients, and locomotives were put out of action by gangs of strikers. The company sued the union, and while the T.U.C. was meeting at Huddersfield in September 1900 the news was received that Mr. Justice Farwell had found for the company. But his judgment was reversed in the Court of Appeal, and the Trade Union movement breathed freely again. The case was then taken to the House of Lords, where the Farwell judgment was restored, C. W. Bowerman, the President of the T.U.C. at the Swansea meeting of 1901, informing the Congress that even a Conservative journal had declared the decision to be a political rather than a legal one.

It was a shattering blow for the Unions, robbing them of rights which they had thought secured to them finally, after their bitter struggles, by the legislation of the eighteen-seventies. Now the Unions could be sued for the acts of their representatives, and the strike weapon in their hands was as likely to be a weapon of suicide as of defence or attack. Support for the new Labour Representation Committee, set up in 1900, grew apace, while the offensive of the employers developed along traditional lines.[2]

In the winter of 1901 a series of articles entitled *The Crisis in British Industry*, and attacking the Unions, appeared in *The Times*. In June 1902 Lord James of Hereford, Chairman of the

[1] *The Times*, 8th January 1901.
[2] Ibid., 15th March 1904, records the presentation to A. Beasley, General Manager of the railway company of " a testimonial in recognition of the services he had rendered to capitalists and employers generally." He received a cheque for £1000, a pair of silver candlesticks, and a diamond pendant for his wife. At the presentation Beasley showed a photograph of the cheque for £23,000 received from the Union as damages.

Coal Conciliation Board, decreed a ten per cent cut in miners' wages. Meanwhile phenomenal prices were being paid for old masters. J. P. Morgan was said to have given £100,000 for the Colonna Raphael, and £30,000 for Gainsborough's Duchess of Devonshire. Hoppner's Lady Louisa Manners fetched £14,752, and a Gainsborough of the artist's daughters, sold in 1888 for 211 guineas, now made 5,600 at Christies.[1]

The new Prime Minister entered upon his responsibilities in the most favourable conditions; a country at peace; a monarch who, punctilious in small matters, did not, as his mother had done, interfere in greater; a substantial majority in a parliament only eighteen months old; an opposition still feeble and disunited.

The Liberal party remained in a sorry state. The Education Bill was still dragging its rather tedious clauses through the two houses, and the force of the opposition in the country was not yet apparent. Chinese Labour was still only a whisper in the press and a secret conspiracy behind the doors of the mining finance houses. The Liberal-Imperialists under the ex-Premier Lord Rosebery remained a thorn in the side of the official leaders, and made Campbell-Bannerman's position as " uneasy as the throne of Poland." [2] Rosebery would neither let go nor resolutely clutch at the crown. " He continues," wrote Raymond Asquith to John Buchan in 1902, " to prance upon the moonbeam of efficiency, and makes speeches at every street corner. . . . No one has the least idea what he wants to effect, and beyond a mild bias in favour of good government and himself as Premier, nothing can be gleaned from his speeches. . . . He has started a thing called the Liberal League, which appears at present to consist of three persons—himself, my father and Grey—backed by a squad of titled ladies who believe that the snobbery of the lower classes is greater than their greed." [3] Of Rosebery, Gladstone had said: " 1. He is one of the very ablest men I have known. 2. He is of the highest honour and probity. 3. I do not know whether he really has common sense." [4] Few would now have any doubts on the third point,

---

[1] See *Annual Register*, 1902, 1904.

[2] The phrase was Lord Rosebery's.

[3] J. Buchan (Lord Tweedsmuir), *Memory hold the door*, 62. Ben Tillett, however, thought that Lord Rosebery was the only Prime Minister except Ramsay MacDonald who can be said to have entered deeply into the life of the poor. *Memories and Reflections*, 170, published in 1931.

[4] Crewe, *Life of Lord Rosebery*, Vol. 2, 661.

to which should be added that he had been ambitious to be Prime Minister, ambitious for the office, not for what he could do with it, as he had been ambitious to marry an heiress and had married Hannah Rothschild, and to win the Derby and had acquired horses that did so.

Campbell-Bannerman called the Liberal-Imperialists " *our* Chartered Company," [1] which perhaps contained a dig at financial connexions. He regarded the arch-imperialist Chamberlain as " the very embodiment of all that is bad in policy and spirit; of all that will wreck and ruin our country, and nothing will bring me to say anything else." [2] But C.-B. was not a dominant figure in political life at this period. His own party tolerated him because there was no rival for the unenviable job of leader of a divided opposition. The Conservatives treated him as a political nonentity. Meanwhile the shrewd, genial, wealthy Scot carried on. He was an optimist by temperament, which was fortunate. He believed sincerely in Gladstonian Liberalism, and although he might be idealistic in his tenets, his attitude to persons was extremely realistic. His favourite apothegm was the Italian: " He who makes himself more agreeable to you than is his wont has either deceived you or wishes to deceive you." [3] He had tart nicknames for his colleagues: Rosebery was Barnbougle (after one of his castles) or The Lord, Morley was Priscilla, Harcourt the Nymph of Malwood. He was a rich man, with a house exquisitely furnished and with some fine French pictures, but he had deep sympathies with the poor, which seem to have had a religious origin. He possessed the common touch. " I have no patience," he said, " with professors of a religion founded by fishermen, who think that the higher posts in the Church must be preserved for the highly born and the highly educated. I have little doubt that St. Peter dropped his h's and that Our Saviour's Sermon on the Mount was uttered in the broadest Galilean dialect." [4]

But, for the present, Balfour had it all his own way. Only one thing he lacked: a policy. For Balfour was a brilliant façade, with nothing behind save a determination to protect the privilege of his class and a pleasure in intellectual contests. Perhaps his ignorance was " judicial " when he asked Mrs. Sidney Webb:

[1] Spender, *Life of Sir H. Campbell-Bannerman*, Vol. 1, 9.
[2] Ibid., Vol 1, 87.   [3] Ibid., Vol. 1, 58.   [4] Ibid., Vol. 1, 57.

" What exactly is a Trades Union?"[1] but he had no sympathy for a working class which did not keep its place.

But if Balfour lacked a positive policy, he did not lack one of the most positive of politicians, Joseph Chamberlain, who shortly after the formation of the new Government decided to visit South Africa. Lucy in *Punch* suggested that the Prime Minister would not be sorry to be rid for a time of his turbulent colleague.[2]

The end of the war had taken the limelight off the Colonial Secretary, and the Colonial Conference of 1902 had failed to fulfil his highest hopes. The net was spread in vain. " Gentlemen, we do want your aid," he pleaded at the Guildhall. " We do require your assistance in the administration of the vast Empire, which is yours as well as ours. The weary Titan staggers under the too vast orb of its fate. We have borne the burden for many years. We think it is time that our children should assist us to support it, and whenever you make the request to us be very sure that we shall hasten gladly to call you to our councils. If you are prepared at any time to take any share, any proportionate share, in the burdens of the Empire, we are prepared to meet you with any proposal for giving to you a corresponding voice in the policy of the Empire." [3]

It was Disraeli's old policy, only more urgently pleaded. British world supremacy could be ensured if the Colonies would pay their share; and if they assisted with the burden, let them be granted a voice in the direction of the Empire.

The response was disappointing. The Conference agreed to increase Colonial Preference, but the sharing of the cost of defence was prevented by Canada. Of her patriotic sentiment there was no question. She had been the largest contributor per head to the Queen Victoria memorial. She now refused the invitation to pay anything towards the cost of Imperial defence, either for army or navy. The shadow of the United States was falling across the Empire.[4]

[1] Lucy B. Masterman, *C. F. G. Masterman*, 61.
[2] *Punch*, 5th November 1902, " A touching scene."
[3] Speech, 11th July 1902.
[4] Disraeli had appreciated this thirty years before. See Monypenny and Buckle, *Life*, Vol. 2, 531, 532.

CHAPTER XIX

COMING TO TERMS WITH WASHINGTON

Although the fundamental decision to hunt with the United States rather than with Germany had already been taken, two important and difficult questions between the English-speaking countries were left over to the reign of Edward VII, with the pro-German groups in Britain still possessing a few shots in the locker.

American competition, although neither ubiquitous nor comprehensive, was serious enough in some ranges of articles for good relations to be difficult for certain sections in each country. The formation of the mammoth United States Steel Corporation, to take over the Carnegie interests at the turn of the century, was menacing to the British heavy industries, particularly when J. P. Morgan, who had arranged the deal, began to acquire a fleet of merchant vessels to bear the company's products to Europe. Threats of tobacco competition were hastily met by the formation of the Imperial Company by Wills and other interests. The development of the London Underground system was largely in the hands of American financiers. When members of the New York Chamber of Commerce came to England, were received by the King at Windsor, and fêted at a banquet at Grocers Hall, at which Lord Lansdowne was present, *The Economist* rather petulantly remarked: "Every toast was proposed and responded to in the spirit of a Christmas hymn . . . it is difficult to believe that we are living in a time in which American competition is becoming a national bugbear." It was however significant that *The Times*, commenting on the competition from across the Atlantic, pointed out that nothing would please the Germans more than that we should quarrel with the Americans.

The two questions which remained for settlement, the boundary of Alaska with Canada and the negotiation of a new treaty in respect of the Central American Isthmus, were difficult and dangerous. The Tsar thought that they would prevent Britain forming a real alliance with the United States against Europe in general and Russia in particular.

Alaska had been purchased from Russia by Secretary of State Seward in 1867. The boundary with Canada had never been settled, and with the discovery of gold in the Yukon, the icy lands of the far north became of increased importance, with American and Canadian prospectors and merchants confronting each other in disputed territories.

The project of a canal across Central America had occupied American engineers and business men for decades. Goethe had noted in 1827: " It is absolutely indispensable for the United States to effect a passage from the Mexican Gulf to the Pacific Ocean, and I am certain they will do it. . . . I should be surprised if the United States were to let an opportunity escape of getting such work into their own hands." [1]

Britain had early realized the importance of the canal which would one day be constructed, and in the Clayton-Bulwer treaty of 1850 had acquired from the United States valuable rights which would have just the effect of blocking that " opportunity." Thus, when the American Government raised the question of a revision of the treaty, Lord Salisbury early in 1899 linked the two questions of Alaska and the Isthmus together; White, the envoy in London, telegraphing to the Secretary of State, John Hay: " I obtained assurances from British Minister for Foreign Affairs that if High Commission (on Alaska) should reach agreement British Government assent to your proposed Clayton-Bulwer treaty would be given at once." [2]

To the United States the canal became of increasing importance as Germany rose to power. If the original treaty with Britain stood, equal international rights would follow, and as Roosevelt wrote to Hay in February 1900: " If Germany has the same right that we have in canal across Central America, why not in the partition of any part of South America?" [3] The British Government, aware that the canal would double the effectiveness of the American Navy, considered the linking of Alaska with the Isthmus a reasonable bargain. In Alaska Britain was in a particularly

[1] 21st February 1827. Quoted by Paul H. Emden, *Money Powers of Europe in the Nineteenth Century*, 54.
[2] 15th February 1899.
[3] Quoted by L. M. Gelber, *The Rise of Anglo-American Friendship*, 53.

difficult position, for here Canadian public opinion was concerned, and the British Government was most anxious not to disturb it. Also, as they well knew, the Canadian case was not a strong one.

But this was before the South African War. Thereafter, American pressure increased, and a weakened Britain was compelled to pay an increased price for American friendship. In January 1900 Congress became busy with an Isthmus Bill. A month later Pauncefote, the British Ambassador, signed a treaty with Hay, granting to the American Government concessions which before the Boer War she had refused; but these now were not enough. A vehement campaign, led by Theodore Roosevelt, Governor of New York, was launched against the treaty, which was drastically amended before the Senate. The position of the British Government was now very difficult; questions of prestige were involved and American opinion was in no mood to compromise. " If England should reject the Senate amendments," wrote Senator Lodge to Henry White, " it is just as certain as the oncoming of day that we shall abrogate the treaty by resolution of Congress and go on with the building of the canal. The American people mean to have the canal and they mean to control it. Now England does not care enough about it to go to war to prevent our building it, and it would be ruinous if she did make war on us." [1] Theodore Roosevelt, now Vice-President, wrote more cautiously (the reference to Germany is significant): " Before we abrogate the Clayton-Bulwer treaty we want to make sure of the position we intend taking should Germany and England combine against us. Of course, such a combination would be one of the utmost folly for England, because she is certain to have her paws burned, while the nuts would go to Germany." [2]

For a brief period the position was rather dangerous. In March 1901 Lansdowne had informed Pauncefote that His Majesty's Government preferred to keep the treaty unaltered. Negotiations were in progress with Germany (perhaps Chamberlain's last attempt, launched in January 1901, owed something to this friction with the United States). There seemed no way out, and then Lord Salisbury decided to start negotiations again. It was an important decision.

All through the summer the negotiations continued. They

---

[1] Quoted by L. M. Gelber, *The Rise of Anglo-American Friendship*, 56. [2] Ibid., 88.

were complete when an assassin's bullet removed President McKinley, and Theodore Roosevelt stepped into the centre of the stage. " There is an impression that he is unusually masterful," wrote *The Economist*, " that he is inclined to Jingoism, that he holds to the policy known as the Monroe doctrine with extreme tenacity, and that he is especially antagonistic to Great Britain." [1] Antagonistic he had been, but the rise of Germany had swallowed up the smaller danger in the greater. He was also influenced by the writings of Captain Mahan, who was beginning to convince many Americans of the value of sea-power, and specifically of the British Navy, in the defence of the United States.

The second Hay-Pauncefote treaty, which gave the United States almost all that the Senate demanded, was signed in November. It was the more readily accepted by the British public, because of the bitterness in Anglo-German relations following Chamberlain's October speech.

There remained the Alaska boundary. In March 1902, Roosevelt sent in American troops. In May, he was telling a member of the British embassy staff that he was " going to be ugly about Alaska." It was in the face of these developments that the negotiations began, but before they were complete a further important event occurred. Venezuela, which had nearly brought Britain and the United States to war in 1896, again produced a dangerous *impasse*, with Germany playing a major role in a triangular situation.

Britain and Germany had financial interests in Venezuela, small in proportion to the total of their foreign holdings, but important enough to the groups concerned. The preoccupation of Britain in South Africa was a factor in precipitating events. *The New York Herald*, no doubt in the interests of American business, had pointed out that the prestige of the British Empire had been destroyed by the Boers.[2] The effect was that debts to Britain, and to other European Governments and groups who sheltered behind British prestige, were ignored by President Castro, to the acute annoyance of the persons involved.

But, as the Americans noted, German interest in Venezuela was not only financial. In May 1901, *The Times*, quoting *The New York Herald*, told that " the German cruiser *Vineta* had completed

[1] *The Economist*, 21st September 1901.
[2] *The Times*, 1st April 1901.

surveys of Margarita Island . . . the German merchants in Venezuela are trying to buy the harbour with several hundred acres of
adjacent land, ostensibly as a private investment, but in reality
to make it a German naval coaling station."[1]

As early as December 1901 Germany informed the United
States that she might be compelled to employ force in collecting
her debts. A correct diplomatic reply was received to the effect
that if force were confined to the object stated no objection under
the Monroe doctrine would be raised. The private opinion of the
American Government was less enthusiastic, and it seems possible
that the British Government was in fact encouraged to act jointly
with Germany in order to keep the situation under control.[2]

A few months later the British Government took the lead,
and in July 1902 Germany officially asked to be associated with her.
In November the Kaiser visited England, and Sir Charles Dilke
was one of those who suggested that the details of the future joint
action were then arranged. Early in December a combined British
and German fleet seized the Venezuelan navy of four ships, and
instituted a blockade. British public opinion did not welcome the
co-operation; soon Kipling was publishing in *The Times* his
violent anti-German poem, *The Rowers*.[3] Feelings rose on both
sides of the Atlantic, particularly after the Germans bombarded
the Venezuelan coast and sank Venezuelan ships. " The outburst
in this country against Germany," wrote the British ambassador
in Washington to Lord Lansdowne, " has been truly remarkable,
and suspicions of the German Emperor's designs in the Caribbean
Sea are shared by administration, the press, and the public alike
. . . it will continue to be fostered by the naval authorities . . .
who wish to increase the navy, and by the powerful shipbuilding
firms of Cramp in the East and Scott in the West, who want more
orders for ships." [4]

On 20th January 1903 American opinion rose to fever heat
when the German ships bombarded San Carlos. The last week
of January found British ministers flying distress signals in every
public speech they made. Lord Balfour of Burleigh described
the joint action with Germany as " a mere casual co-operation for

---

[1] *The Times*, 2nd May 1901.
[2] See Fitzroy, *op. cit.*, Vol. 1, 122.   [3] 22nd December 1902.
[4] *B. D.*, Vol. 2, No. 184. Sir M. Herbert to Lord Lansdowne, 29th December 1902, 163-4.

a specific purpose and for a limited time," to which Asquith for the Opposition retorted that it was " a partnership indefinite to a large extent in its purposes and altogether indefinite in point of time in which we as a nation combined unlimited liability with a strictly limited power of control." Lord Cranborne for the Government admitted that there was a " mess," and referred to "certain arrangements." On 3rd February, Arthur Lee, M.P., Civil Lord of the Admiralty and a friend of Theodore Roosevelt, wrote very critically to *The Times*. On 6th February Sir Edward Grey strongly attacked the Government's pro-German policy. On the following day the British ambassador telegraphed to London: " Our good relations with this country will be seriously impaired if this alliance with Germany continues much longer. The time has come in American opinion for us to make the choice between the friendship of the United States and that of Germany." [1] Lansdowne, who had been the moving spirit in the adventure, now capitulated. A few days later the protocol ending the use of forcible means was signed, and the crisis, this " blunder with the seed of war in it " as Campbell-Bannerman called it, was liquidated. [2]

This was to be the last instance of British-German co-operation, although Lansdowne, impercipient to the end, persisted in his attempts, which seem to have had financial origins. Within a month he had interested the City in the construction of the Bagdad Railway in co-operation with a German group. The storm was immediate and inevitable. Lansdowne later blamed Chamberlain for the opposition and for persuading the financiers to back down. He would have been prepared to fight it out in parliament; but it is improbable that he could have succeeded.

A month earlier, in January 1903, the Alaska treaty was signed, submitting the issue to a tribunal of six, three British, to be appointed by the Canadians, and three Americans. *The Economist* wisely remarked: " The general belief is that the Americans will win . . . that the one Englishman or two Englishmen chosen to sit will decide along with the three Americans in favour of the United States." [3] The British representatives were two Canadian

[1] Ibid., Vol. 2, No. 199. Herbert to Lansdowne, Telegram, 7th February 1903, 172.
[2] J. A. Spender, *op. cit.*, Vol. 2, 85.   [3] 4th April 1903.

lawyers, and Lord Alverstone, Lord Chief Justice of England. The American representatives made Canada gasp. They were distinguished men, but in nothing more distinguished than in their previous advocacy of the American case. The Senate withheld their ratification of the treaty until they saw who was to be nominated.

The Tribunal sat in London in September. " It would be a bad thing for us," wrote President Roosevelt to White on 26th September, " if there were a deadlock in the present commission; but it would be a very much worse thing for the Canadians and the English." [1] On 4th October White had a long talk with Balfour at his home in Scotland: " I left no doubt upon his mind as to the importance of a settlement nor as to the result of a failure to agree . . . he thought it would be little short of a disaster if the Tribunal broke up without a decision. I then explained to him very fully the position of Alverstone and intimated that I thought it would be very desirable that he should be told that the Government, without in any way wishing to influence him, was very anxious for a decision. I never heard directly whether he did anything, nor if so what; but two days afterwards his confidential secretary Sandars, who is a friend of mine, let me know very confidentially that he had had two interviews with Lord Alverstone." [2]

The Lord Chief Justice sided with the three Americans; perhaps there was never any doubt, for the Canadian case was not a strong one, but it would be interesting if we had a note of the *two* interviews. Alverstone was bitterly criticized in Canada. " If you do not want a judicial decision," he retorted at the Guildhall banquet in November, " do not ask British judges to be members of the court." Valuable was the work Alverstone did for Imperial interests, whether the decision was or was not according to the facts of the case. The last unsettled question between Britain and America had been adjusted. Britain now had a firm friend at her back to whom she could safely leave the defence of the Caribbean and of Canada, while she concentrated her strength in the North Sea, or, as Admiral von Tirpitz, *Minister fur Seesfacht*, preferred to call it, the German Ocean.

[1] A. Nevins, *Henry White*, 199.
[2] Dennis, *Adventures in American Diplomacy*, 54.

CHAPTER XX

THE NAVY AND THE ARMY

The British Navy, for historical as well as geographical reasons, occupied a position in the affections of the nation altogether different from that of the army. It had also until recently been the cheaper branch, naval expenditure exceeding military for the first time only in 1895.[1] There had, however, been in operation for some time past a revolution in the national attitude to the Army, which, having its origin perhaps in the uprising of the Volunteers in the sixties to be ready for Napoleon III, slowly changed public opinion, also to be impressed by the series of military actions punctuating the late Victorian period. " Our army is always at war," remarked Lord Wolseley in 1897.[2] A year earlier the War Office had acquired a tract of Salisbury Plain, 15 miles by $5\frac{1}{2}$, for military training.[3] In 1898 the management of the Alhambra, Leicester Square, correctly gauged public taste when they engaged Piper Findlater, the North-West Frontier V.C., whom " Madame Tussauds " modelled in wax.[4] Interest in the Army was certainly growing when in 1899 it met the severe test of the Boer War.

The men did well enough, the officers less well, and as for the War Office, which since 1895 had been under Lord Lansdowne, its performance was pitiful. On the day war began, an order for 250 sets of saddlery could not be met. Two months later gun ammunition was being borrowed from India and from the Navy, while orders for shrapnel were being executed in Germany.[5] The medical services, even after the lesson of the Crimea, were inadequate. It is a measure of the importance of a great landowner in the reign of Edward VII that Lord Lansdowne was not forced out of public life, although to be sure promotion (to the Foreign

---

[1] 1894–5, Navy £17,545,000; Army £17,900,000. 1895–6, Navy £19,724,000; Army £18,460,000.
[2] 17th November 1897, Royal United Services Institute.
[3] Col. C. K. Dunlop, *The Development of the British Army, 1899–1914*, 27.
[4] Ibid., 8, 9.   [5] Ibid., 86.

Office in this instance) had long been the traditional method of rewarding failure in British politics. But if the war in South Africa was the grave of some reputations, it only provided fresh laurels for the two great soldiers whose fame was already secure. Roberts, V.C., of Kandahar, and Kitchener of Khartoum. Roberts was ageing now, his best service was done; but it is worth noting that in his foreword to the official *Combined Training*, 1902, he laid down principles which were to prevent the British Army getting what Churchill in an Army debate in 1903 called " German measles." " Success in war," wrote Roberts, " cannot be expected unless all ranks have been trained in peace to use their wits." We must " break down . . . the paralysing habit of an unreasoning and mechanical adherence to the letter of orders and to routine when acting under service conditions." [1]

Kitchener was still in the prime of life; a queer, solitary figure, more like a business man than a typical general, strong in personality (Lord Milner found himself over-persuaded by the man),[2] and with a dry sense of humour. Thus after the crowning victory of Omdurman he wrote to Cromer in Cairo: " The effect of having killed 30,000 Dervishes is that I have 300,000 women on my hands, and I should be much obliged if you could instruct me how to dispose of them as I have no use for them myself." [3] Campbell-Bannerman was shocked at the callous tone of his South African dispatches, in which he referred to Boer captives as if they were so many head of cattle or brace of game. Lord Esher, the King's confidant, who was to play an important part in Army reform, writes that he " was never seen to address or even notice a private soldier. His mind, with its commercial and financial bent—for like Napoleon he was *homme d'affaires*—had grasped the threat of German competition. He was not a man whom one could love, but he was an admirable organizer, and it was as true of him as of Nelson that those who went to see him came away braver men." [4]

The failures of the Boer War made military reorganization inevitable, but the cleaning of the Augean stable at Whitehall was bitterly resisted in high Army circles, and it was not until two War Secretaries had failed, Brodrick and Arnold-Forster, that Haldane in 1906 was able to carry through the reorganization of

[1] Quoted by Dunlop, *op. cit.*, 226. [2] *Milner Papers*, Vol. 2, 208.
[3] Lord Esher, *The Tragedy of Lord Kitchener*, 29. [4] Ibid., 15, 28.

the War Office, and the preparation of the British Army for 1914.

But it was not only the vested interests that hindered Army reform. More important was the lack of policy, the uncertainty in the official and in the public mind of what the role of the British Army should be in the changing circumstances. It is not accidental that Army reform had largely to wait until after the transformation of Britain's external relations by the Anglo-French Convention of 1904. It was all very well to talk of reorganizing the Army. The experience of the Boer War had indeed shown the need for this; but how did the Army fit into the national and imperial defence as a whole? What was the role of the Navy? Not the least of the obstacles in the way of the Army reformers was the impression that they were competing with the sailors for the public attention and the public purse. Must Britain have a great army as Germany did? Churchill in February 1903 well expressed the Navy point of view: " As to a stronger regular army, either we had the command of the sea or we had not. If we had it we required fewer soldiers. If we had it not we wanted more ships." [1]

But the conflict was by then on the way to solution. A few days previously Balfour had announced to Parliament the setting up of a Committee of Imperial Defence, one of the objects of which was to co-ordinate the activities of the two services. Balfour was always keenly interested in matters of defence,[2] although it seems that the credit for this idea must go to Brodrick.[3]

New ideas were being discussed in progressive naval circles. As early as January 1901 Admiral Fisher had decided that " oil fuel will absolutely revolutionize naval strategy."[4] Messrs. Yarrow, the Jarrow firm, supplied the Netherland's Navy in the following year with an experimental oil-burning vessel.[5] Messrs. Armstrong-Whitworth at about the same time were carrying out research for the Mediterranean fleet under the influence of Lord Charles Beresford.[6] But the day of oil was not yet. It was otherwise with the big-gun ship.

[1] 24th Feb. 1903.
[2] See Sir A. Fitzroy, *Memoirs*, Vol. 1, 137; also Lord Fisher, *Memories*, 210.
[3] See Balfour's speech, House of Commons, 5th March 1903.
[4] Sir R. H. Bacon, *Lord Fisher*, Vol. 1, 157 (28th January 1901).
[5] *Navy Annual*, 1903.
[6] *The Economist*, 29th September 1902, Report of meeting of Armstrong-Whitworth.

New design to make the battleship more formidable was being worked out by many, and notably by Colonel Cuniberti of the Italian Navy, with Britain and America soon following the experiments with the keenest interest.[1] On Trafalgar Day 1904 Fisher became First Sea Lord, and carried through a ruthless and successful reorganization of the methods of naval training and promotion. He had already made up his mind that Germany was the foe whom Britain must inevitably fight. Thus in August 1902 he wrote: " The German Emperor may be devoted to us, but he can no more stem the tide of German commercial hostility to this country of ours than Canute could keep the North Sea from wetting his patent-leather boots." [2] He devoted all his energies to preparing the Navy for The Day. He suggested that it would save trouble if the German fleet were " copenhagened " before it became too strong. He laid down in October 1905 a new type of ship, which he called the *Dreadnought*.

She was not very much bigger than the existing ships of the line, but she developed far greater fire-power, was more effectively armoured and of comparable speed. To Fisher it seemed a death-blow to German naval hopes. The construction was carried through with unusual speed and secrecy. She was launched in February 1906 and began her trials in October. And if she was not very much bigger than previous battleships she was very much more expensive. It may indeed be said to have been the *Dreadnought* that sank the House of Lords.

For a time British sea-power was placed in a predominant position, but as soon as Germany had adopted the new design and began the construction of Dreadnoughts, the effect was to wipe out that part of the British supremacy which was based on the possession of a preponderant number of older battleships. The race would now start from 1906 not from 1896. Fisher has been blamed for this position. He was wiser than his critics. The new design would come sooner or later, better to be the first to introduce it than the second; while, to accommodate the new vessels, considerable dredging would now have to be undertaken by the Germans round their coasts, as well as the reconstruction of the Kiel Canal. It is not without significance that the Canal

[1] E. L. Woodward, *Great Britain and the German Navy*, 107–14.
[2] Sir R. H. Bacon, *Lord Fisher*, Vol. 1, 158.

was not ready until the summer of 1914, just before the war broke out. But the *Dreadnought* was still a blueprint (if that) in 1903 as Britain felt her way towards an agreement with France. New naval decisions were being taken. On 16th February 1903 a public meeting was held at the Westminster Palace Hotel with Haldane in the chair. A resolution was passed expressing " the desirability of creating a North Sea squadron and of establishing a naval base on the East Coast."[1] On 5th March Balfour announced that land had been bought on the River Forth for the construction of a base. The Marquess of Linlithgow had been pleased to sell 1,464 acres with an annual rental of £1,622 for £122,500, a matter of 80 years purchase. It was a good price for the Marquess, not perhaps such a satisfactory bargain for the nation, for when war came, the fleet concentrated at Scapa Flow.

Clear and unmistakable were the signs of British preoccupation with the German threat. It is however to be noted that to the German people, to some of the members of the German government, perhaps even to Tirpitz himself, the German Navy was for defence against a British blow which was genuinely feared.[2]

The naval building race was not confined to Britain and Germany. The *Navy Annual* for 1904 declared that the United States would shortly become the second naval power in the world. In 1907 it announced that she had done so. In Russia, Italy, Austria, according to their means (in the case of Russia, according to other people's means) ships slid down the slipways. Only in France, under a ridiculous Minister of Marine, the fleet languished. It was not the least of the predisposing factors to an Anglo-French agreement.

[1] *Annual Register*, 1903, 35.
[2] H. Temperley in his review of E. L. Woodward, *Great Britain and the German Navy*, comments on Woodward's failure to deal with this point. *English Historical Review*, October 1930.
   See also the Kaiser's comment on the letter from the Prussian Minister at Munich to Hohenlohe, 31st July 1897: The Minister had written " a definite change over by England to Protection indicates that that Empire is losing its pre-eminence in the markets of the world." The Kaiser's note reads: " Now that the superiority of German industry is recognized, Albion will soon make efforts to destroy it, and she will undoubtedly be successful unless we quickly and energetically forestall the evil by building a strong fleet. . . . England herself will not take up Protection but her Colonies will. Since these are all over the world England has ample trade circulation and exchange with them, whilst Germany is excluded from them! *Caeterum censeo naves aedificandas!*"

CHAPTER XXI

THE AGREEMENT WITH FRANCE

Whether Eckardstein's story of his overhearing Chamberlain and Cambon, the French ambassador, mentioning Egypt and Morocco during a private conversation after a state dinner at Marlborough House in February 1902 is to be believed (and probably not), it is certainly true that after the failure of the 1901 attempt at a German Alliance, Chamberlain wasted no time in starting on his new tack. Alliance he was determined to have, if not with Germany then with France, and after France, Russia.

When the storm over Fashoda had subsided, the English press had made it clear that France could have an agreement if she would recognize the British occupation of Egypt. The position remained unaltered, as the persistent, rather unattractive gentleman who presided at the Quai d'Orsay, M. Delcassé, knew well.

He was a skilful maker of alliances, forger of those links of friendship which would enable France to challenge Germany, reverse the humiliation of 1870, and tear the mourning draperies from the statue of Strasbourg in the Place de la Concorde. A *protégé* of Gambetta, the Jewish patriot, who had told his followers to work for the *révanche* but never to speak of it,[1] Delcassé worked with methodical application, rising at five o'clock and retiring to bed at nine.[2] Day after day the ritual continued and the triumphs piled up. In August 1899 the Franco-Russian alliance was strengthened. In December 1900 he did a deal with Italy: support by France for Italian aims in Tripoli; support by Italy for French aims in Morocco; a wedge into the Triple Alliance. In April 1901 the Italian fleet was at Toulon. In September the Tsar visited France, although fear of revolutionaries kept him away from Paris. In May 1902 President Loubet went to St.

[1] O. J. Hale, *Germany and the Diplomatic Revolution: A study in Diplomacy and the Press, 1904–6*, 212, draws the wrong conclusion from the absence of any reference in the French press to the *révanche*.
[2] C. W. Porter, *The Career of Théophile Delcassé*, 111.

Petersburg. And all the time Delcassé kept his eyes fixed on his main objective, an alliance with England, and, through his faithful ambassador in London, Paul Cambon, moved surely though slowly to his goal.

In February 1901 Sir Charles Dilke had written an article in the Paris newspaper *Figaro* urging an Anglo-French alliance, and in July both he and Bryce were expressing similar views in the House of Commons.[1] In April 1901, at a banquet held by the French Chamber of Commerce in London, Cambon made a cordial speech, and the official French paper *Débats* devoted a friendly leader to Anglo-French relations.[2] In August 1901 the International Law Conference at Glasgow, with Lord Alverstone in the chair, unanimously passed a motion by Mr. Thomas Barclay, President of the British Chamber of Commerce in Paris, urging a general arbitration between the two countries, a project which the *Annual Register* considered " certainly had a somewhat millenial appearance."[3] Nor was the movement restricted to small groups. Already at the Trades Union Congress at Huddersfield in 1900 a resolution, regretting " that portions of the British and French press frequently use irritating and dangerous language towards the governments and peoples of these countries " and appointing representatives for a demonstration at which a fraternal address by British to French workers was to be presented, was lost only by 442 to 226, its defeat being probably due to association with the pacifist issue in a time of war.[4]

The movement was under way, expressing the deep economic changes which have already been noted. In January 1902 Monson, the British ambassador in Paris, wrote to Lansdowne: " The meeting of the Association of British Chambers of Commerce during the International Exhibition of 1900 was a great success. The French Government, represented by the Minister of Commerce, treated the representatives of the various British Chambers of Commerce with excessive hospitality, and the visit was undoubtedly the occasion for an interchange of cordiality very advantageous to friendly feelings on both sides of the Channel."[5] In August, Cambon was explaining to Lansdowne that " France

[1] House of Commons, 3rd July 1902.
[2] *The Times*, 27th April 1901.   [3] *Annual Register*, 1901.
[4] Randall Cremer, well-known pacifist, was to be one of the delegates.
[5] B. D., Vol. 2, 26.

and England were not competitors in the economic field, nor rivals in the world's markets, as were England, United States and Germany."[1] Chamberlain, although playing no part in the official negotiations (his part in Fashoda made that inappropriate), gave the movement his blessing as he passed through Egypt that December on his way to South Africa, expressing himself categorically in a conversation which he knew would be reported to Paris.[2]

In March Campbell-Bannerman, at Leeds, spoke warmly of France, the " old ally of Scotland."[3] A fortnight earlier the *Echo de Paris* had carried a story that the King would visit Paris on his way back from the Mediterranean.[4] He had not been there since the outbreak of the South African war. " The moment could not be better chosen," wrote *The Times* correspondent. " I may say, with every confidence, that, should the King choose to visit France, it would have in every respect the most desirable consequences and would produce the best impression among Frenchmen of all classes. . . . There is undoubtedly the commencement of a striking evolution of public feeling towards England in this country which corresponds to that change of popular sentiment towards France which has taken place in England within the last 18 months. We shall perhaps not have so long to wait for an Anglo-French *entente cordiale* as a few incorrigible sceptics may be inclined to think." Soon even the opposition paper *Gaulois* was writing that the King's visit " would contribute to dissipate the last vestiges of that malaise which, so to say, has overshadowed the relations between England and France since the South African war . . . the ever-increasing importance of our mutual commercial relations would, even if there were no other reasons, sufficiently justify the necessity of maintaining all desirable courtesy in the relations between the two countries."[5] *The Times* responded warmly in a leader on 11th March: " Here popular feeling has been altered very decidedly in favour of France, perhaps not without regard to the contrasted attitude taken up by another nation . . . the controverted questions which

[1] C. W. Porter, *op. cit.*
[2] J. J. Mathews, *Egypt and the formation of the Anglo-French Entente of 1904*, 42.
[3] Leeds, 19th March 1903.   [4] *The Times*, 6th March 1903.
[5] *The Times*, 10th March 1903.

agitate the relations of France and England are not of the first order of importance . . . quite trifling in comparison with the great interests which both have in common." On 31st March it was remarked of the forthcoming visit of the King that " nothing more was required to give an impetus to the revival of England's former friendly relations with France." On 4th April that " he is sure to be received with demonstrative evidence of popular satisfaction."

These extracts have been given to correct an impression regarding the King's reception. There had been little doubt that it would be cordial. The ground had been well prepared. And then, as he drove from the station through the Paris streets, a small group of journalists booed him and shouted pro-Boer slogans. It was a small demonstration, and it was not repeated. The King conducted himself admirably. His speech at the Hotel de Ville was happily phrased and confidently delivered, but it is an exaggeration to say that he won over a hostile Paris by his charm.[1]

Two months later, in July, the French President returned the visit, accompanied by M. Delcassé. The ground with Lansdowne had already been prepared by a call from M. Étienne, the French Colonial party leader. At this conversation, Lansdowne reported: " M. Étienne expressed his belief that the most serious menace to the peace of Europe lay in Germany, that a good understanding between France and Britain was the only means of holding German designs in check, and that if such an understanding could be arrived at, England would find that France would be able to exercise a salutary influence over Russia, and thereby relieve us from many of our troubles with that country." [2] A few days later Lansdowne had his first conversation with Delcassé. " As for the French Government," he was told, " they had ceased to desire a wide extension of their Colonial possessions and were intent, not upon adding to them, but upon consolidating them and removing all sources of future trouble within them and upon their borders." [3] Eighty members of the French Chamber came to London to

---

[1] Robert Blatchford's *Clarion*, 8th May 1903, commented on the shortness of the appearances of the King " hemmed in by cuirassiers to prevent his popularity from escaping ".

[2] *B. D.*, Vol. 2, 292–3, No. 356. Lansdowne to Monson, 2nd July 1903.

[3] Ibid., Vol. 2, 294, No. 357. Lansdowne to Monson, 7th July 1903.

confer with British members of parliament on international arbitration. Balfour, Chamberlain and Campbell-Bannerman all attended.[1] In October an arbitration treaty was signed between the two countries, a forerunner of the later Convention.

The negotiations, which were ostensibly directed not towards an alliance but towards a settlement of various points of colonial conflict, soon came down to the bargaining of British interests in Egypt against French interests in Morocco. The prospect of becoming independent of Germany in the Egyptian financial council was tempting, and when the negotiations looked like breaking down, Cromer, from Cairo, insisted on them being pressed forward.[2] In December 1903 he renamed Fashoda, Kodok, a sympathetic gesture.

The outbreak of the Russo-Japanese war in January 1904 overtook the negotiators before their work was complete. It was a difficult test. *The Economist* was anxious, and asked those who were cheering the Japanese victories to " moderate their exultation over Russian defeats. After all they are the defeats sustained by the friend of a friend." [3]

In April the Convention was signed. Outstanding differences in many parts of the world were adjusted. In Egypt Britain's position was recognized in diplomatic language, which meant that France no longer expected Britain to keep her previous promise to withdraw. In Morocco the special position of France was recognized, and by secret articles she was admitted by Britain to be heir presumptive to the country.

In Germany the agreement was received with apparent calm, but it was being carefully noted that no mention was made in the agreement of Germany's interests in Morocco, nor had Delcassé made any approach to the Wilhelmstrasse about them.

In France there was some criticism, but ratification was obtained for the public clauses in the Chamber of Deputies by 435 to 105, and in the Senate by 215 to 37. In Britain the treaty was well received, although the philo-German Lord Rosebery sharply

---

[1] 22nd July 1903. Campbell-Bannerman spoke to the visitors in French. The French deputies also went to the Stock Exchange. " The procession occupied less than five minutes, but it probably left effects that will be felt directly and indirectly for at least as many years to come." *The Economist*, 25th July 1903.

[2] *B. D.*, Vol. 2, No. 387.

[3] *The Economist*, 27th February 1903.

attacked it as obtained at too great a price. It is possible that more opposition might have developed, had it not been for a startling change in domestic politics, following the return of Chamberlain from South Africa.

In April Ritchie removed the corn duty imposed in the previous year. It represented a last-minute decision suggested by the Whips, who were finding it unpopular; but the conflict in the Cabinet on the Free Trade issue had long been growing, only to be postponed by the absence of Chamberlain from England. Now on 15th May he came out into the open, and in an oration to his Birmingham constituents he launched his Tariff Reform campaign.

CHAPTER XXII

CROMER, MILNER, AND CURZON

Whatever judgment may be reached on Chamberlain's campaign, and on Chamberlain's motives in launching it (was it really, as some foreign and colonial newspapers suggested, a bid for the premiership?), his remarkable grasp of the perspectives of his period must be admitted: " No longer," he had declared in August 1902, " have we to read the annals of a kingdom; it is the history of an Empire with which we have to deal." [1] The origins of his Imperialism have already been discussed. There remain to be noted the point reached in Imperial development when he began his campaign, why the campaign failed, and what would have been the consequences of its success.

The decade of the fifties had marked the beginning of the importance of the Canadian and Australian market to the British manufacturer. By 1901, although the market had immensely grown (with Canadian imports £39 millions against under £8 millions in 1851, and Australian £42 millions against £4 millions), competition from American and German sources was exerting unpleasant pressure, while in the Colonies themselves there was the rise of native industries behind immense tariff walls, the portentous embryo of self-sufficiency. To secure an outlet for the accumulating British manufactures, to obtain the raw materials on which industrial supremacy depended, became an ever more urgent need. Some of the important raw materials needed came from, or could come from, the " undeveloped estates." The ingenious financial system based on credit enabled these estates to be developed to the enrichment of certain special interests, and the indirect benefit of the whole " Imperial race." In the eighties came the scramble for Africa among the economically developed powers. That continent, as Lord Salisbury remarked, was " created to be the plague of foreign offices." Agreements were

[1] 1st August 1902. *Speeches*, Vol. 2, 70.

ultimately reached, although international friction was considerable. In the nineties the Imperial race assuaged its guilty feelings by evolving the ideology of the " burden of empire." By the opening of the new century the great imperial powers had reached a situation exactly opposite to that of Alexander. For them there were not " no worlds left to conquer." On the contrary only conquest could bring them new territories, which were no longer to be picked up nonchalantly from natives too weak to resist the arrival of civilization led by that unholy trinity, the missionary,[1] the merchant and the machine-gun.

Chamberlain's Tariff Reform proposals can be properly understood only against the whole Imperial background. The time for true Imperial history has not yet come. One can but be aware of the perspective. It is however worthwhile glancing at three great Imperial figures of the reign, from whose action and ideas something of the nature of Edwardian Imperialism may be gleaned. Cromer, Milner and Curzon, the great proconsuls: were they in fact great men, men of surpassing gifts, or did the circumstances of the time support an illusion? This much is clear. They occupied their positions in Egypt, in South Africa, and in India at a time, and at the last time, when to trust the man on the spot was the accepted policy of the home government. The development of empire had outstripped the development of the Colonial department at home. The bureaucracy had not obtained full control. Although, as each year passed, improving communications were aiding the machine, the circumstances still favoured men capable of exercising autocratic power. Whether they were indeed great men depends upon one's values. They were certainly perfect representatives of the governing class. Curzon was of the aristocracy; Cromer of the financial gentry. As for Milner, although, as he remarked, he was not a man who started life possessed of

---

[1] For the missionary, see F. D. Lugard, *The Extension of British influence and trade in Africa*, Royal Colonial Society *Proceedings*, xxvii, 33. " There is one agency which has done far more perhaps than any other for the development of the British possessions. That is the pioneer work of the missionaries. . . . I put aside the spiritual aspect of such work and am looking merely at its economic advantages to the State. . . . I feel convinced that the Government is wise that will foster and encourage missionary effort for the sake not only of the spiritual advantages but also for the temporal. Mr. Rhodes gave free access to missionaries of all denominations into Mashonaland when that country was first taken over by the Chartered Company, and thereby I consider he showed his wisdom and statesmanship."

the advantages of birth,[1] he was with Curzon one of the products of Jowett's Balliol.

Lord Cromer, who began life as Evelyn Baring of the famous finance family, had entered the army, obtaining his chance when he was sent to India to be the secretary of his cousin the Viceroy. One essential side of his character is expressed by his nickname there of the " Vice-Viceroy," just as later, in Egypt, he was to be called " Over-Baring."[2] He did not suffer fools gladly, and even Kitchener confessed to feeling shy when, summoned to an interview, he approached the door of Cromer's study. His financial acumen was worthy of his heredity. He was also a man of culture, no mean Classical scholar, and a friend of Edward Lear, the humorist.[3] In politics he described himself as a Liberal. He might, had he wished, have been Foreign Secretary in 1905. He was certainly a strong individualist and, as such, a supporter of Free Trade, although not so unqualified a supporter as to be able to feel comfortable as a member of the Manchester Free Trade League after he had discovered that that dangerous Socialist, Ramsay MacDonald, had been admitted.[4] His liberalism had been tempered—some would say diluted—by his early experiences in Malta, where he had taken a poor view of Maltese nationalism. In *Modern Egypt* he quotes approvingly Akenside:

> " Where Order deigns to come
> Her sister, Liberty, cannot be far."[5]

He was among the few military men who foretold the collapse of French arms in 1870.[6] The Prussian or German menace became an *idée fixe* after a careful study of German philosophy and German history. When he went to Egypt in the eighties the opposition of Germany on the financial commission only confirmed his opinion, and made him the most urgent advocate of the *Entente Cordiale*. That he was a religious man cannot be denied. He held that " our relations with the various races who are the subjects of the King of England should be founded on the granite

---

[1] Lord Milner, *The Nation and the Empire*, 441.
[2] Zetland, *Lord Cromer*, 180–1.
[3] Ibid., 186. The following is a letter that Lear sent to him: " Thrippy Pilliwinx, Inkly tinky pobblebockle ablesquabs? Flosky! Besbul trimble flosky! Okul scratch abibblebongibo, viddle squibble tog-a-tog, ferry moyassity amsky flamsky damsky crocklefther squigs. Flinky wisty pomm, Slushly pipp."
[4] Ibid., 330.   [5] Vol. 1, 343.   [6] Zetland, *op. cit.*, 266.

rock of the Christian moral code."[1] He agreed with Lord Curzon that the British Empire was " a pre-ordained dispensation intended to be a source of strength and discipline to ourselves and of moral and material blessing to others." He approved Lord Milner's policy in South Africa.[2] And what of his own? What of the Modern Egypt, with the making of which his name is connected?

" The origin of the Egyptian question in its present phase was financial." Thus Lord Cromer begins his celebrated book. It is a discreet book, not only because it stops long before the years of his stewardship are complete, but because, after this initial admission, there is scarcely a reference to the financial transactions and financial rewards of foreign capitalists in the Modern Egypt provided for them by Lord Cromer.

Whether because, as has been suggested, of Cromer's *laissez faire* Liberalism, or from the natural operation of economic causes, factory acts were unknown in Cromer's Egypt, which " without a Parliament, without trade unions, without a factory act, . . . was a paradise for the investor." Children in 1908 were said to have been worked " sometimes for twelve, usually for fifteen, and on occasion for sixteen or eighteen hours a day " and " in the height of the season . . . were put on night shifts of twelve hours."[3]

Nor was this the only serious charge brought against the régime. Here, as elsewhere in the coloured world under British rule, no effort was made to prepare the population for ultimate responsibility. The expenditure on education was ludicrous. Prussia spent one-eighth of its annual revenue on the children. Even Servia one-fifteenth. In Egypt the proportion was less than one-eightieth.[4] At home the administration was generally approved in both Liberal and Conservative circles. The criticisms of Wilfrid Blunt were considered captious. Only when the Denshawai incident struck the headlines it seemed to some as if a corner of a rich curtain had been lifted to reveal Cromeric rule in an unposed moment of startling clarity.

The first public information was a telegram in *The Times* of 15th June 1906 telling of five British officers who, at the invitation

[1] Ibid., 166.
[2] Cromer to Milner, 26th May 1901. *Milner Papers*, Vol. 2, 250.
[3] H. N. Brailsford, *The War of Steel and Gold*, *1914*, 114.
[4] Ibid., 116.

of a village in the Nile Delta, had gone there to shoot pigeons, had been surrounded by the villagers, deprived of their guns, and assaulted with bludgeons. Captain Bull of the 6th Inniskilling Dragoons had died of wounds aggravated by sunstroke. Major Pine-Coffin and Lieutenant Smithwick had been badly hurt.

Three days later readers of the same paper were advised that the district " bears a bad name, and the fact that cries of ' Death to the Christians ' were raised is of some significance."

Meanwhile a number of arrests had been made, and a special court from which there was no appeal, composed of British and Egyptian judges, met on 23rd June, a Sunday, to try the prisoners, who were accused of " murderously attacking " the five British officers. The defence and the prosecution were in the hands of Egyptian advocates, both of whom thought it necessary to begin their speeches with expressions of fulsome gratitude for the British occupation of their country. All the prisoners pleaded not guilty. On 27th June the trial ended with 4 sentenced to death, 2 to penal servitude for life, 1 for fifteen years, 6 for seven years, 3 for one year with 50 lashes, and 5 to 50 lashes without imprisonment.

No time was lost. Within a few hours a procession consisting of the men to be killed and the men to be flogged, of the gallows and the triangle, of the officials, and of an adequate number of soldiers, was on its way to the little village of Denshawai, where a fortnight before five British officers had gone to shoot pigeons. *The Times* that morning was considerate to those whose conscience might be pricking: " The attack," it declared, " had been premeditated for months." In the Commons Campbell-Bannerman implored a section of his back benchers to trust " the discretion and humanity of Grey."[1] At about the same time at the little village in the Nile delta an hour's performance of imperial power was being enacted. Whether by design or chance the sentences permitted a symmetrical exhibition. Four men were to be hanged, and eight to be given 50 strokes each. " The arrangements," Mr. Findlay, the official acting for Lord Cromer, wrote to Edward Grey, " were admirable and reflect great credit on all concerned." First one man was hanged, then, " owing to the necessity of allowing the body of a man hanged to remain suspended

[1] House of Commons, 28th June 1906.

for some time,"[1] two were flogged. Only the doctor's decision somewhat spoiled the perfection of the arrangements, when he declared that the eighth man due for the lash was unfit to receive it.

The sentences had been carried out swiftly, too swiftly for effective action by progressive opinion, but not too swiftly to prevent its expression. Articles in the native and foreign press in Egypt told a different story about the pigeon shooting at Denshawai. Questions were asked in Parliament, and although Grey with his " discretion " if not his " humanity " was able to hold off the attacks until the sentences had been carried out, and any full discussion until the end of the session prevented it, two White Papers were extracted from him, and these, as Bernard Shaw pointed out in his passionate preface to *John Bull's Other Island*, themselves show that it was not justice that was done on that summer afternoon at Denshawai.

Lord Cromer himself was on official leave at the time, but he had not left Egypt, and fully endorsed the actions of Mr. Findlay, the man whom he had left in charge.

The pigeons at Denshawai were tame pigeons belonging to the villagers. British officers, including Major Pine-Coffin, had been there before, when the destruction of the villagers' property had been resented. Official regulations prescribed that permission must first be obtained from the local chief. The officers believed that this leave had been given, or perhaps they did not care. To the village the arrival of the five officers with guns, and their taking of pot-shots at the pigeons, was the beginning of a drama which was to end fourteen days later in executions and flogging.

Mr. Findlay was particularly pleased at the flogging, although this was strange, since one of the acts on which Cromer based his vindication of British rule in Egypt was the abolition of the lash. " The Egyptian, being a fatalist," explained Findlay, " does not greatly fear death, and there is therefore much to be said for flogging as judicial punishment in Egypt." [2] He must have found it difficult to decide whether the four men who were hanged were fortunate or unfortunate.

The White Papers clearly suggest the motives of official action.

[1] Cd. 3086, 1906. *Correspondence respecting the attack on British officers at Denshawai.*
[2] Ibid.

On the day after the incident Cromer wrote to Grey: " Orders will shortly be issued by the General, prohibiting officers in the army from shooting pigeons in the future under any circumstances whatsoever." [1] The provocation which had led to the situation was then being given full weight; but soon justice began to give way before policy. Three days later Cromer was writing: " They were not only brutally struck and pelted by the infuriated mob, but were robbed of the few valuables they had in their possession." The right of property, more sacred than the right of the person, particularly to a good financier such as Cromer, had been in-fringed. " The facts that the officers were in uniform and that the attack on them was apparently premeditated gives a very serious aspect to the incident." The prestige of the British uniform was at stake. The note of a conspiracy against the British *imperium* had been struck. *The Times* on 28th June significantly pulled out the same stop, and thundered: " It must clearly be ascribed to fanaticism stimulated by the mischievous action of the Turks on the Egyptian frontier and by the incitements of their emissaries in Egypt . . . a revolt upon a small scale on the part of the lowest and most fanatical of the Mussulman population. . . . This is a thing which must be put down at all costs and the more vigorously because our army of occupation is very small." On 5th July in the Commons Grey echoed *The Times*: " All this year a fana-tical feeling in Egypt has been on the increase." It is to the credit of Bernard Shaw that on 7th July he wrote to *The Times* (and to the credit of the editor that the letter was printed), protesting at the " disgraceful, sycophantic and panic-stricken sentences." Mr. Wilkinson, Bishop of Zululand, however, implored the readers of *The Times* to show no weakness in Egypt.

The anger on the Left was the more bitter because Grey, a true Liberal-Imperialist, prevented discussion by the plea of public interest. It was not considered surprising that Cromer soon afterwards resigned because of ill-health, preferring a money grant of £50,000 to the proposed honour of the Garter. [2] The peculiarly financial view he took of the Egyptian situation was thus expressed by him in 1908 after his retirement: " If ever there is an Egyptian parliament," he declared, " persons of

[1] Cd. 3086, 1906. *Correspondence respecting the attack on British officers at Denshawai.* [2] The grant was approved by the Commons by 254 votes to 109.

foreign extraction should be represented on account of their intelligence and the stake they have in the country."

The pressure of Egyptian nationalism was to make Cromerism impossible. His successor, Eldon Gorst, ruled with a lighter hand, and in January 1908 the Denshawai prisoners were released. Great indeed was the power and great the clemency of the British rule, but not great enough to bring back to life the four men who, at suitable intervals, swung on that June afternoon in 1906 at a small village which people in Britain had probably never heard of before, and already are beginning to forget.

Cromer went, Gorst was to die of a painful disease, but the Bank of Egypt remained, with Milner, former High Commissioner in South Africa, as Chairman, and Sir Ernest Cassel occupying a seat on the board.

Alfred Milner was good at figures. He had been Chairman of the Board of Inland Revenue. He was called a Liberal, but although he had unsuccessfully stood for Parliament as a Liberal, he was not at heart a democrat. He was an impressive, autocratic, rather lonely man. He had imbibed the Jowett prescription: " Never explain. Never apologize." He was pleased at being told by an American that he had the hide of an alligator.[1] Lord Rosebery found in him " the union of intellect with fascination which makes men mount high."[2] He went to South Africa in 1897 with remarkably wide political backing.

The main flaw in his character was its lack of flexibility. He was a singularly obstinate man. The conflict with Kruger could perhaps in the circumstances of the case not have been avoided. With Milner as High Commissioner diplomacy was given no chance, and when war did come its end was certainly delayed by Milner's stubborn will. His personal character was of the highest British Civil Service tradition. It is however significant that he objected to Cecil Rhodes because his policy was to " gain prematurely by violent and unscrupulous means what you could get honestly and without violence if you could only wait and work for it."[3] Work Milner certainly did to an extent only surpassed perhaps by Curzon, and with the same phases of hysteria.[4] As

[1] *Milner Papers*, Vol. I, 9, 302.   [2] Ibid., 35.
[3] Ibid., 274. Milner to Selborne, 14th September 1898.
[4] Ibid., 499. Milner to Selborne, 30th August 1899.

for his policy, Milner very soon made up his mind that agreement was impossible and directed his efforts to seeing that when war broke out it should do so in circumstances that would appear creditable to Great Britain. His strongest defence is the character of Kruger, who would not compromise either with Milner or with anyone else.

When peace negotiations ended the war, in spite of rather than because of him, Milner found it " totally impossible . . . to labour for the extension of responsible government in South Africa."[1] He saw all the arguments of the mine-owners on Chinese Labour, and few of the objections. To him the war had resulted in Great Britain coming into possession of a magnificent estate. It was on such a material basis that he built up his Imperialism, which had, as he described it, " all the depth and comprehensiveness of a religious faith."[2] He wished for an Imperial Council, not minding where it might meet, and sharing with Curzon the view that what mattered was to remove Imperial questions from democratic parliamentary control, that " mob at Westminster," to use Milner's own phrase.[3]

On his return home he occupied a detached but influential position in British politics. He had been offered and had refused the Colonial Secretaryship when Chamberlain resigned. He was among those who linked Social Reform with Imperialism. To his mind they were " inseparable ideals . . . you cannot have prosperity without power."[4] " There are," he declared in December 1907, " our great tropical and sub-tropical dependencies which are kept within the Empire solely by the strength of the United Kingdom, by its military and naval power, and by the capacity of its people for the government and administration of the weaker races. If either that power or that capacity fail us, the dominion is at an end.[5] He continued to be interested in figures, both on the Bank of Egypt and on other City boards. Sometimes he gave their Lordships in the Upper House the benefit of his wisdom. Thus " speaking as a financier and a statistician " in 1909, Lloyd George's great Budget year, he declared " that it

[1] *Milner Papers*, Vol. 1, 422. [2] Milner, *The Nation and the Empire*, Preface, xxxii.
[3] *Milner Papers*, Vol. 2, 291. Milner to Muller, 4th January 1902.
[4] Milner, *The Nation and the Empire*, 14th December 1906. Address to Unionist Club, Manchester, " Social Reform and Imperialism."
[5] Ibid., 264.

is evident that we have already reached the extreme limits " of Death Duties.[1] To him Socialism was, as to Lord Rosebery, " the end of everything."[2] After the victory of 1918 he was a supporter of mild peace terms for Germany to prevent her becoming Bolshevist. In a curious letter written in 1903 he seems to have foreseen and not disapproved the emergence of a Fascist dictatorship.[3]

Curzon, Viceroy of India for seven years, shared with Cromer and with Milner the same view of Empire. " Our dominion in India," he told Old Etonians at a banquet on the eve of his departure for Calcutta, " is that of British power sustained by a Christian ideal." [4] His first speech in the country contained a promise to hold the scales even.[5] As the underlying hostility became apparent to him he took refuge in the identification of the Viceroy with a Prime Minister, all Indians being his constituents; a pathetic concept, since against all political reform he resolutely set his face.[6] The speeches continued, hewn into massive periods worthy of a pupil of Jowett. " Let the Englishman and the Indian," he declared to the Convocation of Calcutta University, " accept the consecration of a union that is so mysterious as to have in it something of the divine." Only in his last speeches in the country did he come near to the truth. " If I were asked to sum it up in a single word," he told the United Service Club at Simla in an apologia for his administration, " I would say Efficiency." [7] Efficiency in his view was a synonym for the contentment of the governed.

At least he lived up to his ideal. His was a restless energy, spent freely in pursuit of efficiency. He visited the coal-fields of Bengal, the gold-mines of Kolar, the oil-wells of Burma, and the tea gardens of Assam.[8] He was ruthless where serious lapses among his subordinates were concerned, and did not shrink from

[1] House of Lords, 24th November 1909.
[2] Address to Glasgow Businessmen, 10th September 1909. Crewe, *Life of Lord Rosebery*, Vol. 2, 623.
[3] See Milner to Lady E. Cecil, 24th April 1903, *Milner Papers*, Vol. 2, 447.
[4] Dinner at Café Monico, London, 28th October 1898.
[5] Reply to Address from Bombay Municipality, 30th December 1898.
[6] 9th November 1900.
[7] 30th September 1905.
[8] *Lord Curzon in India, Being a selection from his speeches as Viceroy and Governor-General of India, 1898-1905: Introduction by Sir Thomas Raleigh*, K.C.S.I., xxix.

the unpopular.[1] No detail was too small for him. In an address to the Army Temperance Association at Simla, 6th June 1902, he pointed out that " In one British regiment in India in the month of April last, where the total number of men exclusive of patients in hospitals and members of this Association was 380, the amount of beer consumed was nearly 130 hogsheads. Now this means an average daily consumption of $2\frac{3}{4}$ quarts for every man." Curzon worked to the edge of his strength, and expected others to do the same. When an education conference assembled in Simla in 1901 he made it meet six hours a day for a fortnight to pass one hundred and fifty resolutions drafted by himself.[2] The ancient buildings of the Orient were his special interest. The Taj Mahal was restored. He expelled the Upper Burma Club from King Thibaw's throne room, and the garrison church from the royal audience chamber of the Burmese kings.[3]

When Queen Victoria died he at once determined,[4] against considerable protest, to erect a hall as a memorial, which should be the Taj Mahal of the twentieth century. How was it possible that the western civilization, which he represented, should not equal in artistic expression the eastern, which it had superseded?

Reckless of criticism he proceeded on his magnificent way. Soon light railways were being constructed and electric light installed for a Coronation Durbar to cost £100,000.[5] A vast Indian Art Exhibition was held at which the Viceroy, thinking to persuade the Indian princes to support native industry, made one of his famous gaffes : " So long," he said, " as they prefer to fill their palaces with flaming Brussels carpets, with Tottenham Court Road furniture, . . . I fear there is not much hope." Soon the readers of the local press were entertained by a protest from Maples, the well-known store in that street, who pointed out that they had supplied the furnishings for the Viceregal lodge at Simla.[6] Nor was this the only time that Curzon nodded. In a speech to students of Calcutta University he informed them that

<hr/>

[1] E.g. Demonstration by Ninth Lancers after his disciplinary action when a native cook who had been beaten died nine days later. Zetland, *Life*, Vol. 2, 247.
[2] Zetland, *Life*, Vol. 2, 191.   [3] Ibid., 201.
[4] The Queen died 23rd January 1901. Curzon's memorandum was published 4th February.
[5] Zetland, *Life*, Vol. 2, 232.
[6] Speech at Indian Art Exhibition, Delhi, 30th December 1902.

" the highest ideal of truth is to a large extent a western conception." Soon a careful reader of the Viceroy's books was drawing attention to the description of an incident in his early life as a diplomat in Korea, when in the interests of his craft he had employed deliberate falsehood.[1] He was however sufficiently alert to prevent the inclusion of " Onward Christian Soldiers " in the Durbar parade, so that the assembled Indians did not hear the prophetic words: " Thrones and crowns may perish. Kingdoms wax and wane." [2]

The aim of his policy was autonomy for the Indian government. Could that be achieved he felt that all the reasonable aspirations of the population would be satisfied. The men on the spot understood India. They knew what was good for her. It was the doctrinaires in Whitewall and at Westminster who were the foe. When official visitors from India attended the coronation of Edward VII it was at first proposed that the Indian government should pay the expenses, although in the case of the other great colonies the representatives were treated as guests. When Indian troops were kept in South Africa after the Boer War, an attempt was made to charge the expenses in part to India. Only Curzon's strenuous protests reversed these decisions.[3] Why could not the Indians see that he was their friend? Why must they keep on fighting him? It was so unreasonable of them that he persuaded himself that Congress was a spent force. " My own belief," he wrote home in November 1900, " is that Congress is tottering to its fall." [4]

Agrarian reforms constituted the main feature of his programme, perhaps as a conscious policy of political astuteness designed to split the mass of the population from the educated middle class. For although industrialization was beginning to change British India (the Bengal Iron and Steel Company produced 35,000 tons of pig-iron in 1900; the railway mileage increased between 1891 and 1910 from 17,000 to 25,000; the number of looms in cotton textiles from 28,000 to 44,000), the decline of the former native village industries still continued, and in the last

[1] Zetland, *Life*, Vol. 2, 363.   [2] Ibid., 230.
[3] See articles in *New India*, 20th August 1903 and 15th July 1905. Quoted in Zetland, *Life*, Vol. 2, 421.
[4] Zetland, *Life*, Vol. 2, 151, 152, 18th November 1900. Curzon to Secretary of State.

decade of the century the population engaged in agriculture grew from 61% to 66%. The favourable position of the British manufacturer persisted, the author of a paper read at the Royal Colonial Institute in 1906 thus describing the situation: " The fiscal policy of India being on a free trade basis is very advantageous to the British exporter, whose opportunities of expansion are now so much hampered by hostile tariffs in other countries . . . she actually countervails her duty on imported cotton goods by an equivalent excise duty on her own cotton manufactures so that the Manchester exporter may enter her market on absolutely equal terms with the Bombay spinner.[1] Mr. Romesh Dutt, C.I.E., found that " the first great defect of British administration is its expensiveness, the second great defect its exclusiveness."[2] Both charges are not without confirmation, the above-quoted speaker at the Colonial Institute declaring that " the aloofness of the ruling race is the weakest point in the fabric of the British Raj."[3]

The Viceroy's agrarian reforms included considerable irrigation, but could not avert the consequences of the worst drought for 200 years. This led to the famine of 1900, when 1,000,000 died in British India alone.[4] The average expectation of life at birth was stated by the Census of 1901 to be twenty-six years, but any British readers who might be shocked by this fact were presumably expected to be convinced of the hollowness of Indian nationalism by the scholarly survey of the 147 languages in the country, although puzzled perhaps by the enumeration among the number of Aka with 26 speakers, Bhramu with 15, Kami with 11, Kabui with 4, Nora with 2, and monological Andro with only 1.

Political reform the Viceroy eschewed. It was however a political act which produced the greatest storm of his rule, the partition of the province of Bengal. This gave the Mohammedans numerical preponderance in the Eastern province and was strongly resented by the Hindus. It was repealed in 1911.

Curzon's term was extended in 1904, but in the following year a dispute with Kitchener drove him from power, a disappointed and embittered man. The India Office had had to put up with much from Curzon, who credited it with a " desire to thwart and

---

[1] A. Sawtell, 8th May 1906, Royal Colonial Institute, *Proceedings*, xxxvi, 290.
[2] *British Empire Series*, Vol. I, 127.   [3] A Sawtell, *op. cit.*, 295.
[4] *General Report of the Census of India.* Cd. 2047, 1904, 84.

hinder his work."[1] When the Kitchener crisis arose over the control of military affairs it seems that he might have carried his point had he possessed friends at home. Lord Cromer, whose opinion was asked, declared for Curzon and Civil control, but Curzon's temper and lack of tact had ruined his influence. His resignation was accepted and Lord Minto appointed in his stead.

And if it is asked was there any coherent policy accepted by these three, what answer should be made? Is it possible to detect similar figures in the three carpets on which they sat in their more than princely state?

British Imperial policy was becoming more deliberate. The management of the subject peoples was being developed as a science. Assisted by the possession of exclusive sources of information, the Government controlled the situation which in terms of pure force it could not hope to control. Most priceless among the possessions of the proconsuls was a belief in their own integrity. Without this belief their power could never have been maintained. They were convinced that their rule was in the interests of the governed, and it was the peculiar service of the educational and social system which had made them to have nourished this belief.

How easy for the products of a class society to hold that rule over subject races was in the order of things. How difficult to appreciate the Lincoln dictum: " When the white man governs himself, that is self-government; but when he governs himself and also governs another man, that is more than self-government, that is despotism."

And if the question is asked, were these peoples the better or the worse for British rule, what answer can be given? Only that questions such as this History cannot answer. All that can be done is to explain why Britain acted in the way she did. The unravelling of this tangle is difficult enough. The other is a fruitless quest.

British rule brought these countries into the orbit of the capitalist world. It reproduced in them the same patterns which had emerged at home, with one marked and important difference. The ruling class to a considerable extent was alien. Compelled

[1] *Cambridge History of the British Empire*, Vol. 5, 217. Cf. letter to Lady Curzon, 23rd July 1901. Zetland, *Life*, Vol. 2, 176.

though Britain was in India to share exploitation with native princes and soon with native industrialists, she yet preserved a most valuable position for her own financial and industrial groups, who grew fat as the native industries withered before the blast of Manchester goods.

To the Cromers, the Milners and the Curzons the above analysis would be incomprehensible. As they toiled for their country, which they identified with all that was good in this world, they became more and more conscious of the existence of nations, strong nations, where this obvious fact of British beneficence and exclusive right to colonial rule was not accepted. Imperial consolidation began to become an objective towards which the " mob at Westminster " must be persuaded to press with the utmost urgency. Imperial Federation was still being discussed when Edward VII ascended the throne.

Ever since the eighteen-seventies the idea had been a topic in political circles. In 1884 a number of leading persons, including Lord Rosebery, W. H. Smith, W. E. Forster, Sir Henry Holland and Edward Stanhope, formed the Imperial Federation League.[1]

It was an uneasy group. " The most active members " were later described by Sir Charles Tupper, a prominent member, and sometime High Commissioner for Canada in London, as " mainly intent on levying a large contribution of the revenues of the colonies for the support of the army and navy of Great Britain." This is a motive behind the policy of leading British imperialists, which is often insufficiently stressed. Then there were the various groups, agricultural, commercial and industrial, each with their own particular axe to grind, often for the purpose of cutting each other's throats. Except as a propaganda body the League was ineffectual, and broke beneath the stress of its contradictions in 1893; but as a propaganda body it had been important. One of the many proposals emanating from its varied ranks at least possessed the merit of simplicity: this was the reintroduction of differential duties against the foreigner by Great Britain in favour of the Colonies, which, it was argued, would make the Empire self-sufficient, especially in food and raw materials, in time of war. But this would entail a complete reversal of the free trade policy introduced by Peel, and would raise the price of wool and

[1] See J. E. Tyler, *The Struggle for Imperial Unity, 1868–95.*

wheat. Thus the wheel had come full circle. The old debates of 1846, of free trade and protection, began to recur, faintly at first, for the Conservative managers were scared of the issue, but, as the pressure of foreign competition became more widespread, growing to a significant volume. What statesman would crystallize this movement? It drew support from representatives of the businesses most affected by the competition, from the agricultural interest ever faithful to Protection under whatever name, and from that indiscriminate body of people to whom a closer bond within the Empire meant a stronger front against the country's foes? Perhaps had he not been so wayward and inept Lord Rosebery might have been the leader. When Chamberlain finally assumed the post there were a few days when the Liberal ex-Prime Minister seemed in two minds whether to follow him down the road to Protection, or to remain faithful to the ideas of Cobden and of John Bright.

It was becoming obvious that Free Trade would sooner or later have to fight for its life. One country after another had rejected Cobdenism. The United States was sheltered behind one of the strongest tariff walls. Even the British Colonies, except India, which had no choice in the matter, had become heretics. How long would it be before the issue was joined in Britain? Why was it that Chamberlain launched his campaign in May 1903?

CHAPTER XXIII

TARIFF REFORM—THE SETTING

In the summer of 1902 the Colonial Conference was held in London after a five years' interval. When its ten meetings began on 30th June, Lord Salisbury was Prime Minister and Hicks-Beach Chancellor of the Exchequer. When they ended on 11th August Mr. Balfour and Mr. Ritchie had taken their places. For nearly a month after his uncle's resignation on 11th July Balfour failed to find a successor to Hicks-Beach. What meanwhile was happening at the Conference over which Mr. Chamberlain presided?

Chamberlain had entered the Conference with high hopes. On the day of Lord Salisbury's retirement he thus expressed them at the Guildhall in a public address to the Colonial premiers: " Gentlemen, we do want your aid. We do require your assistance in the administration of this vast Empire, which is yours as well as ours. The weary Titan staggers under the too vast orb of its fate. We have borne the burden for many years. We think it is time that our children should assist us to support it, and whenever you make the request to us, be very sure that we shall hasten gladly to call you to our councils. If you are prepared at any time to take a share, any proportionate share, in the burdens of the Empire, we are prepared to meet you with any proposal for giving you a corresponding voice in the policy of the Empire."

The appeal failed. Although a naval agreement was reached with five of the six colonies, under which payments would be made to the Mother country, the sixth, Canada, refused, not indeed from lack of imperial sentiment (to the Queen Victoria memorial Canadians were the largest per head contributors), but from the facts of her geographical position. Not for her that policy of imperial consolidation, which (as was correctly appreciated in Quebec) would have led inevitably to conflict with the United States, as well as to the subordination of the relatively small populations in the Colonies to the preponderant mass in the United Kingdom.[1]

Independence was valued by the existing Colonies as it had been valued by the thirteen Colonies on the Atlantic seaboard a hundred years before. To British statesmen imperial consolidation appeared as a buttress, a protection of independence against the increasing menace of foreign aggression. To the Colonial it appeared rather as a threat to the progressive development of their independence from British control.

Agreement was possible with all six colonies only on a resolution in favour of the extension of Preference, and of the use of British ships for overseas mails.

Chamberlain's hopes had been disappointed. He was not a man easily to be deflected from his purpose. Soon his thoughts were turning round the possibility of advancing towards imperial unity by the only road approved by the Conference, the extension of Preference.

In 1897 the way had been opened when treaties giving " most favoured nation " treatment to foreign countries had been denounced, and Canada had initiated the system of a preferential rate for British imports. One obstacle and one alone stood in the way of an " extension " of reciprocity by the United Kingdom, but that was a formidable one: the sixty-years-old system of Free Trade. It is a mark of Chamberlain's courage or recklessness that he did not shrink from the challenge, and in September 1902 he wrote to Milner: " I think that the time has come when if a further marked advance is to be made in the relations between the Mother country and the Colonies I must take some step of a rather sensational kind." [2]

In November he left for South Africa, but before he sailed he had suggested to Mr. Ritchie that the Corn Duty should be used to give a Preference to Canada, and on the Chancellor's refusal he had brought the question before the Cabinet, and had carried his point. Only Ritchie and one other were against Chamberlain's policy [3] (or were brave enough to express themselves

---

[1] Cf. Sir Frederick Borden at Ottawa, 23rd February 1906: " unnecessary for Canada to support Imperial fleet. . . . Monroe Doctrine behind which stand the guns and warships of the United States and the whole power of eighty million souls ".

[2] *Milner Papers*, Vol. 2, 427.

[3] Lady Victoria Hicks-Beach, *Life of Sir Michael Hicks-Beach*, Vol. 2, 188.

in that sense). They did not resign. It might have been more honourable had they done so, but it would have precipitated a party crisis, for this was a momentous decision. Hicks-Beach had imposed the duty as a temporary war tax. The Cabinet had now agreed to retain it, and to use it for the extension of Colonial Preference, a definite breach in the Free Trade system. For if corn, the staff of life, might again be permanently taxed, why not any other commodity? Chamberlain must have sailed from Southampton in a mood of keen satisfaction and with dazzling dreams of the political prospect.

Yet it is strange that so experienced a politician should not have realized the danger to his cause of temporary removal from the centre of government. His powerful personality was not relished by his colleagues. *Punch* even went so far as to suggest that Balfour himself was not sorry to be rid of him. He left no strong ally behind him in the Cabinet. Chamberlain was a " one-man firm." Ritchie had made his protest. In the following April he had to open his budget, and if the decision imposed by Chamberlain stood he would have to announce to the Commons a policy with which he fundamentally disagreed; the retention of the Corn Duty and its use for the extension of Colonial Preference. Is it surprising if, not having resigned, he should have sought to reverse the decision?

In March as Chamberlain travelled home he received news that Ritchie was going to abolish the duty. It must have been a staggering blow, and it is not clear if he made any fight for the decision of the previous autumn. In one of his speeches later in the year it is true that he remarked: " We could not afford to lose our Chancellor of the Exchequer just before the Budget was to be introduced," but it seems more probable that he was so confident of himself and of his cause that he dreamed of new political alignments, which would arise when the policy which he had pondered on the veldt burst upon a startled nation.

On 23rd April Ritchie opened his budget and announced the removal of the Corn Duty. On 15th May Chamberlain fired the first shot in his campaign from the friendly platform of his ever-faithful Birmingham constituents: " There is still time," he declared, " to consolidate the Empire; . . . it depends upon what we do now whether this great idea is to find fruition or whether we must for ever dismiss it from our consideration and accept our fate as one of the dying Empires of the world." He placed in opposition trade with the Colonies and trade with foreign nations. " Do you think it better to cultivate the trade with your own people or to let that go in order that you may keep the trade of those who are your competitors and rivals." He made his meaning clear, he declared his determination to raise the issue of Free Trade, and to carry through the struggle, when in a significant passage he flung down the challenge: " I think our opponents may perhaps find that the issues which they propose to raise are not the issues on which we shall take the opinion of the country."

The Free Trade movement, begun by Peel and completed by Gladstone, had destroyed the system of Protection, which had been banished from the programme of the Conservative party as not practical politics; but its association with the rise to prominence of the young Disraeli, as well as the wide adoption of tariffs by foreign countries, including Germany and the United States, made it certain that British politicians and in particular Conservative politicians would continue to have their eyes if not their minds open to the possibility of a change.

The support for Disraeli's onslaught on Peel had come from the landed interest, whose prophecy of the ruin of the British farmer that would follow the introduction of Free Trade, was never near fulfilment until the arrival of cheap prairie wheat in the eighteen-seventies. These landowners, ever faithful to Protection, which before 1846 had given them monopoly profits, now redoubled their efforts as the American squeeze began. But no Tariff campaign could have been launched with any prospect of success had its support been confined to this small though powerful group in the ruling class.

In the same decade during which the competition from American wheat became serious, industrial competition began to be noted as a serious factor, and by the end of the century the consolidation of the Carnegie interests into the great United States Steel Corporation, with the purchase by J. P. Morgan of an ancillary fleet of steamers to bring the products to Europe, raised ugly prospects for the British Iron and Steel industry, whose power and influence in affairs of state had been growing for some time past.

In an important memorandum privately circulated in 1900 among leading public men, W. S. Hewins, soon to resign from his position as Director of the London School of Economics to become Chamberlain's economic adviser, declared for the " substitution in our economic policy of Imperial interests for the interests of the consumer, these interests being measured not necessarily by the immediate or even the ultimate gain of a purely economic character arising from a particular line of policy, but by the greater political or social stability or the greater defensive power of the Empire . . . the highest possible efficiency of the trades subsidiary to a modern navy, particularly the iron and steel industry in all its forms and the coal trade."[1]

No surprise therefore need be felt at the strong representation of the heavy industries on Chamberlain's Tariff Reform League: Sir Andrew Noble, Chairman of Armstrong-Whitworth; Sir Vincent Caillard, Director of Vickers; Charles Allen, Chairman of Bessemer; Arthur Keen, Chairman of Guest Keen.

It is also interesting to note that when Hicks-Beach imposed his Corn Duty in 1902 this was a *pis aller*. He would have preferred to put a duty on manufactured goods, but lacked the necessary statistical data.[2]

Agriculture and Heavy Industry: a powerful combination in the Conservative party. Of more general influence was the financial dilemma of the party in the face of rising expenditure and increasing demands for costly social reform. Who should pay the bill? The yield of the Corn Duty was equivalent to 1*d*. on the Income Tax. The political significance of this tax both in Britain and in the United States has already been emphasized.

But long lingering looks at Protection were not confined to Conservatives. It might indeed be said that some Liberals were now Free Traders largely because they were Conservative in outlook. This surely was a powerful influence even in the case of Mr. Asquith, who was to prove the most deadly platform opponent of Mr. Chamberlain.

It is also difficult to imagine that a tariff was a forbidden

---

[1] W. S. Hewins, *Apologia of an Imperialist*, Vol. 1, 50.
[2] Ibid., Vol. 1, 62, 216.

subject at the Co-Efficients, that small dining club for the discussion of " the aims and methods of Imperial Policy " founded by Beatrice Webb in 1902. The members included Edward Grey, Haldane, H. G. Wells, Bertrand Russell, L. S. Amery, H. J. Mackinder, and W. S. Hewins.[1]

Lord Rosebery was to hesitate when Chamberlain launched his campaign, his speech at Burnley four days later giving indeed a guarded approval.[2] Chamberlain was to tell Hewins that " several important members of the Liberal-Imperialist group had approached him about coming over."[3] Grey it appears was not hostile.[4] Hopes too were held about Labour, that the prophecy of Disraeli, that from the working classes would come the new demand for Protection, might now be fulfilled. Robert Blatchford's *Clarion*, in its first comment on " *Chamberlain's Zollverein* " was quite sympathetic,[5] and when the Fabian Society finally issued its tract in February 1904 [6] the bitterest sarcasm, as Halévy remarks, seemed to be reserved for the doctrine of Free Trade. But these hopes of Chamberlain were not to be fulfilled. There were still those living who could remember the days before the Corn Laws were repealed " when the poor people were very largely fed on barley meal and swede turnips."[7] How could Chamberlain believe that he could answer these memories?

He seems originally to have intended to link his appeal with the delivery of Old Age Pensions, then in the forefront of the programme of the Labour Movement. This surely would be a trump card. In the Commons debate on 29th May 1903 he hinted at this cautiously, but not cautiously enough for his industrialist and financial allies. No more was heard of the proposal, and the incident is important more as a revelation of the forces controlling Chamberlain than as a parting of the ways. It is indeed far from certain that Labour would have responded. Keir Hardie was clear and sharp in his reply: " I am opposed to bribing the

[1] Ibid., Vol. 1, 65.
[2] " He was not one of those who regarded Free Trade as part of the Sermon on the Mount." Lord Rosebery's hopes were for a centre party. This had been the object of his much-advertised Chesterfield speech, 16th December 1902.
[3] W. S. Hewins, *op. cit.*, Vol. 1, 67.
[4] Ibid., Vol. 1, 69.
[5] *Clarion*, 22nd May, 1903.
[6] Fabian Tract 166, *Fabianism and the Fiscal Question: An alternative Policy.*
[7] Mr. G. Chambers of Beaminster, Dorset. *Free Trader*, 21st August 1903.

working classes into accepting principles which, save in young Colonies, have wrought no advantage to Labour. Protection, however disguised, is bad for the worker. It protects rent and interest, promotes trusts, increases cost of living, and demoralizes industry."

The controversy was to be notable for the intervention of University professors through public statements in the press. A. Marshall, Bastable, Bowley, Cannan, Pigou and J. H. Clapham were among those who declared against Chamberlain.[1] Cunningham and Foxwell gave support, while Hewins went further and gave instruction to the leader of the campaign, although he found that " it was rather difficult to help him " and that his speeches " contained many inaccuracies of arguments and statistics." Even after three years tuition Hewins had to confess that Chamberlain " insisted on using figures which I proved to him were wrong, apparently on the singular ground that he has used them before."[2]

It is however doubtful whether the pronouncements of the Economists had much effect on the issue. More valuable to Chamberlain than the picking up of a minority among University teachers to put in the balance against Marshall's cohort was the support given by Charles Booth, the respected editor of *London Life and Labour*. Greater assistance still, of far greater importance than that of any individual, came from a number of facts favouring an onslaught on Free Trade at this particular time.

British agriculture remained in its accustomed distress. Now Industrial depression was widespread, and there was considerable unemployment. The Stock Exchange was stagnant, with Consols slipping towards prices which had not been seen since 1866, and the issue of Municipal loans suspended. Now surely, if ever, the electorate would be willing to consider the possibility of change, as the particular crisis of 1903 came to emphasize that deterioration in Britain's relative world position, which had set in during the seventies, shaking national self-confidence, and with it Free Trade, which had been its religion.

Nor had the faith been preserved in its pristine purity. In 1902 Britain had adhered to the Sugar Convention, under which subsidized sugar imports would be checked, a measure which

---

[1] Cf. F. Benham, *Great Britain under Protection*, 24, and J. M. Keynes, *General Theory* (concluding paragraph), where different views are taken of the effect of theory on events.

[2] W. S. Hewins, *op. cit.*, Vol. 1, 73, 163.

would mean that the British consumer would pay more for his sugar, but the West Indian producer be saved from "unfair competition," ruin and the enticements of United States Tariff concessions. In the same year had come Hicks-Beach's Corn Duty, whose removal precipitated Chamberlain's campaign.

One last question remains to be asked before the course of events of that campaign is traced. What would have been the consequence of success?

Britain's two chief trade competitors were the United States and Germany, and it has already been indicated that German competition was the more serious at this time because it was universal and ubiquitous. United States exports were largely to countries close at hand and were to a considerable extent composed of non-competitive products. Prominent however in the Chamberlain programme was the granting of a preference to Colonial products, and these were largely in those raw materials and foods which swelled the United States export to Britain. Without exaggeration might the *Free Trader* state: "A preferential tariff for Colonial products would leave Germany practically unscathed but would strike heavily at America." [1] Cannan thought that "what advocates of the scheme had in their minds when they spoke of foreign countries was the United States." [2] Leading Liberal platform speakers stressed the same point, most directly of all perhaps Mr. Morley: "We went the other day into a war without calculating, without counting the risks and possibilities. This is most disagreeable ground to tread upon but it is nonsense not to face facts. Let us think twice before we ratify a policy which may lead us into very great difficulties indeed." [3]

It is striking how few are the references to Germany during the campaign, how frequent those to the United States.

Whether Chamberlain was conscious of it or not it seems certain that the inevitable result of success would have been growing friction with the U.S.A., the attempt at a rapprochement with Germany as the only insurance, and the possibility of Britain in isolation when the storm of 1914 broke.

---

[1] *Free Trader*, 31st July 1903.   [2] Ibid., 25th Sept. 1903.
[3] Mr. Morley, Manchester, 19th October 1903. See also Lord Rosebery, Surrey Theatre, 25th November 1903; Mr. Asquith, Ladybank, 8th October 1904; Mr. Haldane, Chertsey, 3rd February 1905; Mr. Chamberlain, Liberal-Unionist Club, 12th April 1905.

CHAPTER XXIV

TARIFF REFORM—THE CAMPAIGN

The Birmingham speech on 15th May opened a new chapter in the political history of the reign. It brought a serious situation for the Conservative party, the prospect of that split which young Mr. Churchill had foretold a year before. Now Mr. Balfour was face to face with a problem, which was the more galling as he was quite unable to understand the passions which Free Trade and Protection kindled among the members of his own party. " I myself," he explained to the Commons on 10th June, ". . . have no settled convictions on the subject." Whether this was strictly true is rather doubtful. Hewins was " never conscious . . . of fundamental differences between Balfour and Chamberlain."[1] But this is certain. The issue between Free Trade and Protection, supposing that a philosopher could accurately define what these conceptions meant, was as nothing to him compared with his dominant aim of keeping the Conservative party together.

Never can he have been more lonely. His uncle, whose shrewd experience (had not Salisbury managed, without harm to the party, to rid himself of that " boil on his neck," Lord Randolph Churchill?) might have been invaluable, died on 28th August. He had been ill for some months, and although, after his death, attempts were made to suggest that he was favourable to Tariff Reform, the whole life of the man is against the supposition, while his last public speech contains a passage which seems unmistakably directed against Chamberlain's impetuosity.[2]

The fissures dangerously widened. Hicks-Beach, still a powerful influence in the party, wrote on 9th June that Chamberlain's new policy " has united the party opposite, divided for the last

[1] W. S. Hewins, *Apologia of an Imperialist*, Vol. 1, 9.
[2] 7th May 1902, Albert Hall. See also Lady Victoria Hicks-Beach, *Life of Sir M. Hicks-Beach*, Vol. 2, 195. Sir M. H.-B. to his son, 16th July 1903: " I went down to Hatfield to see Lord Salisbury—evidently angry with Balfour for allowing Joe to master him so much."

eight years, into a happy family. It is dividing our party . . .
if persisted in it will destroy the Unionist party as an instrument
for good." He declared that his "main object is to keep the
Government together and prevent Balfour from committing himself to Joe."[1] To the Free Trade Conservatives it seemed that
they must wrestle for the Prime Minister's soul. That the situation
should thus appear to party politicians is excellent proof of the
skill with which Balfour was riding two horses at the same time.
It was a feat which looked ridiculous, but in fact contained something of the sublime. As a leader of men Balfour was a failure:
he lacked warmth and conviction; but perhaps only a man whose
heart was not engaged in an issue which roused such strong
feelings could have kept his head and thus kept his party together.

Much depended on the Duke of Devonshire, whose "patience
. . . firmness . . . unselfishness, and . . . practical wisdom "[2] was
one of the great assets of the Government. Chamberlain certainly
strove hard to enlist the Duke on his side. On 25th July he thus
explained in the simple language suitable for this slow-minded
gentleman the argument for Tariff Reform: " 1. British exports
have been stagnant for ten years. 2. They would have shown an
immense decrease but for the increase of Colonial trade and the
large export of coal. 3. British industries will be in the most
serious danger when Germany and America have a large over-
production. 4. Tariffs and Preference, which might remedy the
above evils, are consistent with a growth and progress in protected nations enormously greater than our own."[3] The Duke
pondered and reflected, and then cautiously supported a policy
of inquiry. The Cabinet held together all through the summer.
In September the crisis was reached.

The public were astonished to hear on 18th September that
Mr. Ritchie, Lord George Hamilton and Lord Balfour of Burleigh,
the leading Free Traders, and Joseph Chamberlain, the leading
Tariff Reformer, had left the Cabinet.

The facts of the dismissal of the Free Trade ministers and the
resignation of Chamberlain are still obscure. Ritchie, Lord George
Hamilton and Lord Balfour of Burleigh declared that when they

[1] Ibid., Vol. 2, 191, 192.
[2] *The Times*, 6th October 1903. Leader on his resignation.
[3] B. Holland, *Life of Spenser Compton, Eighth Duke of Devonshire*, Vol. 2,
231.

left they were unaware that Chamberlain had already resigned. The suggestion has been made therefore that Balfour, rather in the way that Robespierre struck down first Hébert and then Danton, rid himself of the extremists on both sides. The version in the Chamberlain papers has still to appear. On the whole it seems most probable that there was not a calculated plan. There is no doubt that there was considerable confusion in the Cabinet at this moment of crisis. No minutes were kept at this time. But, although a carefully calculated plan between Balfour and Chamberlain to push out the Free Traders seems unlikely on the known facts, it is true that Balfour's sympathies were with Protection, as his skilful *Economic Notes on Insular Free Trade* shows.

The Cabinet was reconstructed with the advice of the Duke of Devonshire, who to the surprise and pain of his friends remained at his post. Alfred Lyttleton on his advice went to the Colonial Office, and curious but significant the vacancy at the Exchequer was filled by the promotion from the Post Office of Chamberlain's own son, Austen.

The Tariff Reform campaign now entered a more active phase. Already in August a number of well-known economists, including Marshall, Bastable, Bowley, Cannan, Pigou, and later J. H. Clapham, had signed their letter to *The Times* utterly repudiating Chamberlain's policy. " It is not true," they declared, " that an increase in imports involves the diminished employment of workmen in the importing country. Labour would probably earn lower real wages if there were a tax on food imports." It seemed to them impossible " to devise any tariff regulation which shall at once expand the wheat-growing areas in the colonies, encourage agriculture in the United Kingdom, and at the same time not injure the British consumer." A few days later Hewins and Foxwell made a petulant and rather unsatisfactory reply.[1] Labour had now definitely and almost without exception taken its stand against Chamberlain, and in September the Cobden Club was able to issue a strong Free Trade statement signed by 940 leading members of the movement, including 12 M.P.s, the majority of the Directors of the Co-operative Wholesale Society, the Central Board of the Co-operative Union, and the Parliamentary Committee of the Trades Union Congress.

[1] *The Times*, 15th August 1902, 19th August 1902.

The Liberal party, whatever early hesitations there may have been by some of the Liberal-Imperialists, was now solid for the faith, and when one of their M.P.s, young Richard Rigg, announced himself a convert to Tariff Reform he was brutally assaulted in his constituency and found it advisable to leave the neighbourhood.[1]

Tempers indeed were rising and the violence of language appears now somewhat surprising.[2] Lord Spencer called Chamberlain " one of the most reckless and unscrupulous of statesmen, who never hesitates to use any weapon that would advance his cause."[3] The Bishop of Hereford complained about " this raging tearing Protectionist propaganda manufactured in Birmingham " and declared that " every Bishop has solemnly promised to be merciful for Christ's sake to poor and needy people, but this Birmingham Gospel is all in the interest of the rich and without mercy to the poor and needy. . . . Consequently every Minister of Christ is bound to do his part in banishing and driving it away." Bryce described the policy as " a farrago of fallacies picked out of old dust heaps and compounded of fake figures and imaginary facts."[4] John Burns in his penny pamphlet *Labour and Free Trade* talked of " schemes projected by a political bankrupt in the interests of a distressed bankrupt." Edward Cannan in a letter to *The Times* wrote that " to think that the principal member of the Government which has made capital less abundant in this way (i.e. by the South African War) should be going about the country whining that the wicked foreigner has reduced our exports makes my blood boil. I refuse to take it lying down." To Fredcric Harrison, presiding at " The Festival of Humanity " at the beginning of 1904, Chamberlain was " a tawdry charlatan and impudent demagogue."

But the ex-Colonial Secretary, although on the verge of seventy, put forward stupendous energies, and remained sanguine. In

[1] *Annual Register*, 1904, 230.
[2] The verse produced was poor in quality. For a fair sample see *Tariff Reform Leaflet No. 63, Songs of Reform*, Eva Bright.
    " When wealth and mirth refill the earth,
    Let each man tell his neighbour:
    All this we owe to Chamberlain.
    Hurrah, hurrah, hurrah."
[3] 9th October 1903 at Eighty Club.
[4] Speech at Halifax, 11th December 1903.

November 1903 he visited Windsor Castle and a diarist with inside knowledge recorded: " He was the man of the hour and carried himself as if he knew it. Dilating to high and low on fiscal policy, summoned to explain it at this moment to Kings and the next to Queens, proclaiming to everyone with an easy conviction his certainty of success, he left with the belief, as he boasted on his way up to London, that he had converted the whole Royal family and that the Queen was an ardent Protectionist." [1] In October, before an audience composed largely of working men, he had produced his definite policy: a 2s. duty on imported corn; 5% on foreign meat and produce; 10% on manufactured imports; and the remittance of one-half of the sugar duty and three-quarters of the tea. In his Tariff Reform League were enrolled leading industrialists, and also Charles Booth, and Charles Parsons, the inventor of the turbine. Although he had left the Government his son remained and held a key position. The Prime Minister was sympathetic to the policy, even if he felt strong hostility to Chamberlain's methods, being sensitive to inaccuracies of expression; and there was truth as well as wit in Campbell-Bannerman's remark that Tariff Reform was " now authoritatively approved both by the intra-mural and the extra-mural portions of the Government."[2]

It was true that Asquith, the " sledgehammer,"[3] followed Chamberlain wherever he spoke, meeting sanguine rhetoric with sonorous platitudes, but sound if unimaginative Yorkshire common sense, phrased in Balliol English. It was true that after some hesitation most painful to himself the Duke of Devonshire had followed his Free Trade friends out of the Cabinet, and in December was publicly advising electors to vote against Tariff Reform. It was true that a powerful Unionist Free Food League had been formed with the Duke as President, Lord Goschen, Hicks-Beach and Ritchie as Vice-Presidents, and Lord James of Hereford as Treasurer. It was true that when Chamberlain spoke in the City of London he failed to satisfy financial opinion.[4] But the campaign, supported by the most modern methods of

---

[1] Sir A. Fitzroy, *Memoirs*, Vol. I, 170.
[2] From letter to Organizing Secretary of Cobden Club. See *The Times*, 6th October 1903.
[3] The phrase was Campbell-Bannerman's.
[4] *Annual Register*, 1904–7, 8.

advertising, was making an impression. Harmsworth had brought the *Daily Mail* into the Chamberlain ranks. In November Pearson, a strong Tariff Reformer, bought the *Standard*, hitherto an opponent. *The Times* was sympathetic, and in August 1904 published Kipling's panegyric of Chamberlain " *Now in our time there was a man.*" All through 1903 trade remained poor. Two by-elections at Dulwich and Lewisham in December had certainly shown falls in Conservative majorities, but this could be explained away as the natural swing against a government which had been long in office. It was not until the turn of the year that it was clear that the campaign had failed, and even then it was possible to argue with *The Times* that it was the intervention of the Chinese Labour issue that was losing votes, as when, after an increased Liberal majority at Ashburton in January and a Liberal gain at Ayr Boroughs in February, East Dorset was lost in March. " The yellow Labour cry in particular," it was declared, " had been a perfect godsend to them," and attempts were made not to force the pace on the Tariff issue. " The Unionist party exists for other than fiscal questions. . . . The international situation is such as to make it desirable to avoid a change of Government." [1]

Chamberlain now turned from shock tactics to steady propaganda work, and when during 1904 the trade cycle turned upwards less favourable campaigning conditions had definitely supervened. Even earlier Chamberlain had decided that he must be prepared to take long views. In July 1903 Lodge was writing to Theodore Roosevelt: " It is very interesting politically in England just now. Everybody is talking tariff and nothing else, and Chamberlain is accordingly occupying the entire centre of the stage and has succeeded in stirring England to its depths. I should say he would be beaten at the first election, indeed he told me so, but they look for a weak Liberal government and he believes he will sweep the country on the second trial." [2]

The campaign failed for reasons never better summarized contemporaneously than by Joseph Chamberlain's own cousin Arthur: " I don't think they will vote for Protection because I can't think they will be so silly as to ask the Government to tax the food they

[1] *The Times*, 11th March, 1904.
[2] *Correspondence: T. Roosevelt and H. C. Lodge*, Vol. 2, 42. Cf. *The Times*, 4th November 1905, leading article: " To lose the first fight on a novel issue is nothing."

eat, the clothes they wear and the commodities they use, on the promise of the politicians that their wages will rise." [1]

But if Chamberlain failed, Balfour was to succeed. The Conservative party was to suffer a crushing defeat at the polls. Balfour was to be ridiculed. Later he was to be made a scapegoat. But in his main aim he succeeded. The party was held together. Rarely in history can there have been such a superb example of what brains can effect even in politics.

[1] *Daily Chronicle*, 18th January 1904.

CHAPTER XXV

RUSSIA AND JAPAN

The international situation to which *The Times* referred was the Russo-Japanese War.

Ever since the Sino-Japanese conflict of 1895 Japan and Russia had been face to face, and a trial of strength inevitable. The Anglo-Japanese treaty of 1902 was made with eyes open, and as Jesse Collings, Chamberlain's henchman, remarked in a speech after the war began: " Japan could not have entered into the contest but for the alliance this Government had made with that country." [1]

All through 1903 rumours of war were rife as Russia refused to honour her pledge to leave Manchuria. The delivery of British warships to Japan was accelerated. The Australian wool market was entered for the first time by the Japanese in their need for army cloth.[2] In Russia work on the Trans-Siberian railway went on steadily if not quickly, and obviously one important reason for Japan beginning the war in February 1904 was that when the line was completed Russian military power in the Far East would be substantially increased. Another was the state of the world money market. Trade was suffering from a depression both in the United States and in Europe. Conditions were distinctly favourable for the floating of those loans without which modern war cannot be carried on.[3]

Among those who fully appreciated the course of events was Cecil Spring Rice (at this time Secretary to the Embassy at St. Petersburg), the friend of President Theodore Roosevelt, and later Ambassador to the United States. His warnings to London do not appear to have been heeded, for on 4th November 1903 he was informed from the Foreign Office: " Your letter is interesting but strikes me if you will pardon me for saying so as somewhat

---

[1] Overbury Court, 5th September 1904.
[2] J. H. Clapham, *op. cit.*, Vol. 3, 48.
[3] *The Economist.*

imaginative. The Japanese have not as far as I can see any intention of going to war in order to turn the Russians out of Manchuria." [1]

The Times gave up hope of peace at the beginning of January 1904. On the second of the month a poem, *Dai Nippon*, from the pen of James Bernard Fagan, a name remembered in the history of the English theatre, was printed:

> " Brother give me thy helping hand,
> Brother stand thou by me.
> We are the vanguard of the land
> And the first-born of the free.
> I in the East as thou in the West,
> We are twin—we are twin,
> And our mother's breast
> Is the civilizing sea."

On 4th January it was recorded that " over 400 Canadians have volunteered for service in the Japanese army and navy," and that " American opinion on the merits of the controversy remains inflexibly against Russia "; on 6th January that " the latest information . . . leaves but little room for doubt that Russia means to precipitate a conflict ". On 7th January the public was warned that " circumstances . . . are at least conceivable in which quite apart from the treaty our own direct interests might forbid us to stand idly by. . . . If this war begins the whole question of the balance of power in the Far East will be at stake."

In the event it was not Russia who " precipitated " the conflict. A message dated 5th February, 7.5 p.m., to *The Times* from their Tokio correspondent announced that " the situation is now regarded as hopeless ", and on the night of 8th–9th February Japanese torpedo-boats delivered a sudden attack on the Russian squadron lying in the Chinese roads at Port Arthur. The war had begun and without a declaration.

The Times was not abashed. In a leading article on 10th February it was announced that " the cases in which a formal declaration of war precedes the outbreak of hostilities have been comparatively rare in modern history," the point being made

[1] S. Gwyn, *op. cit.*, Vol. 1, 391.

again on 2nd March: " Our ally put her navy in motion with a promptness and courage that extorted the admiration of the world; and her action in doing so before war had been formally declared, so far from being an international solecism, is in accordance with the prevailing practice of most wars in modern times."

American opinion too was against Russia. Soon 60 volunteers for Japan were reported from Chicago, and *The New York Times* was printing a Russian atrocity story: " To leave them to sink is not war; it is plain murder," the London *Times* echoing the sentiment by declaring that: " It is important to observe that English sympathy with Japan is not merely grounded on the fact that she happens to be by treaty our ally. It draws its strength and justification from the knowledge that in this war Japan is fighting the battle of all civilized nations." The Church of England however was put in a difficult position. The Japanese were not Christians, and the Russians were. The Archbishop of York did not consider it appropriate to offer special prayers for the success of Japanese arms.

The international repercussions of the war might be considerable. It was true that Britain was not compelled by her treaty to intervene unless a second power joined the side of Russia, but in February 1904 the negotiations with France were in their concluding stages, and France was the ally of Russia. In fact the situation which, might have been awkward, turned out advantageous, and when in October the Russian Baltic fleet on its way to the Far East fired on some British fishing-smacks near the Dogger Bank, which it mistook for Japanese torpedo-boats, the Quai D'Orsay played a valuable part in preventing an Anglo-Russian clash.

The war produced an unbroken series of Japanese successes, surprising to those who did not appreciate the rottenness of the Tsarist state. Soon it became clear that the utter defeat of Russia was not to the liking of important groups and interests.

In March 1904 President Roosevelt was writing that " it may be that the two powers will fight until both are fairly well exhausted and that then peace will come on terms which will not mean the creation of either a yellow peril or a Slav peril "; [1] on 13th June that " the Japs interest me, and I like them. I am perfectly well

[1] Ibid., Vol. 1, 398.

aware that if they win out it may possibly mean a struggle between them and us in the future; but I hope and believe not."[1] American military observers found the Japanese insolent in victory, and in December the President was wishing that he was certain " that the Japanese down at botton did not lump Russians, English, Americans, Germans, all of us, simply as white devils inferior to themselves."[2]

The Times continued to support the country's ally unreservedly, and when in October 1905, after the conclusion of the war, the Bishop of South Tokio in a letter on " *The character of the Japanese people* " expressed some hostility to the prevalent romantic view, the Manager of the Publication Department replied: " No one in *The Times* office at any rate can doubt that the standard of integrity among the Japanese is so high that when young men who have bought the *Encyclopædia* abandoned their employment to go to the front their families promptly paid the instalments due, under circumstances of the utmost difficulty." [3]

In March 1905 came the hard-won Japanese victory at Mukden, " the biggest thing that has happened in war since Sedan; . . . the first great victory of the East over the West since the Ottoman conquests of the sixteenth and seventeenth centuries."[4] The lesson was conned by Britain's Indian subjects, and the news excited much interest as it passed through the Eastern bazaars.

The Tsar was now threatened with revolution, and although George Meredith was one of those who appealed for funds in support of it,[5] the more general reaction was one of alarm,[6] and

[1] S. Gwyn, *op. cit.*, Vol. 1, 419. [2] Ibid., Vol. 1, 441.
[3] H. G. Warren, a former missionary, supported the Bishop. See letter to *The Times*, 22nd November 1905.
[4] W. S. Blunt, *op. cit.*, Vol. 2, 121.
[5] Ibid., Vol. 2, 119.
[6] The unbroken series of Japanese victories had alarmed the City. As early as 4th June 1904 *The Economist* was writing: " The continued Japanese successes open up a vista of questions more interesting and also more alarming than those raised by the war itself." Cf. Lodge to Roosevelt, 21st August 1905: " Japan has got all we wanted her to get, . . . it is not our interest or that of the world generally to have Russia too completely crippled. It is better that in the future they should both be strong enough to hold each other in check and keep the peace in the Orient. *Correspondence*, Vol. 2, 176, 177. The " progressive " Spring Rice wrote, 29th March 1905, to Mrs. Roosevelt: " The danger of a Russian revolution is not to be sneezed at, and the army of Germany is a priceless bulwark for Europe. The object of us all should be to have no deadly quarrel in Western Europe which should make it impossible to unite if we were really seriously threatened." S. Gwyn, *op. cit.*, Vol. 1, 465.

the number of those in high places who wished to stop the war steadily grew. As Witte, the Russian Foreign Minister, remarked to Spring Rice in May: " A continuance of the war meant the general paralysis of Russia as a civilized power. It meant also a free hand to Germany in Western Europe. Without losing a man or spending a sou Germany had gained more in the last year than by all the sacrifices and victims of 1870."

The difficulty about arranging peace terms was that the Japanese, ever good imitators, could not see why they should not, as Bismarck in 1871, obtain a fat indemnity. When the naval victory at Tsushima on 28th–29th May followed the military victory at Mukden Japanese intransigence was inevitable, and the request from Tokio to Washington, immediately after Admiral Togo's triumph, was not intended as a sign of weakness but of strength.

But the President was determined to show American power, and in August the negotiators of the two belligerents met at Portsmouth, New Hampshire.

Britain's position was difficult. IIer friend, America, was asking her to put pressure on her ally, Japan. On 24th August the Foreign Office received news of a communication from Roosevelt to the British Ambassador: " The opinion of the civilized world will not support it (Japan) in continuing the war merely for the purpose of extorting money from Russia. . . . I wish your people would get my view." [1]

Lord Lansdowne consulted Mr. Balfour. In June a War Office memorandum had pointed out that: " In the military contingency of the United States being hostile Japanese troops could advantageously be employed against the Philippines and also against the States themselves, thus indirectly assisting in the defence of Canada." [2]

The situation was difficult, but it would have been much more difficult had not a new Anglo-Japanese treaty been signed a few days previously under which an important change was made extending the operation of the treaty to all cases of unprovoked aggression, whether by one power or more than one. No reply seems to have been made to Roosevelt. No pressure seems to have been put by Britain on Japan. There was no need. On

[1] *B. D.*, Vol. 4, 104.   [2] *B. D.*, Vol. 4, 140.

25th August Jacob Schiff of Kuhn Loeb, who had been prominent among those financing the Japanese, saw Takahira, their envoy at Portsmouth. " What I do apprehend however," he politely told him, " is that the money markets of the United States, England and Germany will with the belief of a war *à outrance* no longer be prepared to finance Japanese requirements to any great extent." [1] The Tokio Government dropped their demand for an indemnity and four days later the treaty of peace was signed.

The stage was now set for the next transformation scene: an Anglo-Russian rapprochement. " I am informed that the idea of issuing a Russian loan in England," wrote Baron Greindl, the Belgian Minister in Berlin, " is no longer repudiated in the circles of high finance in London. It is not long since the English bankers would not even have consented to discuss the possibility of such a thing . . . the chief cause of dissension between England and Russia has, for the time being, been removed. I mean Russia's morbid ambition continually to go on extending the boundaries of an Empire that already is much too big. Russia's military disasters, and her internal difficulties, will oblige her to renounce a policy of conquest for a long time to come. . . . Can we expect that Russia, finding herself continually on the rocks and having flooded France and Germany with Russian loans, will long resist the temptation to open up a new financial market to her advantage? . . . The constellations of the political firmament are not everlastingly fixed." [2]

On 8th October Charles Hardinge wrote from St. Petersburg to Lord Lansdowne: " The negotiations which I learn from a private source are in progress for the issue of part of a Russian Loan in London, since the natural desire of the Russian Government to place their paper on the English market, will help to facilitate such an understanding, as it would have a reassuring effect on the British financial public." [3]

[1] Cyrus Adler, *Jacob H. Schiff*. See also Durand to Lansdowne, 24th August 1905, *B. D.*, Vol. 4, 104.
[2] Quoted by E. D. Morel, *Diplomacy Revealed*, 17.
[3] *B. D.*, Vol. 4, 208–10.

CHAPTER XXVI

THE IRISH PROBLEM

Russia had been a problem to the British Government ever since the consolidation of British power in India, and more particularly since the opening of the Suez Canal. The reign of Edward VII was to see its solution in virtual military alliance against Germany. The problem of another country nearer home was to be less tractable: Ireland, *John Bull's Other Island*, as Bernard Shaw was to call it in a play much visited by leading British politicians.

Anyone who reads the parliamentary debates will be impressed by the large amount of space devoted to Irish questions after 1850, and especially after the founding of the Irish party by Isaac Butt in 1870. British politics were affected—on certain occasions it is not too much to say shaped—by the Irish problem.

In 1886 Gladstone's decision to support Home Rule divided the Liberal party, and pushed Chamberlain and Hartington, the later Duke of Devonshire, towards the Conservatives. In 1890, when Home Rule seemed almost assured, Parnell, the Irish leader who had survived in 1881 the forged letters of Piggott published by *The Times*, succumbed to the scandal of divorce and the attacks of Church and Chapel. The Irish party was split and the alliance with the Liberals shattered. Gladstone's Home Rule Bill of 1892, passing the Commons by a narrow majority, was rejected by the Lords.

The problem remained to bedevil British politics for another generation. It entered a new phase with the reuniting of the Irish party under Redmond in 1900.

Now both Liberals and Conservatives cautiously manœuvred for the Irish vote. This was important in Ireland, which sent, election after election (whatever the swings of British politics), a group of eighty strong. It was also important in certain industrial constituencies in England and Scotland, where the Irish were a substantial section and a reinforcement to the far from insignificant Roman Catholic pressure group.

The interest of the Vatican in Ireland was indeed increasing as the number of its adherents declined. There were it appears in 1861 4,505,000 Catholics in Ireland, and 5,955 priests, monks and nuns. By 1911, while the number of Catholics had fallen to 3,243,000, the priest-monk-nun population had risen to 15,397.[1]

The Liberal party still contained a determined Home Rule section. The rank and file seriously held to Gladstone's testament, but the Liberal-Imperialists resisted the raising of the issue, Lord Rosebery, the ex-Prime Minister, in particular being a strong opponent.

The Conservative—the Unionist—party had an even more difficult game to play. To retain the support of Ulster and the British connexion but yet not hopelessly to alienate Irish nationalist opinion. It was in obedience to the dictates of this situation that in 1905 George Wyndham, the Irish Secretary, "tipped" by some as the future Conservative Prime Minister, became involved in an Irish policy whose result was his own downfall.

Wyndham had not liked "the idea of Ireland," but having been appointed he knew what he wanted to do: "To smash the agitation, introduce a Land Bill, get money for a Fishing Harbour policy in the West, and float a Catholic University."[2] Thus, even before the strange appointment of Sir Antony MacDonnell to be his Under-Secretary, George Wyndham was determined to raise the dangerous denominational issue.

His policy was in essence a continuation of the policy of Balfour, with whom he had close personal relations; but circumstances were now more favourable for a constructive approach. Even if the Boer War had aroused strong anti-British feeling, particularly among the intelligentsia, this had to some extent been balanced by the impressive bravery of the Irish regiments in the British Army, which had led the Queen to grant to them, despite the frowns of the War Office, the privilege of wearing the shamrock on St. Patrick's Day. Land Reform agitation might have entered a more strenuous phase with the founding of the League by William O'Brien in 1898, but the reuniting of the Irish members under

[1] Sir J. O'Connor, *History of Ireland*, Vol. 2, 206.
[2] W. S. Blunt, *My Diaries*.

Redmond in 1900 had convinced the landlords of the expediency of meeting agitation with more than a revival of the Crimes Act of 1887. In September 1902, on the initiative of the landowners, a conference was arranged on the question of land reform. Lord Dunraven was elected chairman. Both Redmond and O'Brien accepted invitations to attend. Wyndham conveyed the approval of the Government, and this in effect was all that was needed to make the conference a success.

Previous land purchase legislation had been wrecked by changing prices, since the landlords had been paid not in cash but in government stock. Now it was suggested that payments should be made to the landlords in cash by an immediate Government grant, the Treasury recouping itself from rather smaller payments made annually over a period by the purchasing tenants, with the British taxpayer meeting the deficit. In putting forward these proposals the conference was not in advance of public opinion. The Royal Commission on the Financial Relations between Great Britain and Ireland had given support to those who maintained that Ireland paid more than her fair share of taxation. If the Irish problem could be removed once and for all by a money payment men of all parties in Great Britain would support the solution. Wyndham must have felt that everything was going very well for him. He must have dared to hope that he was destined to occupy a proud position in Anglo-Irish history.

In 1903 he introduced and saw passed into law a land bill embodying the recommendations of the Dunraven Conference. When Halévy, the French historian, visited Ireland that summer he was impressed by " the contentment which prevailed everywhere, the warm welcome given to King Edward in August, the sorrowful admissions of former agitators compelled to live in the obscurity of their villages on the memories of their old struggles that Irish patriotism had apparently found a new outlet."[1] Wyndham was at the peak of his career.

Confidently he moved to fulfil the next stage of his policy: the provision of a Roman Catholic University, a measure which might be expected to enlist the support of Catholics for the Conservative cause in England as well as in Ireland. It was now that the man who, it is to be presumed, was responsible for much

[1] E. Halévy, *History of the English People: Epilogue.*

of the detail of Wyndham's policy took the centre of the stage.

Sir Antony MacDonnell, who had performed distinguished service in India, was unexpectedly chosen in 1902 to be Wyndham's Under-Secretary. He had been recommended to Wyndham by Lord Lansdowne. He possessed the confidence of the King.[1]

MacDonnell was a Roman Catholic. He appears to have accepted the invitation reluctantly. He made his position clear in a letter to Wyndham in which he declared that he stood for " the maintenance of order, the solution of the land question on the basis of voluntary sale, the co-ordination, control and direction of the detached and semi-detached boards into which the Government of Ireland was then subdivided, and the promotion of education, economic reform and administrative reform." He would require, he informed Wyndham, " adequate opportunities of influencing policy and the acts of administration." [2] MacDonnell, like many men who have performed distinguished service in India, was what is called a " strong man." Soon he had involved that literary gentleman, George Wyndham,[3] in a situation from which resignation was the only possible issue.

The Dunraven Conference, flushed with success, moved on to the conquest of other worlds. In August 1904 it put itself on a permanent basis as the Irish Reform Association, and working with great speed issued before the end of September a report suggesting the setting up of an Irish Financial Council, which should control the £6,000,000 of the Imperial Budget that was concerned with the provision of Irish services, and possess the right to pass Bills of purely Irish application. It was an honest attempt to solve the Irish question; with the exception of the Liberal attempt in 1907 the last attempt which might have avoided partition. But it was an ingenuous attempt.

The opponents of Home Rule, who only ten years later were to support armed rebellion, would obviously take fright, and in the Conservative party their influence was strong and determined. Wyndham, who was on holiday, disavowed the report as soon as he saw it, but he was irretrievably compromised. MacDonnell had given official encouragement to the Conference. He had informed his chief, and had apparently been authorized to con-

[1] *D. N. B.*   [2] *D. N. B.*
[3] See his *Shakespeare's Poems* and *Ronsard et la Pléiade.*

tinue. Whether Wyndham was in fact a party to the proceedings, or merely one of those persons not unknown in high places who do not read the letters they receive or the letters they sign, is not quite clear and, historically, not very important. From the moment of the issue of the report the anti-Home Rulers were out for his blood. Were they perhaps really aiming at Balfour through Wyndham? The cross-currents from the Tariff Reform controversy may also have had an influence. This much is clear. Wyndham, whose temperament was not suited to this kind of strain, broke down in health. In March 1905 he chivalrously saved the Prime Minister from a dangerous situation by resigning. MacDonnell remained amid general surprise. Perhaps the confidence of the King was a factor. There was also the approaching General Election. Was it possible that the rising Liberal hopes might suffer shipwreck on the Irish question? Would they not be compelled to outbid the Conservative devolution proposals by offering out-and-out Home Rule? And, if they did, might not the English electorate revolt, and the Conservatives after all snatch victory from the jaws of defeat?

CHAPTER XXVII

WOMEN AND DRINK

If the Government's Irish policy was not perhaps uninfluenced by election considerations, their Licensing Bill passed in 1904 was most certainly welcome to the Trade, which for some years past had been closely allied to the Conservative party. The legal decision of *Sharpe v. Wakefield* had established that public-house licences must be renewed each year, and in the Temperance ranks hopes were raised that now at last there was an opportunity to deal with the Drink Question or Evil thoroughly and drastically.

The Government's Bill introduced on 20th April 1904 was a severe blow to the Temperance group, for whom Sir Wilfred Lawson made a bitter and uncompromising reply. It was in fact a typical piece of Conservative social policy—a compromise between the interests of a section and the desire for reform. The renewal of licences could be refused now not by single magistrates but only by Quarter Sessions, while for an unrenewed licence the publican was to receive money compensation from a fund provided by a levy on the Trade.

The Bill met with keen opposition, the Church of England supporting the Temperance advocates so strenuously that in June the Yorkshire Brewers Association in their exasperation resolved, " having regard to the unfair and illogical attitude of the clergy " to the Bill, to support Disestablishment.[1]

But the Government's majority was safe in spite of the protests of the Lords Spiritual,[2] and the Bill passed through both houses without material amendment. The Conservatives could be sure

[1] *Annual Register.*
[2] Balfour thus dismissed the protest of the Church, House of Commons, 6th June 1904: " But when they come to discuss the purely secular methods by which this House, this Parliament, ought to deal with questions of legislation affecting the public at large, affecting questions of property and all the varied and complicated interests of society, I do not think that any special training which the clergy may have had gives them any special title to give an opinion upon such matters."

that the public houses would as usual be useful aids during the General Election.

The financial situation did not permit any substantial pre-election remission, but Austen Chamberlain did his best in the 1905 Budget by reducing the tea duty by 2d. This was an obvious election move. A more difficult problem was presented by the persistent demand from certain women's organizations for the granting of the vote.

The industrial revolution had led to the destruction of the domestic system in many trades.[1] Women in Lancashire and in Yorkshire had long been accustomed to work outside their homes in the mills. Many of their Southern sisters also went to work outside their homes as domestics in the houses of the richer classes. The women's suffrage movement of Edwardian days, although ultimately the result of the industrial development which had cut the economic roots of the family unit, possessed certain special features. It was in its main origin, as was the importunity with which women were besieging the male citadel of the learned professions, middle class. The large families of Victorian England were of course large for all classes, but the family survival rate was higher in middle-class homes than in those of the working class. There was a real family problem of what to do with the surplus of daughters, whose number more than sufficed for the arranging of flowers and for assistance to the mistress of the house in the superintendence of social and domestic tasks. It will probably be found by the historian who concentrates on this movement that the increased survival rate combined with the elevation into a necessity for the middle-class bride of a marriage settlement were the most important predisposing factors for the increased pressure at this particular time.

Emmeline Pankhurst [2] was born in 1858, the eldest daughter and the third of the eleven children of a Manchester calico printing and bleach works owner. With her husband, who died in 1897, she played a prominent part in early Labour politics, leaving the Independent Labour Party in 1900 because she was unable to persuade it to accept her views on the need for women's suffrage.

[1] This was a continuing process. Thus Olive Schreiner in her *Women and Labour*, 72, writes: " Slowly but determinedly as the old fields of labour close up and are submerged behind us we demand entrance into the new."
[2] See *Life*, by S. Pankhurst.

Her early propaganda was with working-class women in Lancashire, and although later the gentry and the titled were to work in the ranks of the Women's Social and Political Union, which she founded in 1903, the argument that if women had the vote their wages, which always lagged behind those of men, would be improved was frequently heard in the great controversy.

The existing political parties were divided on the issue. W. J. Davis, a representative of the Brassworkers at the Special Conference on Unemployment and the Provision of Meals for Schoolchildren at the Public Expense held in January 1905 (with Keir Hardie in the chair), complained that " the time would come when the man would have to stay at home and mind the baby and the woman would go to work," to which Mrs. Pankhurst retorted that " if men had to stay at home to look after the babies there would not be so many babies." The old Radical M.P. Labouchère, founder of *Truth*, declared that " women were too impulsive, they had too much heart, and were too good for political life. . . . It was said that perhaps women would develop if they had the franchise. According to Darwin they had all developed from worms or monkeys or other lower animals. Were they to give women votes in the hope that in some millions of years they would develop into intelligent voters and proper members of parliament? The mission of a working man's wife was to look after the home, to mind the baby, to cook the dinner, and to do the household washing. She had no time for electioneering." [1] Asquith, Austen Chamberlain and Lewis Harcourt were against granting the vote to women. Balfour, Grey, Lloyd George and Churchill were sympathetic. On the whole the Labour party was the most

[1] House of Commons, 16th March 1904. For an extreme expression of the anti-suffragette point of view, see Sir Almroth E. Wright, M.D., F.R.S., *The Unexpurgated Case against Women's Suffrage*, published in 1913. A few extracts are worth quotation.

35. Women's mind . . . is over-influenced by individual instances; arrives at conclusions on incomplete evidence; has a very imperfect sense of proportion; accepts the congenial as true, and rejects the uncongenial as false.

47 One would not be very far from the truth if one alleged that there are no good women, but only women who have lived under the influence of good men.

71 The failure to recognize that man is the master and why he is the master lies at the root of the Suffrage movement.

81 It is not at all certain that the institution of matrimony—which after all is the great instrument in the levelling up of the financial situation of the woman—can endure apart from some willing subordination on the part of the wife.

favourable and the Conservative the least. Redmond, the Irish leader, was a strong supporter, describing the position of women as akin to that of slaves.

The professional politicians were frightened of the issue. How would enfranchised women vote? Between 1897 and 1904 no motion on the question was discussed by the Commons, and when on 16th March 1904, after a short discussion in a very thin house, a motion in favour of women's suffrage was passed by 182 to 68, this was clearly as the *Annual Register* remarked " a symptom of the approach of a dissolution."

More important was the attendance of Christabel, Mrs. Pankhurst's elder daughter, and of Annie Kenney at Sir Edward Grey's meeting at Manchester on October 1905. When they persisted in their question " What would the Liberals do for women's suffrage?" they were forcibly ejected. A meeting of protest outside the hall received considerable support. The newspapers were full of references to the incident. Mrs. Pankhurst duly noted the propaganda and nuisance value. Militancy was born.

But, although Women's Suffrage was to strike the headlines, and to seem to contemporaries the most difficult of political problems, historical perspective gives greater prominence to the distressing puzzle of the out of work.

CHAPTER XXVIII

UNEMPLOYMENT

As the Oxford Dictionary points out, the word " Unemployment " enters into common use about 1895, and although in 1860 Ruskin in *Unto this Last* had referred to " the vexed question of the destinies of the unemployed," and even before the end of the seventeenth century an author had made a computation of the number of " poor people unemployed " in England and Wales, the turn of the century marks an important change in the position of the question.

It was not of course true that there had not been any substantial number of workless before Keir Hardie, sometimes called the " member for the unemployed," came to Parliament in 1892; nor that periodic crises in the capitalist system began with the great depression of 1873; but, as each trade cycle followed its accustomed course, the fact of an unemployment problem gradually became recognized. Particularly impressive was the deputation, mostly composed of women, which was received by the Prime Minister in November 1905: " The pinch of poverty and hunger brought about by the unemployment of their husbands could easily be traced in their dress and in their white and drawn faces. A large number of the women carried babies in their arms." [1]

The problem sprung ultimately from the necessity under the profit system of a surplus labour force, the prevalent philosophy of the ruling class being expressed by such a categorical reference as that of Mr. Balfour to " fundamental economic laws which are not laws of society but laws of nature, and which no legislation will enable us to overcome." It was also widely held that Unem-

[1] *The Times*, 7th November 1905. The deputation was introduced by Henry Quelch, James MacDonald, Margaret Bondfield, George Lansbury, and Will Crooks, M.P. It was formed by the London Trades Council, and the Poplar Trades and Labour Representative Committee. The banners carried by the several thousands in the procession were inscribed: *Workers of the World Unite, The Poplar Unemployed demand the right to work*, and *Work for Our Men —Bread for our Children.*

ployment was a moral question, that it could be equated with idleness. The Trade Unions were considered by some the villains of the piece. Thus when *The Economist*, in December 1904, supported the suggestion that Borough Councils should stagger their work, it insisted that the Unions should forego disputes.

The Boer War had temporarily solved or come near to solving Unemployment, but the return of the reservists and volunteers and the cessation of war industry dislocated the Labour market. The Government accepted the situation as a matter of course, but the national conscience was not so easily lulled. " When the sufferings of the poor become acute, committees are formed, money is subscribed and distributed, and relief work is provided. But as soon as the crisis is past the distress and danger are forgotten and nothing is done to probe the sources of the disease and to provide a permanent and effective remedy." [1]

A remedy? The Labour Movement was itself undecided on the issue. The Liberal economic writer, J. A. Hobson, adhered to underconsumption theory. John Burns, in an L.C.C. Committee report adopted in October 1903, favoured the expediting of public works in times of depression, and the preparation of schemes in advance. Keir Hardie in February 1904, pointing out in a speech in the Commons that it was " very difficult to convince a large and influential section of the community that there was such a thing as an unemployed class," had nothing more positive to suggest than the appointment of a Minister of Labour and a policy of " Back to the Land."

As the General Election approached the Government deliberately wooed the working-class voters with two measures: The Unemployed Workmen's Act and the Aliens Act. In connexion with the latter, which, making the entry of foreigners more difficult, roused some opposition among Liberals mindful of the memorable exiles to whom Britain in the past had given asylum, the Conservative Central Office attempted to rouse anti-semitic feeling against the Liberal party. The effect of this act on the Unemployment problem was of course negligible. The Unemployed Workmen's Act, sponsored by Mr. Walter Long, a country gentleman of kind intentions who was at this time President of the Board of Trade, was historically important. It made it possible for the first

[1] P. Alden, *The Unemployed: A National Question*, iii.

time for assistance to be given from public funds to persons in distress other than through the Poor Law. But it was a very small measure. No one was eligible who had received poor relief during the previous twelve months. It was confined to London, and applicants must have been within the Metropolitan boundaries for at least a year before they could apply. Men with families were given precedence over single men.

The charitable flavour is obvious. Nor in the election winter of 1905 was direct charity omitted. On 13th November Queen Alexandra issued a public appeal for funds: " I appeal to all charitably disposed people in the Empire, both men and women, to assist me in alleviating the suffering of the poor starving unemployed during the winter. For this purpose I head the list with £2,000." Within a fortnight £100,000 had been subscribed.

With the problem of the unemployed the Labour Movement coupled the provision of meals for schoolchildren. On 25th and 26th January 1905 Keir Hardie had presided over a special conference on these two subjects. The resolution on Unemployment showed an advance in directness: " Unemployment is not caused by scarcity of land, of capital, of national wealth, or by incapacity to consume, because in times of depression, such as this we are now experiencing, the wealth producers are compelled to starve in the midst of plenty; that as the same thing happens in countries where Protection prevents imports this conference declares that neither Protection nor so-called Free Trade is a remedy; further, this conference considers proposals like the Aliens Bill to be misleading and calculated to divert attention from the real causes of the evil, namely, the existence of monopoly and the burdens which the non-producing sections impose on the industrious classes together with the lack of such an organization of industry as will prevent alternate periods of overwork and unemployment."

It was a memorable conference. Mrs. Pankhurt pleaded for equal pay for equal work by women " with a fair field and no favours." Ben Turner declared that " they should not only feed the children but teach the children what to eat." Will Thorne wished to include clothes and boots in the provision for them, but his amendment was lost. It is pleasant to read of the great consideration for the youngsters, even though the context is clearly revealed by the statement of the Steel-smelters' representative, Mr. Hodge: " If they were to be an Imperial race in the real sense of the word it could only be by looking after the children and removing such conditions as had been exposed in London and other large towns."

Physical deterioration indeed was becoming a widely accepted fact. The standard height for admission to the Army had been reduced from 5 ft. 3 ins. in 1883 to 5 ft. in 1900. The Royal Commission on Physical Training in Scotland and the Report of the Director-General of Recruiting both supported those who held that there was a gradual deterioration of the physique of the working classes, from which the bulk of the recruits must be drawn. The number of rejects during the Boer War had been disturbing. Some were of the opinion that not only the quality but also the quantity of the race was threatened. The Bishop of Ripon spoke of a retrogression or retardation of the increase of the population. The Duke of Devonshire for the Government denied this. " It has been suggested," he declared, " that the number of children in the average family is decreasing, but there are no official statistics on this subject, and any statement upon it must be conjecture." [1]

[1] 6th July 1903, House of Lords.

CHAPTER XXIX

LAST DAYS OF THE BALFOUR GOVERNMENT

The misfire of Chamberlain's Tariff Reform Campaign became ever more obvious as business improved. 1904 had marked the lowest point of the Trade Cycle, and the Board of Trade returns for the year, showing improvements in quantity as well as value, damaged the Protectionist arguments. In January 1905 Balfour responded to a challenge by Morley with a statement on a half-sheet of notepaper.[1] It was a skilful statement, although more appropriate to a philosophical society than to an under-educated electorate. Had it been made earlier it might have been more effective. The tide was flowing against the Government. As the year proceeded the only doubt was the degree of the Conservative defeat at the forthcoming General Election.

Balfour clung to office in the hope of something turning up and because of the critical international situation.

In February Arthur Lee, the Civil Lord of the Admiralty, who had influential American connexions, startled public opinion

[1] " First, I desire such an alteration of our fiscal system as will give us a freedom of action impossible while we hold ourselves bound by the maxim that no taxation should be imposed except for revenue. I desire this freedom in the main for three reasons. It will strengthen our hands in any negotiations by which we may hope to lower foreign hostile tariffs. It may enable us to protect the fiscal independence of those Colonies which desire to give us preferential treatment. It may be useful where we wish to check the importation of those foreign goods which because they are bounty-fed or tariff-protected abroad are sold below cost price here. Such importations are ultimately as injurious to the consumer as they are immediately ruinous to the producer. Secondly, I desire closer commercial union with the Colonies and I do so because I desire closer union in all its best modes and because this particular mode is intrinsically of great importance and has received much Colonial support. I also think it might produce great and growing commercial advantages both to the Colonies and to the Mother Country by promoting freer trade between them. No doubt such commercial union is beset with many difficulties. Those can best be dealt with by a Colonial Conference, provided its objects are permitted to be discussed unhampered by limiting instructions. Thirdly, I recommend therefore that the subject shall be referred to a conference on those terms. Fourth and last, I do not desire to raise home prices for the purpose of aiding home production."

at home and abroad by an after-dinner speech which found its way into *The Times*: " There had been a complete redistribution of the British Fleet," he declared, " in order to be prepared for possible enemies. The balance and centre of naval power in Europe had been shifted during the last few years. They had not so much to keep their eyes upon France and the Mediterranean as they had to look with more anxiety though not fear towards the North Sea. . . . If war should unhappily be declared under existing conditions the British Navy would get its blow in first before the other side had time even to read in the papers that war had been declared." Lee later corrected his speech and explained it away, but the reference to Germany was unmistakable. Sir John Fisher was now in charge of the Admiralty, and in October the keel was laid of the new-type battleship, the *Dreadnought*, which was intended to give Britain supremacy over her German rival.

In June Lord Roberts wrote to the press urging that shooting should be made " a national pursuit, and skill with the rifle a national accomplishment, in the same manner that archery and skill with the long bow were so considered in the olden days in England."[1] In July the Volunteers were invited to have a medical examination to see if they were fit for service abroad.[2]

The common people in both countries spoke words of friendship. Herr Bebel, the Social Democratic leader, criticized Navy League propaganda in the Reichstag on 15th February: " I am unable to see what other object this agitation could have," he declared, " than to arm for a war against England. The German Navy is not required to fight France and Russia, as the latter power will be paralysed for many years to come by the effects of its war with Japan, while a war with the United States is out of the question." [3]

At the Socialist Congress at Jena on 17th September a resolution was passed vehemently denouncing as unscrupulous and criminal the attempts to sow discord between the British and German peoples and to incite them to war. At the T.U.C., at Hanley in the same month, approval was given to a similar resolution: " We further desire to assure our German comrades that we know they wish the same relations to obtain between them

[1] *Annual Register*, 1905, 171.   [2] Ibid., 185, 186.   [3] Ibid., 286.

and ourselves, which have been so happily established with France, and that we will do our utmost to induce our Government to cut down armaments systematically on an agreed basis between all nations. Finally we appeal to our German comrades to work continually and cordially with us in a united effort to check the growth of Jingo feelings on both sides of the North Sea, and to bring about a general co-operation between both peoples for the common good of all workers internationally."

Had the workers of the two countries possessed power their fraternization might have been effective. As it was the speeches of the Kaiser and of Herr Bassermann, the National Liberal leader, were more significant. " Every German warship launched," declared the Kaiser at Bremen in March, " is one guarantee more for peace on earth; it means that our adversaries will by so much less be inclined to pick a quarrel with us, while it will render us by an equal amount more valuable as allies. . . . Our Lord and God would never have given Himself such pains with our German fatherland and its people if He had not predestined it for something great." [1] Herr Basserman was more candid when he addressed an election meeting at Essen in September: " Germany, with a population increasing at the rate of a million a year," he cried, " had to abandon a purely ' Continental ' policy and had to find employment for her millions of workers by acquiring foreign markets for her products. This necessitated a mercantile marine with a strong Navy to guard it. . . . England worked for fresh coalitions against Germany in order ultimately to get great forces together for a final reckoning with Germany. . . . We shall not let ourselves be prevented by England's menaces from building the strong fleet which we require. We shall not be hindered by impudent speeches of English admirals and incautious utterances of English diplomatists. . . . We do not desire to make war on England. We only want a pacific development of our foreign commercial relations." [2]

The Anglo-French Convention of April 1904 had set Germany a problem. Was Britain on a road which would line her up with France in a war of revenge for 1870? Germany now mounted all her diplomatic guns against Paris.

On 3rd March 1905 the Kaiser landed at Tangier and made a

[1] *Annual Register* 1905, 291.   [2] Ibid., 293.

speech challenging French claims in Morocco.[1]   M. Delcassé's position was at once threatened. His parliamentary position was not strong, and although King Edward and the British Government gave strong support the Foreign Minister's dismissal became effective in June.

It may seem therefore rather surprising that, when *The Times* came to sum up in December the achievements of the dying Balfour administration, foreign affairs was put first: "A success unexampled in our recent history." But it was so comforting to have obtained two powerful friends, one across the Channel, the other at the other end of the world. The efforts of a group, mostly composed of Liberals, in the cause of Anglo-German agreement were decisively condemned. "This country has no desire to risk losing a good friend in one quarter in order to seek an unproven friendship in another."

[1] Julian Green, in his introduction to the English translation of Charles Péguy's *Basic Verities:* Ann and Julian Green, thus describes the effect of this incident on a sensitive Frenchman. "On 4th June 1905, a German cuirassier, wearing a flashy white uniform, got off a battleship, and entered the city of Tangier on the coast of Morocco. It was the Kaiser. On 5th June Charles Péguy, accompanied by his wife, went to one of the largest stores in Paris, the *Bon Marché,* and bought woollen socks, heavy underwear and other things a soldier may need who is going to the front." The date, of course, is wrong. It must be Delcassé's resignation that affected Péguy, but presumably the story is otherwise based on fact.

CHAPTER XXX

MR. BALFOUR'S RESIGNATION

The life of Parliament was still regulated by the Septennial Act. Balfour was a most loyal observer of constitutional procedure. To him the unmistakable signs that public opinion had turned against his government were irrelevant so long as he had his majority at Westminster. It seems likely that he would have continued in office until the last possible moment in 1906 had it not been that this majority now began to show clear signs of dissolution.

It is true that the situation of the Liberal Opposition had been apparently altered by the sudden removal of Lord Spencer, through a stroke, while out shooting on 12th October 1905. Lord Spencer was the Liberal leader whom *The Times* and other respectable Conservative circles would have liked to see as the next Prime Minister. It has indeed been suggested that Lord Spencer's paralysis was an important factor in the development of events. In fact however there was and always had been only one man whom the Liberal rank and file were determined to have as Balfour's successor, Sir Henry Campbell-Bannerman, of whom *The Times* had written that " although he is called the leader of the Opposition he really leads nobody, never has led anybody, and is never likely to lead anybody,"[1] whom Blatchford's *Clarion* had called " this unhappy old drawler of platitudinous flapdoodle."[2]

It was events within his own party that determined Balfour's actions.

On 14th November he addressed the National Union of Conservative Associations in conference at Newcastle: " The situation with which he has to deal," explained *The Times*, " is a strangely fluid one." Or as young Winston Churchill, rejoicing in the happy prospects held out to him by his new party allegiance, exuberantly declared: " Viceroys resigned in fierce anger, Cabinet Ministers abused, contradicted and disavowed each other. Members of the

[1] *The Times*, 27th November 1901.   [2] 22nd May 1903.

224

same Government and of the same party fought over the Prime Minister as dogs worried over a bone."[1] The Tariff Reformers were growing impatient. Would Mr. Balfour be able to close the Conservative ranks again? He was not left long in doubt. The reception of his speech was chilly and unenthusiastic. On 21st November Mr. Chamberlain, speaking at Bristol, made the further continuance of the Balfour policy of compromise, or, as one member of parliament described it, of " sham, shuffle and shunt,"[2] impossible. *The Times* now wrote in a leading article of " a change in the political situation, which may well induce the Government to revise all its arrangements and to reconsider its position. The Government," it decided, " ought to resign without delay."

The Conservative Administration performed its final acts. On 29th November it announced the names of the Royal Commission on the Poor Law, which was to be bullied by Mrs. Beatrice Webb into accepting her programme of research, although not indeed her own conclusions. On 4th December Mr. Balfour resigned, and Sir Henry Campbell-Bannerman, who had at last been induced by his friends to leave Scotland for London, accepted the King's invitation to form a Government.

Even now *The Times* continued its vendetta. " Sir Henry," it remarked, " takes that place (of Prime Minister) because he is there to take it, but he will make a grave mistake if he imagines that he has any reserve of positive enthusiasm to play with."
" C.-B." however was not probably much interested in enthusiasm. He viewed the political scene with a dour Scottish detachment. He was almost the only leading politician who was impervious to Balfour's charm. He disliked the man because he disliked what he stood for. " Liberals in this matter are fighting not a single proposal but a whole spirit and tone of policy and administration and legislation."[3]

[1] 10th November 1905, St. Helens.
[2] Mr. Black, M.P. for Banff, 18th May 1904. Chamberlain in his speech said: " We are standing on the very brink of a General Election. . . . You must not ask the majority . . . to sacrifice their convictions to the prejudices of the minority. . . . I say that it is perfectly absurd for us to think that we can meet misrepresentations by trying to hide what our policy is. I say you must not go into the battle with blunted swords merely in order to satisfy the scruples of those who do not wish to fight at all."
[3] Speech at Limehouse, 20th December 1904.

There was so much to do after twenty years of almost un-interrupted Conservative rule. But first he must form his government. If he could not satisfactorily accomplish this difficult task all the hopes of himself, and of the army of Liberal supporters who had toiled in the wilderness for so long, would prove but a dissolving dream. Small wonder that he lingered and pondered among his Scottish hills before coming to London to face his problem.

CHAPTER XXXI

THE LIBERAL GOVERNMENT

Campbell-Bannerman's incapacity for oratory blinded the pundits to his considerable political gifts. It was also to be his privilege to preside over one of the most talented of British administrations. Exceptional indeed must he have been had he appeared pre-eminent in such company. It cannot be claimed for him that he was among the greatest of our Prime Ministers, but in the short period of his office he proved equal to every situation, put Balfour in his place and, although not without difficulty, kept his strangely assorted team under control.

Among his qualities were culture and character; reticence and shrewdness; charm of personality and common sense; and, above all, an unquestioning faith in the inspiration of Gladstonian Liberalism. It was this last that enabled him to preserve a singularly optimistic outlook among the many problems with which the twentieth century was confronting his country.

But first he had to solve a personal problem of some difficulty: whom to invite into his cabinet.

Both the long interval since the last Liberal administration, and the splits and divergencies within the party, made the task a delicate one. There was also, still living and intermittently active, a Liberal ex-Prime Minister, that brilliant failure, Lord Rosebery.

It is however a sign of the completeness of that failure that there was no significant demand for his inclusion from any quarter. He had indeed re-emphasized his separation from the true church by his Bodmin speech on 25th November on Home Rule, and it is a good example of " C.-B.'s " shrewdness that he had manœuvred Rosebery into this position. The ex-Prime Minister was replying to " C.-B.'s " Stirling speech on 23rd November, in which the inclusion of Home Rule in the party programme was made clear. " C.-B." had already seen the other Liberal-Imperialists, Asquith, Grey and Haldane, and had obtained their agreement to his formula. The omission of Rosebery from these consultations was no accident. " C.-B." was determined in no circumstances to include him in the Government.

There remained the other Liberal-Imperialists. Their attitude was antipathetic in several respects to that of the Prime Minister. He could form no cabinet without some of them. The General Election lay ahead. The party could not face it with divided ranks. But would it be possible to keep them out of dominating positions? Would it be possible to detach them from each other? It was to avoid this that Asquith, Grey and Haldane made the so-called Relugas compact, under which they agreed not to take office unless all were included in the new government.

The Foreign Office gave " C.-B." his greatest trouble. With Lord Rosebery not in the field, Sir Edward Grey, who had been Under-Secretary in Gladstone's last government, was the obvious choice. Only if someone of outstanding eminence could be persuaded to take office could Grey be kept out. Campbell-Bannerman thought that he saw the way.

Cromer was a Liberal and a Free Trader. Could he be tempted to leave Egypt for such a position? These hopes were disappointed, and since Campbell-Bannerman was determined not to accept the only other possible candidate, John Morley, he was compelled to ask Grey. It was now that the crisis began.

The Liberal-Imperialists were set on controlling the Government. They demanded that Campbell-Bannerman should go to the Lords, and Asquith lead the Commons. On 6th December *The Times* had a leader suggesting this as reasonable, referring to " the general feeling that Sir Henry Campbell-Bannerman is hardly the kind of Prime Minister to make a successful fight against Mr. Balfour and Mr. Chamberlain." It must have been galling reading for " C.-B." Cautiously he did not turn down the demand flat, but determined to abide by the opinion of his wife, who was still in Scotland. The Liberal-Imperialists were in a strong position if they held together, but Asquith, under the influence of Mrs. Asquith, broke from the compact, and decided to accept office. Lady Campbell-Bannerman advised her husband to reject Grey's ultimatum, and, after a brief period of crisis, Grey, under pressure from Lady Grey, became Foreign Secretary.

Asquith went to the Exchequer, an office that he really liked, being on the whole more interested in things than in people.

About his qualities writers have been in singular agreement. " He lacks that capacity to let himself go . . . to rouse energies . . . to fire sympathies," wrote one of his earliest biographers, and defensively added that " although superficial observers would not suspect it Mr. Asquith is known among his friends as the kindest and most considerate of men." [1] In John Buchan's considered opinion " he was immensely intelligent, but he was impercipient. New facts made little impression on his capacious but insensitive mind. . . . He had no serious philosophy to meet the new phenomena in the world of labour and in the national economy. . . . He was a man of wide knowledge and many intellectual interests, but he was essentially the Balliol type of the seventies, rational, sceptical, a devotee of Liberty, which he left half-comprehended as a Schoolman left the mysteries of his Church." [2] A. G. Gardiner many years earlier had said much the same: " Balliol in fact is really atrophy of heart . . . if he is wanting in any essential of statesmanship it is strong impulse to action. . . . He prefers ease to conflict and has none of that joy of battle . . . nor has he that impulse of compelling moral fervour which gave such driving-power to Gladstone. . . . He trusts his intellect where Campbell-Bannerman trusted his faith." [3] Labour circles had never forgiven him for his action as Home Secretary in 1893 during the riots at Featherstone Colliery in the West Riding. He had authorized the employment of soldiers, and two men were shot dead. The *Labour Leader* was to declare him the " most rigid dogmatist and anti-socialist in the House."

In 1894 he had married for the second time, his bride being the remarkable, the irrepressible, Margot Tennant, and his best man Richard Burdon Haldane, a fellow-lawyer and a Liberal-Imperialist, whose loyalty to Milner was so complete that he publicly defended the whole South African policy including Chinese Labour. [4]

Haldane had hoped for the woolsack. Campbell-Bannerman offered him the War Office, where from personal experience he anticipated that " Master Richard " would have his difficulties. In the event Haldane at first puzzled and then pleased the generals,

[1] J. P. Alderson, *Mr. Asquith.*
[2] J. Buchan, *Memory-Hold-the-Door.*
[3] A. G. Gardiner, *Prophets, Priests and Kings.*
[4] J. Buchan, *op. cit.*, 128, 131.

and building on the work of Brodrick and Arnold Forster, his predecessors, made a real success of his office.

The Lord Chancellorship went to Robert Reid, Lord Loreburn, not a brilliant lawyer but a faithful and popular party man. John Morley, disappointed of his hopes for the Foreign Secretaryship, went to the India Office. " I have banished myself to the Bramaputra," he complained.

Morley was hypersensitive, a politician of the study, where his historical and biographical work, which included the life of Gladstone, reached a good level of scholarship. Women could always speak more frankly to him than men. Meredith said of him, " Cut him open and you will find a clergyman inside."

He had inherited something of the old Radical tradition: hostility to power and place. In his attitude to social and economic questions of the time he stood at the point of desire to help the working classes, within the confines of the existing system, to a wider opportunity, but he shuddered at the thought of a society remade in the image of the majority.

Sir Edward Grey, by his acceptance of the Foreign Office, occupied a leading but somewhat detached position in the new Government. He possessed a reputation for character only equalled by that of the Duke of Devonshire, with whom he shared the position of member of the landed gentry (albeit on a smaller scale), slaving at politics out of pure patriotic duty. At Oxford he had taken his studies nonchalantly but had conveyed the impression that nothing was beyond his ability. Politics he had inherited with his name. He slipped into the Liberal party because there were his friends and there Fair Play seemed to him to dwell, but he was never a strong party man who had swallowed the Liberal creed hook, line and sinker. He would never have endured office other than the Foreign Office, where detachment and the avoidance of party recrimination was expected of him. After coming down from Oxford he was elected member for his local constituency in Northumberland, and when Lord Rosebery asked him to be his Under-Secretary and he accepted there was general approval, for Grey was a man who did not excite, because he was careful to avoid, personal or political controversy.

As Under-Secretary he had done everything that was expected of him, his unadorned style providing a pleasant relief from the contrasting impression made by his chief; and now as he returned to take Lord Rosebery's place everyone spoke well of him, as he made it clear that the going of Lord Lansdowne would not affect the general character of British Foreign policy.

He was at once as good as his word. On 10th January, when the ministers were dispersed for the General Election, he received M. Cambon, the French ambassador, and was informed that unofficial conversations between British and French army officers were in progress. Would he, Cambon asked, authorize them himself and thus give them official backing? The two Admiralties were already linked in this way. Why then was there anything startling and important in the present proposal?

The Anglo-French Convention of 1904 was probably understood by Lord Lansdowne as only a clearing-up of outstanding differences between the two countries. But to those of greater comprehension of the contemporary world it possessed the advantages of an alliance without, so it was hoped, the disadvantages. If Germany were to prove the enemy of their fears, how convenient to have the ally across the Channel. It was however important to Britain that so far as was possible a free hand should be retained, that she should not put herself, and the decision of peace or war, in the hands of another government. Nor was French opinion unanimous for a new struggle with Germany. The situation was comfortable for Britain in that now she had an ally in France, but more dangerous in that if that alliance were revealed as a broken reed Britain's position would be exposed as weaker than if there had never been an Anglo-French link. Delcassé had fallen in June. His Morocco policy, which had been the *quid pro quo* for France against the surrender to Britain in Egypt, was now being challenged. How could Britain stiffen the French Government sufficiently to keep her in line, but not support her so far as to put British destinies in her hands?

This was the problem as it must have appeared to Grey, more anti-German than Lansdowne, and equally philo-French.

He received Cambon with cordiality, but explained that he could not commit the Government on his own responsibility. He consulted Campbell-Bannerman and Lord Ripon, the veteran of the Cabinet. He consulted Haldane, the Minister of War, whom he met at an election meeting. On 31st January he saw

Cambon again. He authorized the military conversations, but declared that they must not be considered as having any significance. Parliament alone could take the decision of peace or war. " The Secretary," wrote Campbell-Bannerman to Lord Ripon, " said that Cambon appeared to be satisfied. But I do not like the stress laid upon joint preparations. It comes very close to an honourable undertaking; and it will be known on both sides of the Rhine. But let us hope for the best." [1]

Never in politics can there have been so fond an example of trying to eat a cake and have it. Never was there a better illustration of how Campbell-Bannerman's optimism was able to triumph over his experience. The Cabinet was not consulted, although at one time during the crisis this was mooted. Not until 1912 did the question come before the Government as a whole. For this omission Grey has been blamed, but on 1st February his wife was seriously injured in a carriage accident, and on 4th February she died. It is to be expected that this tragic loss altered the perspective of his conversation with Cambon. It is certain that Campbell-Bannerman and the other ministers were more concerned with the legislative programme for the new session.

Two members of Gladstone's last government, Lord Ripon, who was now 78, and Sir Henry Fowler, who was 75, were included in the Cabinet. Ripon, who was a Roman Catholic, became Lord Privy Seal, Fowler, as Lord Wolverhampton, Chancellor of the Duchy of Lancaster. Lord Crewe, formerly Lord Lieutenant of Ireland, became Lord President of the Council. To Ireland Campbell-Bannerman sent James Bryce, the author of *The American Commonwealth*. To the Education Office, Augustine Birrell, lawyer and man of letters, whose sarcastic wit had been enlivening the pages of the *Liberal Magazine*, of which he had been editor. Gladstone's son Henry went to the Home Office. Harcourt's son Lewis to the Office of Works. Earl Carrington went to the Board of Agriculture, Lord Tweedmouth to the Admiralty, John Sinclair to the Scottish Office. Sydney Buxton became Postmaster-General, Lord Elgin Secretary for the Colonies.

These choices were in accord with the old Liberal pattern. The Cabinet was completed by the appointment of David Lloyd George as President of the Board of Trade, and of John Burns

---

[1] J. A. Spender, *Life of Sir Henry Campbell-Bannerman*, Vol. 2, 257.

to the Local Government Board. In spite of King Edward's support, and because of Nonconformist opposition, no place was offered to Sir Charles Dilke, whose political career had been wrecked by his connexion with a divorce case in 1885.

Lloyd George had made a local name as an apostle of Welsh nationalism. He had become a national figure by his violent attacks on the Boer War, and by his leadership of the non-payment of rates campaign against Balfour's Education Act. " He was," declared *The Times*, " the most conspicuous of the militant spirits below the gangway." [1]

The appointment of John Burns was calculated to satisfy working-class opinion that this was a government worthy of their support. His acceptance of office marked final separation from his previous Labour colleagues. " Mr. Burns," declared Keir Hardie, " has the opportunity of showing he can be a statesman as well as an unemployed demagogue. From a political point of view I regret that Mr. Burns should have accepted office." [2]

Soon the new minister was informing his Battersea constituents that they should eschew " pauperizing palliatives that were illusory and extravagant . . . they must not sterilize men's self-reliance, undermine their character, and destroy their capacity to make strong men and citizens." [3] The officials in Whitehall, who had been afraid that he might have intended to do something for the poor and the unemployed, must have smiled with relief.

It was a cabinet of considerable strength, but the power of the government was best illustrated by the junior appointments which Campbell-Bannerman was able to make. Many who were to make their mark on the record of the British people now took office. Reginald McKenna [4] became Financial Secretary to the Treasury. Herbert Samuel [5] became Parliamentary Secretary to

---

[1] *The Times*, 5th December 1905.
[2] *The Times*, 18th December 1905. Speech at Manchester.
[3] *The Times*, 27th December 1905.
[4] R. McKenna, after holding many important Cabinet posts, President of the Board of Education, First Lord of the Admiralty, Home Secretary, Chancellor of the Exchequer, became Chairman of the Midland Bank in 1919, and one of the most influential figures in the City of London.
[5] Herbert Samuel, in addition to holding important Cabinet posts, Postmaster-General, President of the Local Government Board, Home Secretary, was the first High Commissioner in Palestine, and Chairman of the Royal Commission on Coal, 1925. A leading figure in the Liberal party and in public and political life for many years.

the Home Office. Walter Runciman [1] went to assist John Burns. Winston Churchill became Under-Secretary for Colonies. He had hoped for more. " A small post, a humble post," he called it two days later. " An Under-Secretary," he complained, " is a mere stipendiary echo." [2]

[1] Walter Runciman, in addition to holding important Cabinet posts, President of the Board of Education, of the Board of Agriculture, of the Board of Trade, and Lord President of the Council, led the British Mission to Czechoslovakia in 1938. He was linked with the City through family shipping connexions.

[2] *The Times*, 15th December 1905. Speech at City Liberal Club. The definition of an Under-Secretary was quoted from Lord Hugh Cecil.

CHAPTER XXXII

THE ELECTION OF 1906

Campbell-Bannerman's Cabinet-making was conditioned by the fact that it preceded and not succeeded the General Election. The leading Liberal-Imperialists have left on record the interesting fact that only the need to present a united front to the Electorate if Liberalism was to triumph at the polls induced them to accept " C.-B.'s " terms.[1]

The Liberal party was indeed a collection of disparate elements united only by a dislike of the Conservatives and a wish for power. Surprise has been expressed at the contrast between the great Liberal majority of 1906 and the handful of Liberal members in 1918. The War Coalition has been blamed. The legislative record of 1906 to 1914 has been adduced as proof of the driving force of Liberalism, which—so the argument runs—proves that Liberalism was betrayed, stabbed in the back, and did not die because its course was run. The question awaits the examination of the record of the Campbell-Bannerman and Asquith governments, with which we are not now concerned. It is however worth glancing at the public statement of the policy of the new government made at the Albert Hall on 21st December 1905 by the Prime Minister.[2]

He informed his audience that he had " no new pronouncement to make," a statement which was received with assent except by the now usual group of women suffrage interrupters. Foreign Policy, he explained, would be unaltered. " There had been no shudder through the Chancelleries of Europe " because Edward Grey had succeeded Lord Lansdowne. The Conservatives " by renouncing those undesirable characteristics we have formerly detected in their Foreign policy . . . have made it possible for us to pursue a substantial continuity of policy without departing

[1] See J. A. Spender and C. Asquith, *Life of H. H. Asquith*, Vol. 1, 174, 175. Cf. Lord Grey, *Twenty-Five Years*.
[2] *The Times*, 22nd December 1905.

from the friendly and unprovocative method " of the Liberal tradition. The City had accepted the change of Government without anxiety: " Consols . . . have actually risen." India was prominently mentioned. It was a " wise rule . . . to keep questions of the internal administration of India outside the area of party politics." In matters of Finance a cautious policy would be followed. There might be " something from the land . . . a rate on ground values . . . and from licences," but he placed his main hope in a reduction in the expenditure on armaments, that " great danger to the peace of the world."

The workers were promised that the Law of Combination would be amended; the unemployed that the Government considered that " an experiment, carefully conducted and constantly watched, may be with advantage entered upon with the view of finding out how best to mitigate the evils of non-employment," the gloss on which was supplied by John Morley, replying at Arbroath to a Labour and Socialist deputation on 6th January: " The proposition that the State was bound to provide work at a standard wage for those to whom private enterprise did not supply it was unsound and dangerous." [1]

Old Age Pensions were not mentioned in this speech by the Prime Minster, but when he was asked a question at Dunfermline on 29th December [2] he replied that this was " not so simple as Mr. Chamberlain told us it was. . . . Before you can have any big scheme for old age pensions the national finances must be put into a better position."

In view of the claims made for the Liberal party on the basis of the legislation up to 1914 it is worth comparing this speech with the statements put before the Electorate by the various Labour groups. [3]

The Labour Representation Committee condemned the late Conservative Government on the ground that it refused to the Trade Unions the liberty enjoyed by Capital, and neglected the aged poor; that the slums remained and overcrowding continued; that shopkeepers and traders were overburdened with rates and taxes, whilst the increasing land values benefited people who had

---

[1] *Annual Register*, 1906, 5.   [2] *The Times*, 30th December 1905.
[3] Summaries are given by B. G. de Montgomery in his *British and Continental Labour Policy, 1900–1922*.

not earned them; that when the unemployed asked for work the Government gave them a worthless Act; that underfed children at school were neglected; that Chinese Labour was supported in the interests of the mine-owners; that Protection was no remedy for poverty and unemployment.

The Independent Labour Party stood for the abolition of the House of Lords and of property qualifications; was in favour of Women's suffrage; against slums, private liquor traffic, denominational education, and the capitalist press.

The Social Democratic Federation asked for State maintenance for children, the organization of the unemployed, and old age pensions.

The Parliamentary Committee of the Trades Union Congress issued a comprehensive programme: A Trade Disputes Bill to wipe out the injustice of the Taff Vale decision. The extension of Workmen's Compensation. The amendment of the Truck Act. Employment at Trade Union rates for the unemployed. Better housing for the working classes. The end of Chinese Labour. Pensions for those over 60. Adult suffrage. An eight-hour day for industry.

The Times in an article on *The Working Classes and the Election* [1] referred to fears that sufficient Labour members might be returned to put the group in the balancing position formerly enjoyed by the Irish. Local agreements approved by Liberal party headquarters were noted, which might result in the return of some Labour members, but, the writer concluded: " So far the safety of the Ministerial position is not seriously imperilled by Labour disaffection."

The prophets became busy with forecasts of the result. " There were," said Morley in a speech on the eve of the first polling,[2] " three predictions about the composition of the new Parliament. Either the Liberals would be equal to the Conservatives and the Irish together, which would give the Irish members the balancing position; or there would be a Liberal majority over all other parties of about 80; or of about 30 or 40."

The second alternative alone would put the Liberals in a safe parliamentary position. It is interesting to note that no mention was made in these predictions of an independent Labour group.

[1] 9th January 1906.   [2] *Annual Register*, 1906, 9.

In wintry weather the Election campaign was fought. Thousands of workers with tired fingers but tireless spirit addressed thousands of envelopes. Floods of oratory submerged the voters. In the breasts of candidates hope struggled with despair.

Not for many years had there been so few unopposed returns, only 30 compared with 159 in 1900. It was significant that no one dared to oppose Campbell-Bannerman at Stirling Burghs, while news came of a hard struggle by Balfour against a young Liberal lawyer in Manchester.

Polling was not all on the same day at this time and on 12th January the first return was received, a Liberal gain at Ipswich. On the next day, a Saturday, the landslide began. The Lancashire and Yorkshire boroughs were almost solid for Free Trade. Balfour had been defeated. Churchill was in. It was a gloomy Sunday at Conservative headquarters.

After the week-end London followed Manchester. Scotland was even more hostile to the Conservatives than England. In Wales not one of their candidates was returned. The swing over to Liberalism in the counties was only slightly less pronounced than in the towns. Only, in Birmingham, Chamberlain's machine and Chamberlain's personality triumphed.

The final results showed 377 Liberals out of a House of 640, an absolute majority of more than 100. 157 Conservatives were returned, and of these over 100 were supporters of Chamberlain. For Balfour it was a heavy blow.

On 14th January he arrived at Lyme Regis from Manchester, and Lord Newton recorded in his diary: " This was the first occasion on which I had ever seen him seriously upset." [1]

The Irish Nationalists came back 83 strong as was expected. It was the remaining 53 members who were the surprise of the Election. 30 were supporters of the independent Labour Representation Committee, the remainder being the Miners, who still adhered to the Liberal-Labour alliance.

Keir Hardie, Will Crooks and Arthur Henderson were all returned with increased majorities. Ramsay MacDonald, J. R. Clynes, Philip Snowden, Will Thorne, Stephen Walsh, C. W. Bowerman, G. H. Roberts, G. N. Barnes and F. W. Jowett entered Parliament for the first time.

[1] Lord Newton, *Retrospection*, 146.

The Times lightly remarked that the Labour members had " chosen their time with great judgment and patriotism " [1] but Balfour was deeply moved: " If I read the signs aright what has occurred had nothing whatever to do with any of the things we have been squabbling over the last few years. C.-B. is a mere cork dancing on a torrent which he cannot control, and what is going on here is the faint echo of the same movement which has produced massacres in St. Petersburg, riots in Vienna and Socialist processions in Berlin." [2]

It was to Russia particularly that he was referring. The defeats by Japan had released active discontent. On 22nd January 1905 a peaceful procession led by Father Gapon to the Winter Palace in St. Petersburg had been shot down on " Bloody Sunday." In June the sailors of the battleship *Potemkin* mutinied, hoisted the Red Flag, and steered their ship into a Rumanian port. In October Soviets of Workers' Deputies made their appearance. In November a revolutionary who worked under the name of Lenin arrived in Russia. A few weeks later he met for the first time a fellow-conspirator who called himself Stalin, at the conference at Tammerfors at which the plans for armed insurrection were made. In December the attempt was launched with a political strike in Moscow. Barricades appeared in the streets and a bloody struggle began. Only after nine days fighting were the revolutionaries defeated and the safety of the throne assured.

These were the events that were in Balfour's mind with all the freshness of recent memory.

What affinities, one may ask, would History show between the defeated Russian revolutionaries fleeing in disguise from the Tsarist police, and the group of Labour M.P.s who, after making themselves duly known to the friendly but firm policeman at the door, were now admitted to that Palace of Westminster in which the Parliament of the British people held its sessions?

[1] *The Times*, 16th January 1906.
[2] Blanche Dugdale, *Arthur James Balfour*, Vol. 1, 335.

Hicks Beach, Sir Michael (Lord St Aldwyn), 1837–1916, Chancellor of Exchequer, 87; Financial policy, 110–112; Resignation, 147; And Tariff Reform, 194, 198; Mentioned, 186, 188.
Hobhouse, Miss Emily, On British Concentration camps in South Africa, 96.
Hobson, J. A., Economist, author of *Imperialism*, 65, 71; Unemployment policy, 217.
Holland, Sir H., 184.
Hours of Work, In Edwardian Britain, 33, 34.
House of Lords, 40.
Hyndman, H. M., 1842–1921, Leader of Social Democratic Federation, 46.

Imperialism, Chapter IX, *passim*.
Income Tax, 29, 108.
India, Expectation of life in, 27; Morley-Minto reforms, 15; Winston Churchill and, 68; Keir Hardie and, 72, 73; Ramsay MacDonald and, 73; Lord Curzon and, 179–183; Mentioned, 14, 19, 34, 42, 66, 70, 84, 88, 133, 230, 236.
Infant Welfare, 27, 28.
Ireland, Chapter XXVI, *passim*, Irish Nationalists, 48, 82, 124, 237; Irish-Americans and South African war, 80; Mentioned, 84, 85, 86.
Isolation, 130.

James of Hereford, Lord, 1828–1911, Conservative politician, Chairman Coal Conciliation Board, 148, 149; Free Trader, 198.
Japan, Trade competition, 50; Navy, 58, 59; Alliance, 130–134; Russo-Japanese war, 201–206.
Jowett, F. W., Labour politician, 238.

Kaiser, See Wilhelm II, German Emperor.
Kenney, Annie, 215.
Khaki Election, 1900, 88, 89.
Kitchener, Earl, 1850–1916, And South African War, 96, 97, 160; Dispute with Curzon, 182, 183.
Kipling, Rudyard, author, 1865–1936, 69, 157, 199.

Labouchere, Henry, Liberal M.P. and journalist, 214.

Labour Movement, Origins, 45, 46; Opportunism of, 47; And Imperialism, 72, 73; And Chinese Labour, 99, 105; And Education, 124, 125, 126; And France, 165; And Tariff Reform, 191, 192; And Unemployment, 216, 217, 218; And Germany, 221, 222; And Liberal government, 231, 233; And Election, 1906, 236–239.
Langer, Professor W. L., 130, 132, 133.
Lansdowne, Lord, Conservative politician, Foreign Secretary, 87, 88; And Germany, 142, 143, 157; And U.S.A., 154, 156, 205; And France, 165, 167; Mentioned, 129, 138, 159.
Laurier, Sir Wilfrid, Canadian politician, 70, 111.
Lawson, Sir Wilfred, Liberal M.P. and Temperance advocate, 212.
Lee, Arthur (Lord Lee of Fareham), Conservative politician, 157, 221, 222.
Lee, Sir Sydney, 13.
Lenin, 239.
Liberal party, Basis of, 44; And Imperialism, 65, 66, 71, 72; And South African war, 96, 102, 105, 106, 107; And Education, 117, 118, 119, 120, 127, 128; And Foreign policy, 129; And Tariff Reform, 190, 191, 193, 197, 198, 199; And Ireland, 207, 208, 209, 227; And Government, 1905, 228–234; And Election, 1906, 235–239; Mentioned, 42, 48, 54, 55, 89, 91, 112, 149, 150, 172, 173, 223, 224, 225.
Liberal Magazine, 127.
Linlithgow, Marquess of, 163.
Liverpool, 27, 37.
Lloyd George, David, 1863–1945, Prime Minister, 1916–22, Liberal politician, King Edward and, 16; And South African war, 90; And Education Act, 1902, 120; President of Board of Trade, 232, 233; Mentioned, 41.
Lodge, Henry Cabot, American Senator, and friend of Theodore Roosevelt, 51, 199.
London, 28, 33, 36.
Loreburn, Lord, See Reid.
Loubet, President of France, 10.
Lowndes, G. A. N., Author of *The Silent Social Revolution*, 117, 118.
Lowther, James, Conservative politician, 111.